W9-ACX-588

Designing Employee Assistance Programs

Designing
Employee
Assistance
Programs

Dale A. Masi

amacom

American Management Associations

This book is available at a special
discount when ordered in bulk quantities.
For information, contact Special Sales Department,
American Management Associations, Publications Group,
135 West 50th Street, New York, NY 10020.

Library of Congress Cataloging in Publication Data

Masi, Dale A.
  Designing employee assistance programs.

  Includes index.
  1. Employee assistance programs. I. Title.
HF5549.5.E42M37 1984   658.3′82   83-73034
ISBN 0-8144-5616-2

© 1984 American Management Associations, New York.
All rights reserved.
Printed in the United States of America.

This publication may not be reproduced,
stored in a retrieval system,
or transmitted in whole or in part,
in any form or by any means, electronic,
mechanical, photocopying, recording, or otherwise,
without the prior written permission of
American Management Associations, Publications Group,
135 West 50th Street, New York, NY 10020.

Printing number

10 9 8 7 6 5 4 3 2

To
David and Daniel Masi
with faith, hope, and much love

Preface

The excellent companies treat the rank and file as the root source of quality and productivity gain. They do not foster we/they labor attitudes or regard capital investment as the fundamental source of efficiency improvement. As Thomas J. Watson, Jr. said of his company, "IBM's philosophy is largely contained in three simple beliefs. I want to begin with what I think is the most important: our respect for the individual."

Thomas J. Peters and Robert H. Waterman, Jr.
In Search of Excellence: Lessons from America's Best-Run Companies

The worlds of business and of professional counseling have not traditionally been considered compatible. Business has often chosen to ignore the personal problems of employees; in a similar vein, employees often viewed their personal lives as separate and distinct from their jobs. The employee's salary indicated a cooperative contractual agreement to perform a specific service or function. Business believed it was the individual's responsibility to perform the job and produce a quality product while continuing to manage his or her personal life. The American worker was satisfied with this arrangement and certainly accepted the employer's lack of involvement in personal matters.

This arrangement sufficed for years, until society changed dramatically in the 1970s. The number of alcoholics, drug abusers, divorced couples, and single parents rose. The majority of these people were employed in one capacity or another. American productivity declined, and health insurance claims increased by 11.2 percent per annum.

Enlightened managers viewed these changes in relation to the workplace. It soon became apparent that the personal life of an employee did affect his or her job performance. Business realized the importance of the job to the employee. The value of work to the individual became a force in itself; work, as a manifestation of ego, accomplishment, and human drive, provided the employee with a crucial sense of identity. The security of this livelihood was threatened by problems that manifested themselves in the workplace.

The traditional split between the work life and personal life of the employee began to disappear, although the shift developed gradually and cautiously. Businesses, upon realizing the link between the personal life and the productivity of the employee, had no choice but to become concerned and involved.

Employee counseling and employee assistance programs represent a positive method for such intervention. These professional and confidential programs furnish an alternative for employer and employee to improve performance through a positive mechanism rather than through punitive measures. Most importantly, the employee receives help for his or her distress.

I have worked directly in the welding of business and human services for more than ten years. In many ways my diverse background enabled me to be compatible with both worlds. As the daughter of a Republican ward leader for 30 years in Westchester County, New York, I grew up in an atmosphere inspired by a philosophy of business and the work ethic. My academic training in Catholic schools kindled a human services interest. As an officer's wife of 22 years who lived in eight states and two foreign countries, I was exposed to the military and the engineering sectors. Raytheon, Control Data, and Stanford Research Institute were household words. At the same time, as a professional in the human services field, I organized a prisoners' program with businessmen in California and a homemaker's program in Massachusetts, and I fought racial discrimination in housing under the dual auspices of the Urban League and the Department of Defense.

There are other areas in the workplace for human services to merge with corporate responsibility, but since my expertise is in employee counseling I will not address these areas of change. Employee assistance is a major professional specialty in itself.

This book discusses how employees' personal problems cause enormous financial and human loss in the workplace. It describes in detail the approach of handling such problems through employee assistance programs (EAPs). Such programs have proven cost-effective to companies and are a valid way of reaching all employees whose productivity is suffering, from no matter what cause.

I first became aware of this field in 1973 when I was a professor at Boston College, chairing the Master in Social Planning program. An alumnus informed the dean that Kennecott Copper was running a program for employees in which the university might be interested. I was assigned the responsibility of following through with the suggestion and expanding on it by exploring company programs that provided human services for employees. Coincidentally, at about the same time the *Boston Globe* had a feature story on a meeting sponsored by alumni of Harvard University who were concerned because alcoholism was incapacitating so many of their classmates who held very responsible company positions. I attended the meeting and saw the implications of alcohol problems in the workplace. I then learned that other companies were also beginning to reveal their concerns through programs designed to reach their employees by offering constructive assistance rather than punitive action.

I spent the next year visiting such programs and studying the field, and I realized that trained professional staff were essential to administer the programs and to counsel the employees. Since I needed to obtain locations to provide training for my graduate students at Boston College, I began to negotiate with numerous companies in the area. This culminated in five locations, serving a total of 51 companies. It was at these locations that I designed and implemented employee assistance programs (EAPs), using faculty and graduate interns as staff personnel. Companies were initially skeptical. Many did not acknowledge the increasing prevalence of the problem but were willing to start the program and await the results.

Hanscom Air Force Base—the home of the Electronic Systems Division, which includes federal officials with sensitive clearances—became one site. The sensitive clearances represented much more than top security; they included scientists dealing with nuclear weapons, the Airborne Warning and Control Systems, and sophisticated radar sites. The slightest association with personal problems would mean a loss of clearance and, of course, employment. Various commanding officers, including several generals, confided that they recognized the presence of such problems and that perhaps the university's sponsorship of this confidential program would effectively assist the troubled employees. The second site was the New England Telephone Company. The corporate medical director had sponsored a counseling program, but it had not been successful in reaching executives and women. A cooperative approach with both programs was designed. The third site was a program with the chambers of commerce in the cities of Brockton and Taunton, Massachusetts, which comprised 19 companies, including Reed & Barton Silversmiths, Coopercraft Guild, Rand McNally Company, and Morton Hospital. The next site was a pool of 32 federal agencies located in the Boston Regional Center, including the Internal Revenue Service, the Army Corps of Engineers, the General Accounting Office, and the Department of Housing and Urban Development. The last site allowed me to develop a program at my own university for faculty and staff. Six years later, when I left to direct the model program for the federal government, these programs had seen thousands of cases, and each had become permanently installed in the company. The employers saw a return in dollars as well as a decrease in the size of the problem.

In the mid-1970s I was asked by a group of multinational corporations (Exxon, Bechtel, Westinghouse, Standard Oil Company, Morgan Guarantee Trust, and Charter Medical) to join them in a not-for-profit corporation that they had formed—the International Occupational Program Association (IOPA). Its purpose was to jointly study the problem of overseas employees and to develop strategies for intervention. (This work is described in greater detail in Chapter 11.) I became their executive vice-president and planning consultant and worked for them until my departure for Washington, D.C.

In 1979 I was honored to be asked by the secretary of health, education, and welfare to come to Washington to administer the EAP for 150,000 employees of the Department of Health and Human Services (DHHS), which was to be the model program for the federal government. With 16 offices, a professional staff of over 50 in house plus 7 consortiums, and a budget of over $2 million, it is one of the largest programs in the United States. The federal government was well aware of the cost of personal problems of employees. The costs of troubled employees to DHHS were calculated at $148.5 million per year, based on the 150,000 employees earning an average salary of $22,000. The total costs to the federal government were close to $2 billion per year, based on a total of 2,142,400 federal employees, with an average federal salary of $20,258.

Since the fall of 1982, I have been teaching and developing an EAP curriculum as part of the master's and Ph.D. program at the University of Maryland, my present employer, as well as continuing to consult on the DHHS effort. I am also the senior EAP consultant for IBM and for the Sheppard Pratt division of professional and public education.

I have relied strongly on my DHHS and Boston College experiences in presenting here my conceptualization of the human services field and my recommendations for the future. Otherwise, this book would have been just another "how-to" manual. I express opinions on the state of the art as well as where the field is headed. These are clearly my own thoughts and are interspersed throughout the book. It is my hope that the book will help direct the field to a more conceptual framework.

This book contains 13 chapters. After discussing the human factor in productivity loss in the Introduction, I present in Chapter 1 a history of EAPs. Chapter 2 focuses on designing EAPs and includes such issues as staffing, company policy, case maintenance, record-keeping procedures, and legal questions. Chapter 3 discusses the role of managers and supervisors and the critical issues that surface in their training. The consortium design, a cooperative agreement between small companies, is highlighted in Chapter 4. Chapter 5 focuses on alcoholism counseling in industry by discussing the special problems of the alcoholic; the types and patterns of alcohol abuse; the defense mechanisms, such as denial; and various special populations, such as working women and the families of alcoholics. Chapter 6 provides an overview of the pervasive problem of drug abuse in industry through a discussion of the incidence and scope of the problem, the types of illegal drug abuse, legal drugs and women, the use of urinalysis, and the EAP as an effective method to intervene and confront the employee. Chapters 7 and 8 cover the areas of mental health counseling and health promotion, respectively, and include the topics of executive stress, sexual harassment, and the development of health promotion programs. Chapter 9 is devoted to a specific analysis of women in industry. The special problems faced by working women, the stresses on them, and how to reach such women through EAPs are addressed. Chapter 10 looks at other special populations in the workplace—minorities (blacks, Hispanics, and Native Americans) and the handicapped—and discusses appropriate strategies for reaching these groups. Chapter 11 covers international employee counseling relating to Americans employed overseas, industrial social work in Europe, and the EAP movement in England, Scotland, and the West Indies. Chapter 12 focuses on the evaluation component of the EAP. It explains personnel items and health insurance costs and discusses cost-effective models for the delivery of human services programs. The final chapter presents three case studies that describe unique programs, including the DHHS evening and weekend treatment program in the workplace, the General Motors (GM) program, and the peer referral model of the union program for flight attendants.

Acknowledgments

No book is written as a single effort. Other people in an author's life contribute directly and indirectly to its creation. In reference to those persons who contributed indirectly to this book I wish to acknowledge the many people across the country who supported and encouraged me. I am grateful to the companies who had the courage to hire me, to accept my consultation, and to regard my work with respect and professionalism. For many, employee counseling was and is a new concept; working with a human services provider and university professor who also happens to be a woman is not typical of the corporate world.

For those directly involved, my friend and associate Crystal Palmer deserves a special thanks. She has been there to criticize, to suggest, and always to support. Her unselfishness is something that humbles me.

My two immediate staff members at the Department of Health and Human Services, Lisa Teems and Elina Peoples, need to be recognized for putting up with such a "boss" for the past four years. Their good work in the program enabled me to conceptualize and create further vistas to explore. I will always remember the many times they said, "No new ideas, we can't handle any more!" Yet they always did.

Robin Masi and Carl Eisen deserve recognition for mastering the Apple IIe computer and the PeachText® word processor and typing the manuscript. As printers, disks, and new computer languages were learned, a new method for producing a document was born before my eyes.

Special appreciation and recognition must go to Maura O'Brien, research associate. Maura's multidimensional role culminated in the background research and editing of the manuscript. She made a major contribution in helping put this book together. Her ability to grasp a new field while continuing her graduate program at the Georgetown Kennedy Institute of Ethics was amazing. She has, in her own right, become knowledgeable in the area far beyond the work of a research associate.

I am also grateful to Thomas McFee, the assistant secretary for personnel administration (ASPER) at the Department of Health and

Acknowledgments

Human Services, who continually supported the EAP concept and the belief that productivity is being dramatically affected by employees' personal problems. I also wish to recognize the former secretary of health, education, and welfare, Joseph A. Califano, Jr., who appointed me, as well as former secretaries Patricia Roberts Harris and Richard Schweiker and the current secretary, Margaret Heckler. All these people exercised their special roles under the law to cooperate with the Office of Personnel Management in developing EAPs throughout the United States by continuing the model program.

Lastly, grateful thanks to Dr. William Denham from the National Institute of Mental Health (NIMH), who gave the personal support I so badly needed. In his subtle, thoughtful, and intellectual way, he met the challenge and enabled the work to succeed.

Contents

Introduction

The Human Factor in Productivity Loss

Because of personal problems that affect the employee, 18 percent of any work population is losing 25 percent of productivity;[1] in other words, 18 percent of any work population is working at only 75 percent capacity. For example, for a company with 100 employees at an average salary of $20,000:

$$(18\% \text{ of } 100) \times (25\% \text{ of } \$20{,}000) =$$
$$18 \times \$5{,}000 = \$90{,}000 \text{ cost to the company.}$$

Similarly, for a company with 1,000 employees at an average salary of $40,000, the cost is much greater:

$$(18\% \text{ of } 1{,}000) \times (25\% \text{ of } \$40{,}000) =$$
$$180 \times \$10{,}000 = \$1.8 \text{ million cost to the company.}$$

This 25 percent figure is a conservative estimate based on such measurable items as absenteeism, sick leave, accidents, and rising health benefits claims. It does not include the hidden costs of poor decisions, corporate theft, decrease in quality of work produced and costs of adverse action, early retirement, and workers' compensation claims.

The most difficult factor in dealing with this problem is the massive denial that everyone shares—including the employee, employer, co-workers, managers, and supervisors. Although statistics reveal the startling incidence of such problems, these factors cannot be absorbed. So people deny them.

Personal problems include alcohol abuse and drug addiction (which concerns both legal and illegal drugs), as well as emotional

1

stress resulting in depression, crisis behavior, family breakup, suicide, and violence. These problems have reached epidemic proportions at all levels of our society:

- Alcoholism is costing U.S. industry more than $20.6 billion a year in lost productivity.[2]
- The cost of lost productivity because of drug abuse is nearly $16.6 billion a year.[3]
- Illness, both mental and physical, resulting from occupational stress costs U.S. business an estimated $20 billion a year in the white collar job sector alone.[4]
- The total costs to industry, based on the conservative dollar estimates of lost productivity listed above, surpass $55 billion for alcohol, drug, and mental health problems.

In addition, it was projected that in 1983 alone U.S. companies would pay $77 billion in health insurance premiums, which is more than those companies will pay out in dividends.[5] Many of these claims are due to alcoholism, drug addiction, and mental illness. The manifestation of personal problems at the workplace is evident in the extensive personnel costs, health care costs, and hidden costs listed below:

Personnel Costs

- Sick leave taken.
- Absenteeism (not including earned annual leave).
- On-the-job accidents.
- Leave without pay.
- Absence without leave.
- Suspension related to emotional or addiction problems.
- Replacement costs.
- Termination costs.

Health Care Costs

- Health insurance claims.
- Sick benefit payments.
- Accident benefits paid.
- Outpatient medical visits.
- Inpatient medical days.

- Disability retirement and early retirement related to personal (addiction and psychological) reasons.
- Workers' compensation claims related to personal (addiction and psychological) reasons.

Hidden Costs

- Bad business decisions.
- Diverted supervisory and managerial time.
- Friction among workers.
- Damage to equipment.
- Personnel turnover.
- Damage to public image.

Additional Costs to Industry

- Discipline and grievance action (legal action).
- Productivity losses (decline in performance functioning).
- Corporate theft.
- Threat to public safety.

The employee assistance field must now accommodate itself not only to a high rate of employee alcohol abuse but to the dramatic increase in drug abuse and its effects on industry. Cocaine is in the boardroom and in the stockbroker's office. Marijuana is smoked in the parking lot and during coffee breaks. Pills are carried in employees' purses and pockets. This has been the focus of much recent publicity, as such magazines as *Newsweek, Time,* and *U.S. News & World Report* have realized the critical nature of the problem and devoted cover stories to it. In August 1983, I appeared on *The Phil Donahue Show* to discuss drugs in industry. Telephone calls came in from across the United States, as employees, including a stockbroker and a nurse, described the pervasiveness of drug abuse in the workplace and the enormous financial toll it is taking on companies. Besides drug abuse, emotional problems caused by stress, divorce, and financial difficulties are a few of the additional concerns that are affecting the worker today.

Employee assistance programs cannot solve all the troubles of human productivity loss. The key is good personnel management and supervision, not massive denial. It is also very important to develop appropriate personnel policies that complement the employee

3

assistance program and allow both the program counselors and the personnel department to work cooperatively.

By building a strong employee assistance program, an organization reaps several kinds of benefits. It significantly reduces the many costs, financial and otherwise, that it would have incurred because of employees' personal problems. The saving in human happiness and relief from distress can never be measured—but this saving can certainly have a positive effect on overall morale (even among untroubled employees), team spirit, loyalty to the organization, and public image.

REFERENCES

1. Dale A. Masi, *Human Services in Industry* (Lexington, Mass.: Lexington Books, 1982), pp. 2–18.

2. James E. Royce, *Alcohol Problems and Alcoholism: A Comprehensive Survey* (New York: Free Press, 1981), p. 198.

3. "Taking Drugs on the Job," *Newsweek*, August 22, 1983, p. 55.

4. Michael Roddy, "Overcoming Stress on the Job," *Business Magazine*, May 15, 1977, p. F-3.

5. *The Washington Post*, August 21, 1983.

Chapter 1

History and Definition of Employee Assistance Programs

As just described in the Preface and Introduction, employee assistance programs have evolved because of changes in modern society and industry's response to those changes. More and more employees are hindered from doing their jobs productively by personal problems, and industry is realizing that it is not only humanitarian but cost-effective to take more responsibility than it has in the past for helping employees solve these problems. This chapter will describe in more detail exactly what an employee assistance program is and how the concept has developed since the early days of occupational alcoholism programs in the 1940s.

The intentionally broad title of employee assistance programs achieves two major purposes:

1. It conveys that the program focuses on assisting employees, regardless of the type of the problem from which they may suffer.
2. It avoids the stigma that may be attached to a more narrow program, specifically identified as for alcohol or drug problems.

The term *employee assistance program* (EAP) is frequently used interchangeably with *employee counseling services* (ESC). Each reflects the same program concept, but the latter avoids the financial connotation of the term *assistance* to which federal unions raised objections. Thus, ECS is used more often by federal agencies.

An object of the EAP is to avoid the problems experienced in alcoholism programs, where supervisors become diagnosticians who attempt to identify people in need of help. In addition to alcoholism, other problems, including drug addiction and such emotional disturbances as depression, are often the cause of unacceptable job performance. All troubled employees in EAPs are offered assistance and referred for whatever appropriate counseling and care is available.

The idea of the EAP is relatively new. A brief history of occupational alcoholism programs in the United States, beginning with the emergence of formal counseling and referral programs in the early 1940s, will provide the necessary framework underlying the conceptual evolvement of the EAP as a successful response to the failures and inadequacies of previous program strategies. This chapter will also discuss the role of the National Institute on Alcohol Abuse and Alcoholism (NIAAA) and the Association of Labor–Management Administrators and Consultants on Alcoholism (ALMACA), which led to the emergence of the EAP job performance model. The stage is then set for the next chapter, which describes the essential ingredients of an EAP.

HISTORICAL BACKGROUND

According to John Helzer, M.D., professor in the Department of Psychiatry at The Washington University Medical School, current estimates are that "one in seven adults 18 years of age or older in the United States have met Diagnostic and Statistical Manual (DSM III) criteria for alcohol abuse or dependence in their lives."[1] Yet, as a 1980 Institute of Medicine report states:

> The research investment in alcoholism is not commensurate with the research effort mounted against other major diseases . . . research investment in alcoholism is not commensurate with the burden of illness on any basis of comparison one chooses (research dollar per patient, per cost of illness, per industry dollar, per tax revenue dollar).[2]

And although alcoholism is one of America's most serious public health problems, comprising a large percentage of employee-related troubles, only recently has special attention been focused on the largest single subpopulation of alcoholics—the working alcoholic.

In the early 1940s, Alcoholics Anonymous (AA) became prominent, offering an effective method of recovery from alcoholism by achieving total abstinence. Many alcoholic employees who had been terminated were rehired when, with the help of AA, they demonstrated that they could maintain sobriety. Their extraordinary improvement in work productivity prompted many organizations to develop alcoholism programs. For the most part, these early occupational alcoholism programs were staffed by recovered alcoholics who were either current or former employees of the companies. The aim of these programs was to help the recovery process by recognizing the alcoholic employee and enabling him or her to get help before poor job performance resulted in termination.

For many, the job was the last hold to ego functioning; some had lost families as well as friends years before. Threat of job loss was the final lever that could be used against the alcoholic's denial, and amazingly this had excellent results. Jobs mean more to people, including alcoholics, than had been previously realized. This is important knowledge for human service workers, who often have seen the workplace as a negative rather than an ego-reinforcing environment.

The mid-1940s witnessed a scattered growth of alcoholism programs in major industrial firms, including E. I. DuPont de Nemours Company, Kodak Park Works of Eastman Kodak Company, and Kemper Insurance. Such programs were also encouraged by the establishment in 1944 of the National Committee for Education on Alcoholism (NCEA), sponsored by Yale University. In 1945, Ralph M. Henderson joined the NCEA staff as assistant to the executive director. In 1949, when the NCEA separated from Yale sponsorship and became the National Council on Alcoholism (NCA), Henderson remained with the Yale group in New Haven, Connecticut. The program document entitled "Yale Plan for Business and Industry" was the product of a collaboration between Henderson and Seldon Bacon, a colleague at Yale, and led to the recognition of Henderson as the first industrial consultant in the alcoholism movement.

An example of Henderson's outstanding achievements as a consultant was the development and installation in 1949 of the alcoholism program at the Milwaukee operation of the Allis-Chalmers Manufacturing Company. Henry A. Mielcarek, manager of the personnel services section of the industrial relations department, and George J. Stracken, director of the Milwaukee County Alcoholic Information Center in the county hospital, both had an active interest in the problem of alcoholism. Henderson recommended an in-plant study of alcoholism prevalence, disciplinary cases, and absenteeism for the 18,000 employees in the Allis-Chalmers Milwaukee operations. His recommendation was actualized as an operational alcoholism program, which soon became known as the most sophisticated and fully staffed attempt to date to integrate alcoholism assistance within the broad scope of personnel services. It was this approach, which related active alcoholism to poor job performance (absenteeism, lateness, and so on), that philosophically justified business involvement in such programs.

However, this rationale became clouded: An overemphasis on reaching the alcoholic and not enough emphasis on cost-effectiveness led some of the programs to develop an evangelistic flavor that alienated businesspeople. Job performance must be a key issue, or the program could be eliminated as company budgets tighten.

Further interest in alcoholism within the work site is represented by the following major events during 1947–1950:

- In 1947, the development and implementation of the alcoholism policy administered by the medical department of the Consolidated Edison Company of New York and the Great Northern Railway Company.
- The first national conference on alcoholism in industry, held in Chicago on March 23, 1947.
- In 1949 and again in 1950, the Industrial Medical Association devoted a section of the program of its annual meeting to a presentation and discussion of alcoholism as a medical problem in industry.
- In 1949 the Western Electric Company developed a document called "Policy and Program in Alcoholism."[3]

LIMITATIONS OF OCCUPATIONAL ALCOHOLISM PROGRAMS

Although a growing interest began to mount, the majority of innovative alcoholism programs failed to get off the ground, primarily because of industrial apathy, social stigma, and the denial of alcoholism as a major problem. The supervisory identification approach was designed to train supervisors to recognize the symptoms of alcoholism among subordinates and to encourage these people to get help. Since first-line supervisors were usually the people trained to be the diagnosticians, seldom was anyone above that level identified. Such a system enabled management to view alcoholism as an affliction of the lower echelons of the corporation. The approach came to resemble a witch-hunt and forced alcoholics simply not to show their

8

symptoms while working.[4] This was possible, since most employees did not exhibit the late-stage symptoms, which were the focus of the program.

Despite the inadequacies of this model, many worthwhile programs emerged yet failed to be implemented because of the stigma attached to alcoholism, the lack of resources available, and the lack of trained professionals who knew how to administer the programs. An example of an aborted effort was the plan developed at Yale in the late 1940s. This proposed plan was designed for 75,000–90,000 employees in five to six plants in Pittsburgh, where the Western Pennsylvania Committee for Education on Alcoholism (an affiliate of the NCEA) was based. The total budget for the one-year project was estimated at a modest $23,700.[5] Although this plan was well documented, it never went beyond the early stages of design.

For many years after the initiation of psychosocial research on drinking behavior in the 1940s, virtually all descriptive data on problem drinking were based on either the captive populations of jails and mental hospitals, the conspicuous populations of skid rows and other sites of public inebriation, or the self-selected populations who presented themselves for help. All these groups are characterized by fairly long histories of heavy drinking and little or nothing in the way of long work histories. It was also believed that there is an identifiable line that differentiates alcoholics from nonalcoholics. Stereotypes, misdefinitions, and false assumption regarding the drinking behavior of alcoholics and people with related problems affected the treatment opportunities as well as the development of occupational alcoholism programs in the 1940s.

THE 1950s—THE DISEASE MODEL

It was not until the late 1950s that alcoholism was recognized in professional magazines and journals as an occupational health problem. Such recognition was encouraged by the emergence of the disease model of alcoholism, pioneered by E. M. Jellinek, which reoriented traditional attitudes toward alcoholism and alcoholics. The model was officially accepted by the treatment community in 1956 when the American Medical Association (AMA) defined alcoholism as a disease, thereby reducing the stigma previously associated with its treatment as a moral weakness. According to this model, the alcoholic was viewed as a person who was not responsible for his or her behavior and was worthy of rehabilitation and treatment. The concept focused on alcoholism as a cumulative process that allowed a person gradually to increase his or her consumption over a period of years, leading eventually to a complete physiological and psychological dependence on alcohol. The disease is accompanied by marked stages of social deterioration, family and marital disruption, antisocial acts, and work and financial troubles. The similarity between the disease model and the philosophy of AA stems from the fact that pressure from AA prompted the AMA to classify alcoholism as a true medical disease.

It is this disease model that continues to cause confusion in the philosophy of EAPs: If alcoholism is viewed as a physical disease over which the alcoholic has no control, how does one justify confrontation? Should it not then be treated as other diseases, with the victim placed in disability retirement as if suffering from cancer? This is why the Department of Defense and the Department of Health and Human Services both define alcohol abuse in their official policy as a condition and as a treatable problem, respectively. However, if alcoholism is seen as a predisposition to a disease or a psychological addiction that can result in a physical disease such as cirrhosis of the liver, intervention and threat of job loss can be justified. It is then possible to place the program in the personnel area, not the health area—the essential difference between an occupational alcoholism program and an EAP. This is tied to the basic definition of alcoholism, which is an extremely controversial subject in the field.

It is important to clarify that I am not attempting to discredit the disease model of alcoholism. I am discussing EAPs, not treatment philosophy. The use of the word *condition* in EAPs relates these programs to job performance and justifies the placement of EAPs in personnel. As George Vaillant states in his book *The Natural History of Alcoholism,* alcoholism has "an unstable, chameleon-like quality that makes it difficult to pin down at any given time, thus, the professional literature of alcohol abounds in controversy; and controversy, if unresolved, may add to uncertainty and actually detract from knowledge."[6] Vaillant contends that one must acknowledge the psychological as well as the physical manifestations of alcoholism in order to develop a rational and effective method of addressing its incidence in the workplace.

Leo Perlis, the former director of Community Services Activities, sparked a national interest in counseling for employees when he spoke out on behalf of the interest of labor and management. In 1958 Perlis reported the results of a survey to which 74 out of 137 unions affiliated with the American Federation of Labor and Congress of Industrial Organizations (AFL-CIO) responded. Questions were designed to assess union attitudes and actions concerning alcoholism. One union, the United Brick and Clayworkers of America, replied that it had officially adopted a program for dealing with alcoholism among its members.[7] According to a survey conducted in 1959 by the Christopher D. Smithers Foundation, only 35 corporations in the United States acknowledged that they had implemented some formal, therapeutically oriented action in response to alcoholism.[8] Limitations of survey sources, in addition to varying conceptions as to what constitutes an alcoholism program, resulted in the wide discrepancies that are characteristic of the early programs. Nonetheless, it is apparent that during the period from 1944 to 1959 few unions and corporations in the United States developed programs to treat alcoholics.

THE 1960s—GROWTH OF OCCUPATIONAL ALCOHOLISM PROGRAMS

The early 1960s witnessed the initial steps toward a merger of programs that focused on alcoholism with those that focused on behavioral problems, including problems of an emotional or a financial nature. The number of industrial, or occupational, alcoholism programs was beginning to grow as the people who pioneered these early programs gradually joined forces. They were willing to speak about their own alcoholism and develop a philosophy to reach other alcoholic employees. These people revealed that if the companies had not been so kind to them—that is, had not ignored their alcoholism—they may have achieved sobriety sooner. They wanted the opportunity to work with other employees who were suffering from alcoholism and believed it was necessary to break through the manipulation and alibis of the alcoholic. Their approach was to intervene with "tough love," a confrontational method based on positive concerns for the employee's well-being, which focused on cracking the alcoholic's denial. This proved to be the first successful method for alcoholism treatment.

The passage of the Comprehensive Alcohol Abuse and Alcoholism Prevention, Treatment and Rehabilitation Act (the Hughes Act)

11

by the United States Congress in 1970 was perhaps the greater impetus to the development of occupational alcoholism programs.[9] Senator Harold Hughes, a recovered alcoholic, had the courage to speak out in the Senate on behalf of the act. It was this law that established the NIAAA in the Department of Health, Education, and Welfare to guide the national efforts in combatting alcohol problems in the public and private sectors, and mandated that alcoholism programs be instituted in all federal agencies and military installations. It was amended on March 21, 1972 (Public Law 92-255) to include drug abuse. The Occupational Program Branch of the NIAAA offered technical assistance and guidance to organizations interested in implementing programs and provided an impetus to the occupational alcoholism movement.

THE 1970s—JOB PERFORMANCE AND FEDERAL LEGISLATION

In the 1970s the focus of programs shifted from alcoholism per se to identifying impaired job performance. Two forces were at the root of this change. Alcoholism counselors realized that their recovered alcoholic employees often had other problems to deal with as well (for example, marital or legal). This raised an important ethical concern: How could they help one employee who had an alcohol problem with his or her marital and legal problems but not another employee who did not have an alcohol problem but whose job was affected by serious marital and legal problems? The other rationale was pragmatic—the term *alcoholism* was stigmatizing. In some cases, changing the name was all it took to make the program more palatable.

This change had one powerful, unanticipated result. In the early 1970s, I participated with a group of occupational alcoholism program administrators who met periodically under the auspices of the Occupational Program Branch of the NIAAA. When this shift was explained, I pointed out that opening up the program to employees who were not alcoholics would justify other professions entering the field and claiming expertise. This statement was disregarded at the time, but today the EAP field is becoming dominated by human service professionals, many of whom are without training in alcoholism. Although I advocate the broad-based model, I acknowledge that the lack of professionals trained in alcoholism remains a critical issue and source of tension in the field.

The new concentration on job performance was less stigmatic, indicated a better understanding of the alcoholic's use of denial, and released the supervisor from the role of diagnostician. Although the reasons for the shift in focus were valid, there was one critical flaw when the concept was applied to the work setting. Supervisors continued to be trained to recognize the symptoms of alcoholism rather than to concentrate on the deteriorating job performance. Furthermore, the only resource to which an employee was referred was an alcoholism counselor, since alcoholism was the only problem for which a formal system of referral and rehabilitation existed. Therefore, supervisors tended not to refer employees unless the symptoms of alcoholism were present. Even though the name was changed, the programs themselves remained similar to the original occupational alcoholism model until fairly recently.

The NIAAA estimated a total loss to society in 1971 of $25.37 billion due to alcoholism. A large part of this represented the cost of lost production of goods and services by alcohol-abusing members of the nation's workforce. To address the prevalence of alcohol misuse by the economically productive members of society, the NIAAA endorsed the broad-based employee assistance concept as the ideal successor to occupational alcoholism programs.

In mid-1972, the NIAAA provided grants to each state authority to hire two occupational program consultants to develop programmatic approaches for every conceivable type of employment setting. The NIAAA estimated that during the period of the early 1970s, over 400 new programs were initiated in both the public and private sectors. Yet because of the vast number of national employment settings that did not have formal programs, the occupational program consultant idea still had a long way to go.

The number of programs continued to grow in the mid-1970s. By 1974, the Alcohol and Health Report to Congress indicated that 344 major private organizations had developed some form of program to provide assistance to employees with drinking problems.[10] Early identification of problem drinkers in business and in industry was encouraged, as Elliott Richardson, former secretary of health, education, and welfare, recommended in a special report to the Congress on alcoholism and health:

> The magnitude of the costs to the Nation's economy stemming from problem drinking and alcoholism is staggering. It is imperative to encourage the wider establishment, in government as well as in the pri-

vate sector, of types of programs that, with the cooperation of labor and management, have successfully restored substantial majorities of affected personnel to health and normal function. The economic benefits of effective early identification and treatment programs demonstrably outweigh the costs, and the human benefits are beyond evaluation.[11]

The scope and depth of interest in programs and the emergence of this area as a distinctive specialty are reflected in the growth and activities of ALMACA, which was established in 1971. Its membership was composed of occupational program consultants, EAP administrators in work organizations, labor representatives, and researchers, and indicated a trend toward professionalization. ALMACA serves in a limited fashion as a clearinghouse for job opportunities, provides information about pending legislation, and provides members with monographs outlining the results of research or other trends in the occupational field. Although in the early years, part of the organization's administrative functions were supported through an NIAAA grant for occupational program research, it is now financially self-sufficient and has gained strength through the establishment of over 50 local chapters. ALMACA's leadership is concerned with the development of standards for both EAP programs and programmers; it has recently begun a concerted effort to increase the quantity and quality of research needed to enhance the structure, functioning, and diffusion of occupational programs.

The adoption of programs, stimulated by the formation of such professional organizations as ALMACA, had considerable impact in terms of education and attitude changes that paved the way for the acceptance and maintenance of EAPs. Testimony to the critical role of ALMACA was given by the NCA in June 1983, when it dissolved its labor–management division, stating that ALMACA had the leadership role in the occupational area and to continue NCA's effort would be a duplication.

THE DHHS MODEL PROGRAM[12]

In August 1979, under the direction of Joseph A. Califano, Jr., former secretary of health, education, and welfare, a major initiative was launched to combat alcoholism and alcohol abuse. The Employee Counseling Services (ECS) program was established as a model for the entire federal government and served the approximately 150,000 employees of DHHS. A significant focus of the initiative was to encourage state and local governments, businesses, labor organizations, and others to establish EAPs to address problems that interfere with an employee's job performance.

The Office of the Director of ECS (under the assistant secretary for personnel administration) was given responsibility for the program's overall administration and policy direction, technical assistance to the ECS units, implementation of special demonstration projects, and evaluation of the program. Sixteen ECS operating units were set up in the ten regions and six headquarters offices in the Baltimore/Washington area. These units were made responsible for such day-to-day operations as supervisory training and employee assessment and referral. Each unit had its own unit director.

In 1980 an agreement was signed with the Office of Personnel Management (OPM) that designated the DHHS ECS as a model federal program and outlined the following responsibilities for it:

1. The implementation of a model evaluation system to estimate the cost benefits and the cost-effectiveness of the program. (This is described in Chapter 12.)

2. The development of consortiums (as discussed in Chapter 4).

3. The development of a management information system (MIS) to track ECS efforts in providing information, technical assistance, speeches, meetings, and publications to individuals and organizations outside of the DHHS ECS. From the start of data collection in March 1980 until March 1983, the ECS responded to 3,875 requests for information from federal agencies, congressional offices, the White House, private industry, treatment facilities, local and state governments, and interest groups.

4. The development of the following six special demonstration projects to enhance the delivery of services. The result of these six projects will be made available to the field.

- *A Model Supervisory Training Package.* This 3.5-hour presentation includes a film entitled "ECS: A Supervisor's Alternative." The purpose of this package is to train managers to identify, confront, and refer troubled employees whose work performance is deteriorating. It is the first film that was specifically designed for use in the federal sector. Funding was provided by NIAAA.
- *An ECS Model for Drug Abuse.* The purpose of this project was to develop new outreach strategies for employees with both legal

15

and illegal drug problems. In addition, guides have been developed to help federal supervisors deal with drug abuse and assess drug treatment facilities. This project was conducted in the Chicago region, and funding was provided by the National Institute of Drug Abuse (NIDA).

- *An Evening and Weekend Alcoholism Treatment Project.* This project provides treatment to federal employees in the Washington, D.C., area whose work performance is deteriorating because of alcohol-related problems. It is unique in that the treatment takes place in the evenings and weekends at the workplace, with minimal disruption to the employee's normal work schedule. In addition, child care is available. Funding for the treatment is being provided by the Blue Cross/Blue Shield Federal Employee Program. (This program is described in Chapter 13.)

- *An ECS Model for Indian Health Service (IHS) Employees.* This model is currently being developed to provide ECS services to all employees of the IHS nationwide. It will be implemented on a regional basis, with consultation and training from the ECS director and unit directors. The ECS will evaluate the effectiveness of the program in the IHS. Funding will be provided by the IHS.

- *An ECS Model for Senior Executive Service Members.* This model is being developed to define appropriate strategies for the identification and referral of Senior Executive Service (SES) members to ECS programs. With the cooperation of OPM, SES members in the Washington, D.C., federal government departments will be provided ECS services.

- *An ECS Model for Field Employees.* Because of the diverse geographic locations of many employees in DHHS, especially those in Social Security Administration (SSA) offices, a special project to reach these employees is currently being developed. DHHS held a demonstration in cooperation with AT&T's Picturephone Meeting Service to test the possibility of using video counseling as a technique for reaching troubled employees in remote areas. In this demonstration the counselor was in Philadelphia while a staff person acting as a client was in Washington, D.C. Numerous officials from the National Institute of Mental Health (NIMH) and SSA viewed the demonstration, and it was decided such a method might be feasible in the future. To test the validity of video counseling, a research project is being designed jointly by DHHS and AT&T.

The problem of companies with offices in many different locations is a common one. Such companies find it difficult to overcome logistics in delivering EAP services fairly and equitably to all employees regardless of where they are located. Some companies are using telephone counseling; however, according to NIMH, no study has yet been done to test the validity of telephone counseling. Other companies have contractual agreements with "affiliates," professionals whom the company pays to spend a certain percentage of their time counseling employees in their own communities. The implications for the counseling field of the various approaches described here could be enormous.

President Ronald Reagan has established an initiative for the private sector, which includes cooperative efforts between both the public and private sectors. Several ECS projects have been selected for inclusion in the President's private sector initiative. For example, the training film "ECS: A Supervisor's Alternative" has been adapted for use in private industry. The new film entitled "It's Your Move" was developed by the ECS, DHHS, and the Hazelden Foundation and will be presented to companies nationwide. Also, two ECS consortiums (Dallas/Ft. Worth and Puerto Rico/Virgin Islands) will be expanded to include employees in private industry.

The ECS program is currently exploring its potential relationship with workers' compensation to determine the possibility of reducing the cost of workers' compensation by offering ECS services to claimants.

The SSA headquarters ECS unit in Baltimore has initiated a demonstration project to develop alternatives to disability retirement. The project was undertaken in cooperation with OPM and the National Institute of Handicapped Research.

APPROACHES FOR
REFERRING EMPLOYEES TO THE EAP

The employee assistance program, unlike its predecessors, has emerged as a successful method for dealing effectively with employees whose alcohol, drug, and mental health problems are eroding their job performance. Today over 60 percent of the *Fortune* 500 companies have programs. There are now over 5,000 EAPs, and the number is increasing at an unprecedented rate.[13] Absenteeism is a behavior that industry can no longer afford. Not only is it costly in terms of dollars and productivity, it represents a waste of a company's most valuable resource, a trained employee. Leave abuse is also a clear indication of a troubled employee.

Many organizations still suspend employees who have performance problems. It is naive, however, to think that a simple removal from the work site for a specified number of days will cure the employee of the problem that initially caused the suspension. This misguided strategy is similar to that used by schools that suspend a student in the hope that such disciplinary action will remedy the underlying reasons for disruptive behavior or poor academic performance. What in fact happens is that the employee returns not only with the original problem intact but often with anger toward the suspending supervisor and feelings of guilt, embarrassment, and lowered self-esteem. These findings, in addition to the high cost of suspending an employee, prompted the Employee Counseling Services (ECS) at DHHS to propose a referral to ECS when the employee returns to the work site. The success of this proposal is also contingent on educating supervisors about possible employee assistance intervention and referral as a more constructive alternative to suspension.

Described below are organizations—General Motors Corporation, the Social Security Administration (Baltimore), and the Office of Personnel Systems Integrity (DHHS)—whose work in the area of leave abuse and EAPs is significant.

General Motors Corporation

The findings of a three-year company-wide study of absenteeism (work missed) and time and attendance (time spent working) at General Motors Corporation (GM) were considered a clear indication that abuse of leave time required direct intervention. As a result GM instituted an irregular attendance control program. The GM model for the program was developed by management and approved by the union in contract negotiations. The accepted agreement stipulated that an employee must see the attendance control counselor, which in the GM structure comes under the labor relations function, if the number of absences without leave and leave without pay the employee has taken is 15 percent above the leave earned. This referral is considered a warning. If this number is 20 percent above the leave earned, the employee is automatically referred to the employee assistance program. Formal disciplinary action may or may not be taken.

Social Security Administration (Baltimore)

The ECS at the Social Security Administration (SSA) has developed a computer search to identify employees who are abusing leave without pay and those who have been away without leave. A list of these employees is sent to the deputy commissioner, who then notifies the first-line supervisor. This supervisor reviews the problem with the identified employee and makes a referral to employee counseling, if appropriate.

Office of Personnel Systems Integrity (DHHS)

The Office of Personnel Systems Integrity (OPSI) releases a sick leave report to personnel officers of DHHS. It provides comparative data on the salary cost and time expended for sick leave. This enables the division to compare itself with other units as well as against its own record. It also allows the abuse of sick leave to be expressed in terms of salary dollars. The OPSI sick leave report released in April 1983 stated that in 1982, sick leave cost DHHS $670 per employee. The report recommended that employees with chronic leave problems be referred to the ECS.[14]

THE QUESTION OF SELF-REFERRALS

The question of self-referrals is one of the most provocative concerns to EAPs in the 1980s. Self-referred employees are those who approach the counselor of their own accord, not because a manager has referred them. On the one hand, it can be argued that while a self-referred employee may not be operating at a productivity loss as extensive as that of the employee referred by a supervisor, no doubt any personal problem will have some negative effect on an employee's ability to work. In addition, the EAP approach opens the door for employees who have family members that are addicted to alcohol or drugs; certainly the job performance of these employees will be adversely affected. Employees who are apt to seek help on their own are also sometimes in financial trouble; in fact, these types of cases are on the increase in EAPs. Financial hardship may reflect the economics of the times, but it may also be a sign of an expensive drug or gambling addiction. Some program administrators contend that self-referrals mean people are being reached at earlier stages of addiction and hence justify their prevalence in EAPs. However, this may be only a rationalization of administrators who are more comfortable with self-referrals and not skilled in outreach case finding.

A disproportionately high number of self-referrals rather than referrals made by managers and supervisors to EAPs may indicate further shifting from the key issues of cost-effectiveness and job performance. The enormity of costs to industry caused by addictions has already been documented. Denial, which is the nature of addictions as well as of many emotional problems, blinds individuals from recognizing on their own that they need help. Most of these cases will go undetected for prolonged periods of time, with attending prolonged industrial costs, unless supervisors and managers who are trained in the signs of declining job performance initiate these referrals. A predominance of self-referral cases is already evident in many EAPs, and the EAP will lose the uniqueness of its design unless this is carefully watched. To compound matters, many programs are being staffed with more and more mental health professionals not trained in addiction. Such programs are beginning to resemble typical community family counseling agencies. The United Way family agencies are already available to workers on a self-referral basis and are supported by both employers and employees, so funding a duplicate service effort is unnecessary.

I discussed the trend toward self-referrals in EAPs with Bertram Brown, the former director of the NIMH, in the 1970s. He wisely stated that the number of cases did not prove anything; he could put a counselor anywhere, and certain types of cases would arise. Some types of people gravitate toward counselors. The important question, he said, was what kind of cases I wanted to reach. Were they, indeed, the groups the program was designed to reach? He claimed that many self-referred cases could use community counselors and did not necessarily need the EAP method. However, addictions and certain types of emotional problems that use denial as a defense did require the EAP approach, and the supervisory referral was then crucial.

In my opinion, program managers should carefully monitor the self-referral trend in their programs. I have also found that certain counselors have more self-referrals than others. Invariably a counselor with a strong foundation in the area of addiction will have a higher managerial referral rate.

CONCLUSION

The EAP is a method of intervention that focuses on the decline in job performance, not on the nature of the employee's problem, to restore the worker to full productivity. Careful documentation of the declining job performance justifies the employer's intervention, and the threat of job loss can be used to break through the alibis, the denials, and the excuses that troubled employees, especially alcoholics, often exhibit.

The combination of early assessment and referral services allows the employer to confront the troubled employee when a documentation of performance changes warrants such intervention. Such confrontation is the most effective technique that can be used with executives. It provides a strong motivation for employees to do something about their problems before dismissal results. Raymond Kelly, president of his own consulting firm in Chicago, stated in a conversation with me that the greatest motivation for executives is the threat of job loss; for some strange reason executives are ready to sacrifice their homes, health, and families for their drinking, but not their jobs.[15] It is these factors, which will be discussed in more detail in the following chapters, that have made the EAP successful where the traditional models proved inadequate.

As noted, the current trend in EAP programs appears to be toward the more traditional social service model and away from the job performance supervisory referral. The years ahead will be critical for EAPs, as either the job performance model or the broad-based, self-referral human service approach becomes dominant. I hope both dimensions will be kept and the swing toward self-referrals will be tempered by an equal emphasis on supervisory referrals. Then I believe we will truly have a broad-based EAP service.

REFERENCES

1. Cited in "The Alcoholism Report," The Johnson Institute, Vol. 12, No. 1 (Washington, D.C.: October 31, 1983), p. 7.
2. Institute of Medicine, *Alcoholism and Related Problems: Opportunities for Re-*

search (Washington, D.C.: National Academy of Sciences, July 1980), p. 22.

3. Cited in Lewis F. Presnall, *Occupational Counseling and Referral Systems* (Salt Lake City: Utah Alcoholism Foundation, 1981), pp. 5–7.

4. James T. Wrich, *The Employee Assistance Program* (St. Cloud, Minn.: Hazelden, 1980), p. 11.

5. Files of Ralph M. Henderson, Research Library, Center for Alcoholic Studies, Rutgers University, New Brunswick, N.J.

6. George E. Vaillant, *The Natural History of Alcoholism* (Cambridge, Mass.: Harvard University Press, 1983), p. 1.

7. Cited in Presnall, *Occupational Counseling*, p. 10.

8. *A Basic Outline for a Company Program on Alcoholism* (New York: Christopher D. Smithers Foundation, 1959).

9. Pub. L. 91-616, 42 U.S.C. 4582, 1970.

10. National Institute on Alcohol Abuse and Alcoholism, "Alcohol and Health Report to Congress" (Washington, D.C., 1974).

11. Elliott Richardson, Department of Health, Education, and Welfare, "Second Special Report to the Congress on Alcoholism and Health" (Washington, D.C., 1973).

12. This section is based on the DHHS "Summary Report of the Employee Counseling Services Program," August 1979 to March 1983, Washington, D.C., pp. 1–6.

13. Paul Roman, "Executive Caravan Survey Results," *Labor–Management Alcoholism Journal*, November/December 1981.

14. DHHS Memorandum on "The Mandatory Referral to ECS for an Employee Returning to the Worksite Following Suspension," from Virginia Venable to Dale A. Masi, Washington, D.C., August 8, 1983, pp. 1–2.

15. Raymond Kelly, in telephone conference with Dale A. Masi, November 16, 1983.

Chapter 2

Essential Ingredients of an EAP

Once a company has decided to start an EAP, it must decide on the type of delivery model. An in-house model is one in which the entire EAP staff is employed by the company. In an out-of-house model, a consultant firm is contracted to provide the total EAP staff. However, variations and combinations of the two models are possible; it is not a strict either/or decision. A company may use in-house staff to oversee the program, to evaluate it, and even to train the supervisors and educate the employees. The contractor provides only the actual referrals and assessments and, sometimes, short-term counseling. The reverse is also possible; the contractor may do the training, and the company provides the counseling. Another variation is that some units or divisions of a company might have a completely in-house operation while other units contract for EAP services. DHHS has an in-house program for monitoring and evaluation; however, counseling and supervisory training programs vary, depending on the region. New York contracts out all parts of its program, Kansas City is completely in house, and Dallas has a combination.

It is difficult to ascertain which is the best approach. When starting a program, many companies prefer the contractual approach because the commitment need not be long-term and because it is easier to cancel a contract than to terminate members of the staff. On the other hand, the in-house approach helps a company conceptualize what it needs. Regardless of the approach selected, I recommend that the company conduct a separate evaluation for the program and monitor it very carefully. If the company trains its supervisors, the contractor needs to be involved at least in a consultative capacity because supervisory referral and management consultation depend on the effectiveness of the training. Once the approach has been decided, the designing of the program begins.

When an EAP is being designed, certain ingredients are essential to ensure an effective, smoothly operating comprehensive program:

1. Program support.
2. A program plan.
3. A policy statement.
4. An information assessment and referral service.
5. Appropriate staffing.
6. A confidential record-keeping system.
7. A community referral network.
8. Appropriate location of the EAP.
9. Funding.
10. Resolution of the legal questions.
11. Training of supervisory and union personnel.
12. Program evaluation.
13. Employee education and outreach.

This chapter will discuss the first ten components; the last three are discussed in Chapters 3 and 12.

DEVELOPMENT OF PROGRAM SUPPORT

The support of the organization's key personnel is vital to the program's existence. This includes those people who make decisions that affect the EAP either directly or indirectly and those who operate as political allies to the EAP. Top-level support for the program must be ensured before its actual start, since program support is apt to "trickle down" but not "trickle up." Placing responsibility for the EAP at a high level in the organization demonstrates top-level endorsement. Such endorsement may also take the form of a signed announcement from the company president or vice-president for personnel. Management and supervisors must continue to show their support through program development.

Financial support must also be considered. The company must be willing and able to fund the EAP at an adequate level. This component is essential for assessing the company's commitment. Adequate staffing is also important. Programs with one staff member in corporate headquarters for tens of thousands of employees nation-wide are without a feasible method of providing adequate employee services. For every 3,500–4,000 employees, one professional full-time staff member is needed. I arrived at this ratio after counsulting with the staff of the accrediting organization for the national counseling organizations, which are the Family Services Association of America, the Child Welfare League of America, the National Conference on Catholic Charities, the Association of Jewish Family and Children's Services, and the Lutheran Social Services System. The ratio is for information referral and assessment, which consists of between one and four interviews. For short-term counseling, which consists of more than four interviews, the proportion of EAP staff members to employees must be increased. The ratio also applies when family members of employees are included in the program.

DEVELOPMENT OF A PROGRAM PLAN

A projected plan (for example, a three-year plan) for the program's development is important. The plan should be a fluid instrument, to be changed as appropriate and updated annually. An accepted plan that circulates through upper management also enhances the EAP's viability and purposes. The plan should delineate the values, assumptions, and goals, as well as the strategies for achieving the goals. The process for designing the plan should include:

- Having EAP staff visit a sample of the organization's various sites or plants. For example, when the DHHS program was being planned, visits were made to the National Institutes of Health (NIH) where some of the world's top medical researchers work; the Social Security Administration, where enormous amounts of data are collected routinely; and the Indian Health Service (IHS) reservation, where employees work in a very different system. Designing an appropriate EAP for such varied work sites was a real challenge.
- Studying the organization's existing systems and reviewing all existing policies to learn the potential interface with EAPs. For example, this will include the personnel system, the performance management program, the equal employment opportunity office, and the medical operation.
- Completing a demographic study of the employee population, including age, sex, level in the organization, and other appropriate information.

• Conducting interviews with the company's key personnel for their input.

DEVELOPMENT OF A POLICY STATEMENT

One of the early concerns in formulating any program is the development of a written policy statement. Some EAP personnel advocate that a policy be written before a program is implemented. If this is not possible, a letter of intent from the company president and a supporting letter from the union official, if there is one, are sufficient to start.

A policy must have appropriate input from those people of critical importance to the program. The DHHS policy statement, which is ten single-spaced pages, took two years to develop. The procedure for approving the policy was comprehensive and unique. After its initial formulation, the policy statement was circulated first to headquarters, then to the union, personnel, and each DHHS office throughout the country. The offices participated by sending back some 400-odd pages of comments, which served as the guidelines for a policy revision. The revised statement was recirculated to DHHS headquarters for final approval.

Too often policies focus on alcohol and drug problems, neglecting the broad-based role of the EAP in serving troubled employees regardless of the nature of their problems. The policy statement should include:

• The purpose of the policy. This is based on the organization's recognition that the work performance of employees who demonstrate problems may be lacking and that they may potentially be suffering from an alcohol, drug abuse, or mental health problem, as well as on the recognition that these problems are treatable.
• Organizational mandates for such a program and the source of authority under which the policy is being written.
• Location of the program.
• The eligibility of employees for the program's services. Whether to include families is an extremely important policy issue. The first question to be decided is how *family* will be defined. Will only those families sanctioned by marriage or by eligibility for insurance coverage be included? Many significant

relationships other than the legally defined family can cause dramatic changes in job performance. If family members are included, how will records be kept? If they are under the employee's name, then does the employee have access to these records? Would all family members be eligible? What about a minor child or a teenager or a wife who is separated and seeking a divorce? Clearly there are no easy answers to these questions. What is important is that the company's personnel, including the staff of the legal office, grapple with these issues before making quick decisions that can later result in problems.

- The integration of the program into the overall management systems of the organization.
- The roles and responsibilities of the various personnel in the organization.
- A delineation of the procedures for the program's use, especially the use of leave time to participate in the program.
- The record-keeping procedures, which must emphasize confidentiality.
- The criteria for professionally staffing the program.
- The importance of and procedures for supervisory training.
- Provisions for an evaluation of the program.
- The statement that an employee's participation in the EAP will not jeopardize his or her future opportunities.

It is imperative that the policy statement be signed by the organization's top management and, where appropriate, include a joint union support statement.

The guidelines for the DHHS Employment Counseling Services are given below.[1] All policy statements do not have to agree with these guidelines, but each company must deal with the questions they raise. Too many policies are only statements of intent and never address the serious questions relating to implementation.

- The DHHS ECS policy guidelines define alcohol and drug abuse as treatable problems in which the employee's work performance or conduct may be impaired as a direct result of the use of alcohol or legal or illegal drugs. Emotional and behavioral problems are defined as

    . . . personal problems which may impair job performance. Such problems include depression, anxiety, stress or psychiatric ill-

27

nesses, and those stemming from the alcohol or drug abuse or emotional problems of *another* person, such as a spouse, a supervisor, or a co-worker. Such problems can also stem from working conditions or the nature of the job itself.

- Employees who suspect they have an alcohol, drug abuse, or emotional problem, whether or not it currently affects their work, are encouraged to use the ECS voluntarily on a confidential basis.
- Self-referred employees who wish to inform their supervisors of ECS participation as well as employees referred by their supervisors may use work time to attend ECS for assessment without being charged with sick leave.
- Managers and supervisors play a critical role in the effective implementation of ECS programs. They are responsible for learning about ECS policy and procedures, for informing their employees about the services available, and for referring employees to the program on the basis of poor performance or misconduct.
- Manager or supervisor referral to ECS should be written as well as oral. The manager or supervisor may also wish to discuss the employee's situation with the employee relations office but is not required to do so.
- Regardless of the nature of the referral, the ECS counselor may not disclose any information about a participating employee to the employee's manager or supervisor without the employee's written consent. If the employee keeps an appointment during working hours, the ECS counselor is permitted to inform the manager or supervisor of that fact; information regarding the nature of the appointment or the employee's problem, however, may not be revealed.
- Whenever outside referral to a community agency or practitioner is deemed advisable for an employee, the ECS will refer the employee to the appropriate treatment services. The ECS will attempt to assure that the costs of such treatment are kept within the employee's financial means by using third-party payments, community resources with sliding fee scales, and self-help groups to the extent possible.
- Counseling records and information from employee visits, as well as all medical records, will be kept in a confidential manner, in accordance with Sections 122 and 303 of P.L. 93-282 and

implementing regulations; the Privacy Act of 1974; 42 CFR, Part 2, "Confidentiality of Alcohol and Drug Abuse Patient Records"; and the ECS case maintenance system.

INFORMATION ASSESSMENT AND REFERRAL SERVICE/SHORT-TERM COUNSELING

During the information assessment and referral component of the EAP, the counselor assesses the particular problem(s) of the client and makes a diagnosis. The counselor, as the key person, must possess the specialized professional skills requisite for an informed referral and diagnosis. Too many counselors view this component as merely listening to the client's statement of the problem and referring him or her to an appropriate community facility. This is the equivalent of a physician letting a patient self-diagnose. No reputable physician would refer a patient to a specialist without adequately examining the patient and making a diagnosis. It is just as critical that the counselor take the necessary time to render a proper diagnosis. This will spare the employee the anguish of being sent for inappropriate treatment. The real problem, as opposed to the apparent problem, which is often what the employee presents, must be determined. Although this often represents a difficult task, it cannot be sacrificed for the sake of expediency.

Some EAPs have considered extending the information and referral functions to include short-term treatment, which is normally contracted on a separate basis. This would be directed at the client who prefers the continuity of remaining with the same counselor throughout the various program phases. I see this as a major new development in EAPs. As staff members acquire more professional training, they can handle short-term counseling for a variety of problem categories. This approach may also be more economical because the company has more control and can measure the number of interviews more easily. I feel this approach merits attention because it makes sense from the standpoint of counseling as well as from a financial perspective. The assessment model originally was developed because many EAP counselors were not professionally trained and could not work with employees who had emotional or drug problems. In my opinion, the question of EAPs competing with community services in providing short-term counseling needs to be weighed, but short-term counseling should still be considered.

STAFFING

Staffing is perhaps the most critical issue in an EAP. The staff positions must be filled by practical professionals. By this I mean people practicing psychology, social work, psychiatry, and psychiatric nursing—the recognized mental health professions. However, because the field is so new, there are no degrees that automatically qualify a person to work in an EAP. Many social work schools try to cover the waterfront and train students for all phases of the human services in industry, but EAPs are a specialty and need appropriate courses and internships. However, senior facility who have actually run programs, and are therefore able to teach relevant courses, are extremely rare.*

Many programs separate the administrative and the counseling functions. Finding a professional who can do both administration and counseling in an EAP is difficult, although it may be necessary for smaller programs that cannot afford two positions. When in-house staff are being selected, it is important to consider the balance between administrators and counselors. It would be a serious mistake to emphasize only the counseling aspect of the program, since a large amount of staff time will be spent on such administrative and coordinating functions as policy development, training, and employee education. When considering staff for these functions, a professional with strong administrative and planning skills who has an understanding of business and systems analysis would be the most appropriate.

In addition, an EAP is a human services program usually located in personnel. Administrative skills are needed, and experience in running other human services programs can prove invaluable. Among my previous experiences before entering the EAP field were my positions as director of a community council in California, a family services agency, and a homemaker's program. These experiences

---

* I am currently developing at the University of Maryland an M.S.W. and Ph.D. program specializing in EAPs. The master's program will contain three core courses: "Human Services in Industry," "Administrating Employee Assistance Programs," and "Addictions: Counseling in the Workplace." Courses in personnel management and a variety of courses in the business school are electives. A one-year internship in an EAP in which the student specializes in counseling or administration, as well as a research project in the EAP area, will be required. The doctoral program will also have a core set of courses, and students will be encouraged to write dissertations concentrating in the EAP area.

provided excellent training grounds for administrating EAPs. However, I do not share the opinion typical of many business schools that management and supervisory skills can be applied to all fields and that knowledge of the subject—in this case, addiction and emotional problems—is not necessary. On the other hand, personal experience alone in administering a program for alcoholics does not qualify a person to be an EAP manager or supervisor. Administrative experience, knowledge of human services programs, and expertise with drug and emotional problems are all necessary.

Counselors must have demonstrated the ability to work in an industrial arena and to advise and assist managers, supervisors, and unions. They must possess excellent counseling and assessment skills, particularly in addiction, and have a thorough knowledge of the treatment resources in the community. All staff must exhibit professionalism, or respect for the organization will be lost.

ESTABLISHMENT OF A CONFIDENTIAL RECORD-KEEPING SYSTEM

All EAP administrators give lip service to the concept of confidentiality. The real test, however, is the implementation. How many programs train secretaries in confidentiality? How many keep files open during the day? Is case information typed into word processors? Where is the case coding system kept? Who in the organization has access to the files, and is this clearly delineated?

All individual case files must be confidential and be kept in a manner that ensures maximum security. The EAP staff, including secretaries and volunteers, should be advised on how to maintain confidential records and should be knowledgeable about the company procedures that outline the location and accessibility of records. The training of volunteers, then, becomes critical. There are very few in EAP programs, but they do exist and if utilized must be oriented properly. All files should be locked and, as much as possible, not identify the employee or give diagnostic information. Only the minimal amount of data needed for a counselor to work with an employee should be maintained, and only EAP staff should ever have access to the employee files. And procedures for accessing the files should be made perfectly clear. A professional associate of mine was forced to leave a program when she refused to make her records available to the director of personnel, because the company policy did not clearly state that only EAP staff would have access. Reports and statistical information should never contain identifying information on employees. I recommend that records be kept according to a coding system rather than by name of employee. In addition, procedures must be established for destroying closed files.

To foster the goal of confidentiality, the federal government has taken an increasingly pervasive role in the regulation of the release of medical records maintained by federally financed health care providers, especially those records that focus on patients treated for alcohol or drug abuse. In March 1972, Congress passed Section 408 of the Drug Abuse Office and Treatment Act, which regulated the release of information from medical records relating to drug abuse patients. Congress subsequently amended the Comprehensive Alcohol Abuse and Alcoholism Prevention, Treatment and Rehabilitation Act of 1970 so that the system for regulating the release of medical records of drug abuse patients was extended to cover the records of alcohol patients also.[2] Recent initiatives concentrate on extending this system of regulation to all medical records.

Because the federal regulations are mandated by law, they clearly depict the most stringent policies of confidentiality. If an EAP wants to ensure that its procedures fall within such stringent requirements, it can use these regulations as guidelines. Most companies, in fact, receive some federal money under government contracts and therefore fall within the boundaries of this legislation. In my experience companies prefer to be careful and to follow the regulations rather than to disregard them.

DHHS attorneys reviewed all case-coding and record-keeping procedures for the program before the policy was signed. The DHHS ECS Case Maintenance System provides for the confidentiality of employees' identity, diagnosis, prognosis, and treatment in connection with the ECS program.[3] The DHHS, therefore, uses a system of case coding that ensures the anonymity of each employee who participates in the program. The system maintains the degree of records security set forth under the provisions of the Privacy Act of 1974.[4] The highest professional standards are expected to be adhered to by ECS staff regarding client confidentiality.

The case-coding process allows the ECS counselor to assign an individual case code number to one employee's files and to enter the code number into the ECS system. In the case of a family member who uses ECS services, the record is made in the name of the DHHS employee. The counselor then reports the enrollment of the individual employee by case number to the ECS unit director, who later reports new enrollments and case terminations to the ECS central office in Washington. The case file standards require that each case file include only the information that is essential to the counselor in handling the case. All case files are labeled only with the identification number and are kept in a locked file cabinet to which only properly trained staff have access. Only the unit director, the counselor, and the designated ECS secretary for that program shall have direct access to all unit records maintained and are responsible for controlling all access to and release of information from these files in accordance with the provisions of the Privacy Act of 1974.

COMMUNITY REFERRAL NETWORK

It is critical that an EAP develop a network of community treatment resources to use in referring employees. It is the responsibility of the EAP staff to evaluate the available agencies or practitioners on their quality and adequacy of services. When evaluating a treatment facility, consideration must be given to its location, fees, and philosophy. For instance, when implementing a program for a highly professional clientele, I was informed that the employees wanted to use psychiatrists. I knew that many at that time did not support an EAP approach, so I had the staff interview the psychiatrists in the local community. They were asked questions concerning their philosophy on alcoholism and Alcoholics Anonymous. If they refused to be interviewed or did not support a philosophy of abstinence, they were not used as referrals.

When EAPs do not maintain an in-house staff and instead contract for assessment and referral services, they should ensure that the contractor refers to services other than its own. Careful scrutiny of the referrals used should be maintained by the EAP staff. Some treatment facilities offer free EAP services and training to companies because they are looking for business. It is a rare agency or facility that can handle all types of problems in all treatment situations. Some can, but this needs to be spelled out very clearly by the facility. As discussed earlier, setting limits for short-term counseling may also be feasible.

Once a network is developed, the EAP should establish a liaison with the key staff at each agency to ensure smooth coordination or referrals and follow-up activities. It is also important to update the network periodically. Staff changes occur frequently, and a good referral source one day may not be so good the next day. In addition, diversity in referrals is necessary. Too often psychologists refer to psychologists, social workers to social workers, and so on. A company must also beware of appearing to favor certain community facilities.

LOCATION OF THE EAP

The location of the EAP, both organizationally and physically, must be considered. Organizationally, it is vital that the EAP be located under the personnel functions. This follows from the basic premise that EAPs are connected to job performance, which is clearly the concern of personnel. Some companies place their programs in the medical units. In most instances, however, the medical units are under the company's personnel functions, so the relationship to job performance is still present.

It is also critical to consider the physical location of the EAP. First of all, every employee should have access to it. This means making provisions for handicapped personnel. Second, the program should be located so as to maximize confidentiality. In other words, it should be placed inconspicuously, so that employees cannot be identified as going to the EAP. It needs to be well furnished and located in good surroundings. Some EAP offices are inconveniently located and clearly make a comment about the company's opinions of the program.

FUNDING

There are basically four funding alternatives open to a company that implements an EAP:

1. The company assumes all expenses by maintaining an in-house staff.
2. The company performs all functions except for information and referral and/or short-term counseling, which are contracted on a fee-for-service basis and covered by the company insurance.

3. A flat administrative fee (approximately $3 to $5 per employee) may be levied by the contractor to the employer in addition to the fee for service. This administrative fee might cover such areas as supervisor training, start-up costs, and administrative overseeing by the contractor.

4. The company contracts out for a flat fee to the provider, who is not reimbursed by an insurance carrier. The fee typically ranges from $12 to $22 per employee. Services can include assessment and short-term counseling and may also include supervisory training and employee educational sessions. The fee varies according to the geographic location and the size of the client group (penetration rate). A company that is considering the per capita method would want to be certain that the costs are not higher than what their insurance company will pay out for mental health counseling. The company should negotiate for the per capita rate on the basis of an expected penetration rate and should not leave the fee open-ended.

LEGAL ISSUES

A number of legal issues are relevant to the EAP. Questions concerning malpractice and liability to the employee and to the company represent serious considerations that must be addressed when designing an EAP.*

Disclosure of Records

The federal regulations against disclosing records of alcohol or drug abuse clients are extremely broad. The rules apply to records of identity, diagnosis, prognosis, and treatment of any client and to the location of such records in connection with an alcohol or drug abuse program that is directly or indirectly assisted by a federal agency.[5]

---

* I have always had an attorney as a consultant to my programs. I am grateful to Frank J. Parker, an attorney on the faculty of the Boston College School of Business. Frank was the first attorney on my staff and trained my interns and staff well in the legal pitfalls of an EAP. Since then, attorneys on the staff of the Office of the General Counsel at DHHS have served as consultants for a variety of questions, from policy design to evaluation. Richard Friedman, in particular, has provided the expertise on the application of the Privacy Act regulations and accessibility to records.

Indirect assistance by a federal agency is difficult to determine. Each corporation should check with its own legal office before making such a determination.

Several types of communications are excluded from the coverage of these rules:

- Communications among personnel who need the information in connection with their duties.
- Communications in which the client involved is not identified in any way.
- Communications between the hospital and an organization performing such services as data processing, dosage preparation, laboratory analysis, or legal, medical, accounting, or other professional services.[6]

Federal law mandates that all records be confidential and be disclosed only as authorized by the regulations. No information is to be released unless the recipient has demonstrated a need for it. The regulatory prohibitions apply to all personnel of the program or anyone having access to these records and continue even after a person terminates his or her employment or relationship with the program.[7] Thus, anyone who obtains access to records covered by these regulations must abide by the restrictions in making any further disclosure of the contents.

Generally, the rules require that the records or information be disclosed either (1) with the consent of the client; (2) without the consent of the client, under certain circumstances; or (3) pursuant to a court order. Disclosure with consent requires that such consent be in writing and be specific to the release of records to the person or organization to which disclosure is made.[8] Disclosure without consent can be made (1) to medical personnel to meet a bona fide medical emergency; (2) to relatives of a seriously ill medical patient who is incapable of rational communication; and (3) to qualified personnel for the purpose of conducting scientific research, management audits, financial audits, or program evaluation. Disclosure pursuant to a court order requires that the applications for such orders do not use the real name of the client. This type of disclosure also requires that the order be given to the person whose records are requested so that he or she will have an opportunity to respond to the request.[9]

Right of Privacy

Although individuals are granted a right of privacy against improper dissemination of personal information, this protection rarely applies to routine disclosures of human services information. In general, invasion of privacy involves four primary causes of legal action:

- Intrusion by prying into a person's physical solitude or seclusion, such as invading a home or eavesdropping on private conversations.
- Appropriation of a person's name or likeness for commercial gain.
- False attribution of a statement or opinion to a person, which results in harm to his or her reputation.
- Public disclosure of private facts concerning a person—perhaps the most widely applicable cause of action for the invasion of privacy.[10]

Public has been interpreted broadly, with some cases holding that communication to one person is public.[11] The strict test to safeguard privacy necessitates that "not only must the fact be private, but the disclosure must be offensive and objectionable to a reasonable person of ordinary sensibilities."[12] Courts have refused to apply the protection of personal privacy to wrongdoing in connection with data collection on individuals. However, since much of the information stored in data banks and government files is personal in character and potentially embarrassing or harmful if disclosed, the U.S. Supreme Court has recognized a possible constitutional right to privacy involving a person's interest in avoiding disclosure of personal matters.[13]

These emerging legal mandates for disclosure of information to clients and third parties have important implications for an EAP. The issues of security, relevance of information recorded, accuracy of information, consent for disclosure, access by clients, and the process of informing clients as to the reasons and methods for the collection of data, retention of records, and liability insurance each represent crucial areas that demand analysis before the record-keeping system is designed and implemented. An EAP that is not careful about these issues may find itself in legal trouble.

Code of Conduct

The organization's code of conduct presents another area of legal concern. Company policy must explicitly delineate the code of conduct expected from its employees in addition to the punitive action that may be taken upon a violation of such a code. Breach of conduct can warrant a referral to the EAP even if the level of job performance has not been affected. Such a referral can often prevent an immediate suspension or firing.

For example, the code of conduct for all DHHS employees is publicized in a handbook published by the DHHS. The introduction states:

> Employees, supervisors, and management officials all share the responsibility for ensuring that high standards of ethical conduct are maintained within the Department. The employee is required to become familiar with the Standards of Conduct regulations and to exercise judgment to avoid misconduct and conflict of interest situations. Supervisors and managers must become familiar with the Department's Standards of Conduct regulations and apply the standards to the work they do and supervise. They also must provide advice and guidance about the HHS Standards of Conduct regulations to all employees.[14]

It is the responsibility of the organization to make this information available to its employees, but it is the responsibility of each employee to familiarize himself or herself with the material and seek the appropriate guidance for further information when needed. The code of conduct applies to employees both on and off the work premises. If an employee breaches the code after work hours or off the company premises and causes embarrassment to the employing organization (for example, by driving while intoxicated and behaving in a bizarre manner in public), then action may be taken whether it be in the form of a referral to the EAP, a censure, or a probation without pay.

Liability

Anyone can sue anyone, but whether one has a case or can win is another matter. It is important that all EAP counselors carry professional liability insurance besides relying on their company to protect them. Liability questions are so tricky today that it is prudent for the company as well as staff to be insured with appropriate and maximum protection. Although large companies do insure their full-time, permanent staff, they should also decide how to cope with the problem of coverage for volunteer workers. Smaller companies should make provisions for coverage for all in-house staff, including secretaries.

If staff are not professionals—that is, not social workers, psychologists, psychiatrists, or psychiatric nurses—how to adequately protect the company as well as the individual is a serious question. A number of recovered alcoholics without mental health training make EAP referrals for people who are not alcoholics. It is impossible to make a referral without first determining the problem, and a wrong diagnosis by a staff person not trained in such areas as mental health may expose the company and staff person to increased liability.

CONCLUSION

It is essential to raise new policy questions concerning the legality, efficacy, and ethics of new and emerging areas. The following are issues that EAPs will have to address:

- The use of social security numbers for employee identification in confidential record keeping.
- The use of the mandatory urinalysis and breathalizer test.
- The accessibility of employees to their own EAP records.
- The registration of a family member's record under the employee name or ID number.
- The use and abuse of sick leave, which, although a function of the personnel department, should include involvement of EAPs when appropriate.
- The application of the code of conduct off the work premises.
- Legal concerns of a confidential record-keeping system, especially in regard to computer accessibility to material for bona fide evaluation.

Each of the preceding areas must be analyzed according to relevant legal groundwork, ethical considerations, and efficacy to the functioning of the organization. The modifications that must be made when the analysis warrants change will undoubtedly have an effect on all the essential ingredients described in this chapter.

REFERENCES

1. These guidelines are based on the DHHS ECS *Personnel Manual*, DHHS Transmittal 82.16, August 13, 1982, pp. 2–8.

2. Pub. L. 91-616 303, 42 U.S.C. 4582, December 30, 1970, as amended by Pub. L. 93-282 122(a), 88 Stat. 131, May 14, 1974.

3. DHHS ECS, "Case Maintenance System," DHHS Exhibit 792-2-B, *Personnel Manual*, DHHS Transmittal 82.16, August 13, 1982, pp. B1–B3.

4. Privacy Act of December 31, 1974, 5 U.S.C. 522(a).

5. 42 C.F.R. 212 (1980).

6. 42 C.F.R. 3.221(p) (1980).

7. Daniel L. Human, "Release of Medical Records of Alcohol and Drug Abuse Patients: The Regulatory Maze," reprinted from *Journal of a Missouri Bar* in *Journal of AMRA*, January 1983, p. 21.

8. Ibid., pp. 23–27.

9. Ibid., p. 25.

10. Carol J. Schrier, "Guidelines for Record-Keeping Under Privacy and Open Access Laws," *Social Work*, Vol. 25, No. 6 (November 1980), p. 454.

11. Charles L. Egan, "Psychotherapist's Liability for Extra Judicial Breaches of Confidentiality,"*Arizona Law Review*, Vol. 18 (1976), pp. 1064–1094.

12. Schrier, "Guidelines for Record-Keeping," p. 454.

13. Whalen v. Roe, 429 U.S. 589, 599, 605, 51 L.ed. 2d 64, 97 S. Ct. 869.

14. "Standards of Conduct . . . in Brief," DHHS *Handbook*, Personnel Pamphlet Series 7, p. 2.

Chapter 3

Managers and Supervisors: Consultation, Training, and Referral

The manager/supervisor maintains a critical role in the EAP; the success and effectiveness of the program hinges on the availability of management consultation, proper supervisory training, and documented referrals. After a brief discussion of the characteristics of managers/supervisors, this chapter will address their role, supervisory training, the DHHS model training package, management consultation, intervention and confrontation, managerial and supervisory referrals, the supervisor's Bill of Rights, the role of labor unions, and employee education and orientation.

CHARACTERISTICS OF THE SUPERVISOR

The manager/supervisor, who is basically concerned with the behavior of the employees, is responsible for other people's work and must operate within an agency setting. The value of the manager/supervisor to the agency is, not in his or her doing the job, but in the enabling of numbers of others to do their jobs, thereby multiplying his or her effectiveness. According to Peter F. Drucker, the word *management*

> denotes a function but also the people who discharge it. It denotes a
> social position and rank but also a discipline and field of study. . . . It
> is an objective function and ought to be grounded in the responsibil-
> ity for performance. It is professional—management is a function, a
> discipline, a task to be done; and managers are the professionals who

practice this discipline, carry out the functions, and discharge these tasks.[1]

Throughout the rest of this book I am using the word *supervisor* to refer to a manager as well, even though there are slight differences in meaning between the two terms. However, regardless of whether the person is called a supervisor or a manager, he or she has the same responsibility for the effective performance of employees, and thus for my purposes either term is appropriate. I am aware that the word *supervisor* is not commonly used in university or high-tech settings.

THE ROLE OF THE SUPERVISOR

Perhaps the greatest single problem in implementing an EAP is to get supervisors to identify their subordinates with job performance problems. A combination of self-interest and sympathetic concern for the employee often leads many supervisors to feel it is their responsibility to handle the problems of the employees who report to them. In addition, many supervisors often feel that the need to bring such problems to the attention of management is a failure on their part.

The supervisor's role is to identify the troubled employee through poor job performance and to motivate the employee, through intervention and confrontation, to acknowledge that there is a problem and to seek help through the company counseling program. The supervisor alone possesses one of the most effective tools used to motivate the employee to seek help—the leverage of the job. One utility company states:

> The key to successful motivation of employees to seek help lies in the fair and constructive use of the supervisor's authority. . . . A mere offer of treatment is as ineffectual as giving lectures or repeated "chances." The employees must be made to understand that unless the problem (whatever it is) is corrected and job performance is brought up to standard, they will be subject to existing procedures for unsatisfactory job performance. They will also need assurance that utilization of the program will not jeopardize their job or opportunities for promotion.[2]

It is important to note that the decision by an employee to use the EAP is a voluntary one. The supervisor may threaten to start disciplinary action if an employee's job performance does not improve, but should never threaten to do so because an employee does not use the EAP. The employee may elect to go elsewhere for assistance that results in an improved performance on the job. The supervisor can strongly urge use of the EAP but cannot force it.

The supervisory responsibilities may be outlined in three steps:

1. Knowing EAP policy procedures.
2. Informing employees about the EAP.
3. Referring employees to the EAP.

The supervisor must learn to recognize job deterioration as the possible result of an employee's personal problems. The nature of a problem is irrelevant; the supervisor does not possess the necessary qualifications to diagnose or treat the disorder. But when these problems affect the employee's work capabilities, then it is time for the supervisor to intervene. As one farm equipment company policy states: "Referrals for diagnosis and treatment will be based strictly on unsatisfactory job performance which results from an apparent behavioral-medical problem in a previously competent worker."[3]

Perhaps the role of the supervisor may best be outlined in the following steps, as reported to The Conference Board by an insurance company:

1. Monitor job performance and attendance.
2. Document any deterioration.
3. Informally discuss with employee a need for improvement.
4. Give a time limit by which improvement must be demonstrated.
5. Discuss case with department manager.[4]

SUPERVISORY TRAINING

Supervisors sometimes cover up for a problem employee for many years before taking action. They may deny, promote, transfer, ignore, or become overly involved. However, supervisors rarely underestimate a problem. They will observe an employee's severely disturbed behavior and rationalize it. For example, a male employee was jealous of the attention given a female secretary. The office tolerated this behavior until he began to be rude to the other men who paid her compliments. The employee had no relationship with the secretary, and, although the secretary was married and complained to the manager when the employee started following her home, the manager did nothing. Not until the employee put up a "hit list" with the names of other men who had been nice to the secretary did the manager seek help.

Another example of inappropriate managerial behavior was when a young man was deserted by his wife, who left him with a newborn infant. In this case the manager was so upset by the employee's dilemma that he took the baby home to be cared for by his wife. As could be expected, this quickly became a problem, and after only a weekend they realized this was not the way to handle the problem and sought EAP assistance.

Allen R. "Pete" Martin, of the North Carolina Department of Human Resources, states that "the ultimate success of the EAP rests in the supervisor." Martin offers the following reasons for training supervisors:

1. Supervisory training provides supervisors and the program administrator with the opportunity to:

   A. Examine their own feelings.
   B. Develop positive attitudes.
   C. Become acutely sensitive to changes in job performance.
   D. Through active participation, become completely familiar with their company's EAP policy and procedures.

2. It is the supervisor, second only to the troubled employee, who has the most to gain from the program:

   A. The supervisor is responsible for meeting production quotas assigned to his or her section.
   B. Excessive absenteeism creates a need to locate a temporary replacement, and often the quality of work suffers.
   C. Many troubled employees create internal tensions which affect the attitudes and morale of co-workers, which in turn frequently results in increased mistakes, spoilage, and a general decrease in production.
   D. It is the supervisor who may ultimately have to make the painful decision to terminate a once valuable employee because an untreated and often unrecognized personal medical problem destroyed his or her ability to function at acceptable employment standards.

E. It is also the supervisor, through day to day monitoring, who is first and most aware of deteriorating levels of job performance, excessive absenteeism, and/or personality problems characteristic of employees with personal–medical problems.

F. Troubled employees often ignore or rationalize the efforts of family and friends, but it is not easy to ignore or rationalize the possibility of losing one's job.

G. In the past, supervisors relied on "gut feeling" or chance, or waited until a crisis developed to confront a troubled employee. Or the entire situation may have been ignored.

H. With an EAP, supervisors are provided with a tool they have not had before—a specific set of procedures that will be uniformly applied throughout the entire employee population.[5]

EAP training should always encourage the self-sufficiency of the participants, not their dependency on the trainer. Effective training must encourage problem-solving skills, with the EAP staff member as a backup resource until those skills become second nature.

THE DHHS MODEL TRAINING PACKAGE

The DHHS ECS supervisory training package was developed to provide a standardized format and sophisticated resource for the training of supervisors, who maintain perhaps the most pivotal role in the EAP. It is described as one example of a training package. Each program needs to design a curriculum of its own as a prototype that can be used as a reference.

The DHHS package includes a trainer's manual to be used as an aid in the training sessions, and is divided into three modules, each with instructions, time guidelines, and objectives. In addition, a film and a videotape, both entitled "ECS: A Supervisor's Alternative" are included. Other segments of the package are graphs and handouts. Finally, brochures for publicizing the ECS program are included.

The comprehensive training package is the result of months of dedicated efforts by many people at DHHS. It seeks to provide systematic training for:

1. Motivating supervisors to seek ECS support when confronted with an employee whose deteriorating job performance may indicate serious personal problems.

2. Enabling supervisors to understand the policy and procedures that apply to efforts to address the employee problem situation.

45

3. Equipping supervisors to recognize the performance and behavior indicators of employee problems and to respond to them effectively.

The three modules of the DHHS training plan are designed to build on one another in sequence: Module 1—introduction and case study; Module 2—film and discussion, followed by a statement of performance issues; Module 3—practical application and conclusions.

During the introduction, participants are welcomed and necessary administrative details are accomplished. The focus is to give participants a clear idea of why they are attending the session and what they can expect to get out of it. Participants should begin to understand the rationale for the ECS approach, to grasp key issues surrounding the program's use, and to have some idea of how the process works. The introduction is succeeded by a case study, whose objective is to stimulate participants to:

1. Recognize that they are strictly responsible for offering employees assistance through ECS, in lieu of or as part of a disciplinary process.
2. Recognize their critical role in motivating employees to seek help from ECS.
3. Analyze how they would respond to various manifestations of a troubled employee.
4. Begin considering possible indicators of serious personal problems and thus get a clearer picture of who can be helped by ECS.
5. Question their ability to single-handedly diagnose and deal with a troubled employee.

The case study is based on the salient facts of a case decided by the Merit Systems Protection Board (MSPB) entitled *Ruzek* v. *General Services Administration*, dated August 20, 1981. The case, which is discussed in detail in Chapter 10, involves an appeal to the board by an employee who had been removed from his employment following a history of poor attendance and performance.

Module 2 uses a training film entitled "ECS: A Supervisor's Alternative" as the central instructional and motivational vehicle. It demonstrates the ECS process in action and underscores the value of support from ECS, as it depicts the supervisor's struggle to come to terms with an employee whose job performance is affected by personal problems. This second module assists participants in learning how to:

1. Approach the dynamics of a troubled employee crisis with greater detachment and objectivity, and thus greater ability to take effective action. More specifically, they will be equipped to:

   • Recognize manipulative behaviors the employee may use to keep control of the situation.
   • Identify supervisor responses to employee problems and see that they are normal, even legitimate, responses to a difficult situation.
   • Appreciate other factors that tend to have an inhibitory effect on the supervisor.

2. Discern performance and behavior indicators of employee problems.
3. Appreciate the desirability of intervention in the early stages of a crisis.
4. Recognize that the ECS program affords an alternative to the traditional personnel management method of dealing with a job crisis.
5. Understand how the ECS program works.
6. Understand their own critical role in making the process work.

Following the film and discussion, participants are taught how to identify the manifestations of performance problems and how to state these manifestations in a clear, succinct manner.

Module 3 focuses on the practical application and is intended to help participants take effective action concerning a troubled employee. A role-play of the confrontation interview is done, followed by a discussion emphasizing the value of the referral memo. This conclusion of the session enables participants to raise questions and concerns, and makes them aware that ECS is present to assist the supervisors as well as the employees.

The total training session should enable participants to (1) develop greater confidence in their ability to confront the employee and make the referral; and (2) grasp the purpose, function, and contents of the supervisory memo that describes the performance problems and refers the employee to ECS.[6] Perhaps most important, the DHHS training process should leave participants with the knowledge that they can turn to ECS staff for advice on confronting the employee, drafting the memo, and making the referral.

A critical factor in supervisory training is to ensure that the supervisor has an outlet, whether it be his or her supervisor or the agency program coordinator, who will provide support and assistance.

MANAGEMENT CONSULTATION

The supervisor often experiences feelings of anxiety and uncertainty when faced with the task of referring a troubled employee to the EAP. The system itself discourages supervisory intervention in a number of ways:

- Complicity of other employees (covering up).
- Peer pressure to "tough it out."
- The supervisor's reluctance to admit failure.
- A prohibitive maze of rules, regulations, and procedures.
- Threat of discrimination complaints, grievances, or other retaliation.
- The supervisor's fear of harming employee's career or "making things worse."

The supervisor, like the troubled employee, must be encouraged to talk about the anxiety or negative feelings that he or she may experience in dealing with the troubled worker. Just as the EAP addressed the problems of the employee, the supervisor must have access to the appropriate agency person so that his or her concerns and questions may be aired in confidence. Talking with a counselor can help the supervisor come to terms with his or her emotions and achieve the detachment and objectivity needed to take constructive action.

The consultation between the supervisor and the EAP counselor is a vital component of the supervisory training package. The counselor can lend an ear, decide if the EAP can help, help prepare the supervisor for the confrontation, help the supervisor document problems and prepare a referral memo, and work with the supervisor and the employee until the problem is resolved. When seeking such help, the supervisor should be prepared to discuss job performance deficiencies and negative behavior (for example, employee personality change or breaking work rules). The supervisor must be assured that:

1. A visit with the ECS does not commit the supervisor to any action. The decision to confront, refer, or take action against the employee remains the choice of the supervisor.
2. The discussion of the case will remain confidential.
3. Asking others for help is not a cop-out or a failure on the part of the supervisor. On the contrary, it is good management.[7]

These consultation sessions help the supervisor determine if the employee should be referred, and if so, they prepare the supervisor for the intervention with the employee. The supervisor is helped to get in touch with his or her feelings toward the employee and the problem, and to accept those feelings as normal responses to the stressful situation. In addition, any apprehensions about meeting with the employee need to be accepted as legitimate; the supervisor, with the help of the EAP counselor, must learn to accept that the task is never easy or pleasant, and that there is no way that it can be made so.

INTERVENTION AND CONFRONTATION

Confronting an employee whose job performance has deteriorated is never easy. It is especially difficult when previous efforts to handle the situation have not worked, when tensions have built, and when communication has been strained or blocked. Writing a memo can often be the best way to handle it. If the memo is handed to the employee in the interview, it emphasizes the seriousness of the situation. It also shows that the supervisor means what he or she is saying. The following is an example of an approach the supervisor may use:

> I know you feel that you've been singled out for punitive treatment and that I'm out to hurt your career. You may even feel that I'm interfering in areas that don't concern me. . . . So in order to be objective and factual about your concerns, and to get my concerns out in the

open too, I've written this memo. I feel it is an honest appraisal of your situation. . . .

This approach allows the supervisor to introduce written documentation to silence any protests and futile arguments that are made by the employee.

Perhaps the crucial element of confronting the employee may be best summarized by the following list of do's and don'ts:

DO focus solely on declining job performance, and the offer of help.

DO have on hand written documentation of the declining job performance, so you can let the record speak for itself.

DO maintain a firm and formal, yet considerate, attitude. If the interview becomes a casual or intimate conversation, the impact of the message will be lessened.

DO explain that help is available through the EAP.

DO emphasize that all aspects of the program are completely confidential.

DO state that the employee's decision will be considered in reevaluating his or her performance at a later date.

DON'T try to find out what is wrong with the employee, and don't allow yourself to get involved in the employee's personal life.

DON'T make generalizations or insinuations about the employee's performance.

DON'T moralize. Restrict your criticism to job performance.

DON'T be misled by sympathy-evoking tactics. Stay focused on your right to expect appropriate behavior and satisfactory job performance.

DON'T threaten discipline unless you're willing and able to carry out the threat.[8]

SUPERVISORY REFERRALS

Supervisory referrals comprise the necessary mechanism to address the troubled employees who choose not to seek assistance on their own. Supervisors can be trained to help make a sensitive referral. The quality of the referral is determined by how early the problem is recognized, how the employee is confronted with the facts of his or her declining job performance, and how supportively the EAP and the coordinator's assistance are offered to the employee.[9]

Supervisory referrals are one of the ways in which an organization can measure the effectiveness of its program. The thoroughness and tactfulness with which the EAP staff trains its supervisors and provides outreach strategies is a measure of that staff's skill. Leadership and communication skills contribute to the quality of supervisory referrals.

EAP staffs depend on supervisors or union personnel to make referrals to the program. Supervisory referrals may be made for a number of appropriate circumstances. Karen Annette Lewis conducted a survey to determine these circumstances and their frequency.[10] In some organizations, supervisors are instructed to make referrals only on the basis of deteriorating job performance; in others they are given considerably more latitude in determining when to refer employees. Lewis's survey found the distribution of reasons for referrals indicated in Table 3-1.

Although 100 percent of the organizations surveyed refer employees for decreasing work productivity, only 78 percent refer the troubled employee who is suspected of alcoholism and drug abuse. It is not as frequently considered appropriate for workers facing other job-related crises to be referred—only 25 percent suggest referral for dismissed employees and 10 percent for employees troubled about being transferred.

Table 3-1

Frequency of Circumstances for Supervisor Referrals

Circumstance	Number	Percentage
Deteriorating work performance	68	100.0
(Frequent) tardiness/absence	63	92.7
Worker–manager/supervisor conflicts	45	66.2
Preoccupation with personal problems	56	82.4
Emotional upset	56	82.4
Retirement	16	23.5
Relocation/transfers	7	10.3
Dismissal/displacement	17	25.0
Suspected alcoholism/drug abuse	53	77.9
Others	3	4.4

NOTE: Multiple responses permitted.

SOURCE: Karen Annette Lewis, "Employee Assistance Programs; The State of the Art of Mental Health Services in Government and Industry" (Ph.D. diss., Northwestern University, 1981), pp. 47–48.

THE WRITTEN MEMO

Since intervention and referral are interrelated issues, there is an increasing emphasis on the written documentation by the supervisor. The specific incidents of inadequate job performance that led the supervisor to identify the employee as in need of help are recorded, and this documentation provides a clear basis for employee referral. This allows the supervisor to confront the employee with his or her deteriorating work performance and to inform him or her that refusal to cooperate with the EAP will result in normal disciplinary procedures designed to handle poor job performance. The referral memo serves to detach the supervisor from involvement in the employee's personal problems, provides essential written documentation of a consistent decline in work performance, and acts as the supervisor's record that an offer of counseling has been made to the employee.

The counselor assists the supervisor in preparing this during supervisory consultation sessions. It should (1) document the inadequate work performance; (2) specify that neither the documentation nor the referral to EAP constitutes a disciplinary action; (3) indicate that the supervisor has spoken to an EAP counselor; and (4) offer EAP services to the employee. If the memo is part of a system of records kept by the supervisor, the Privacy Act prevents its disclosure beyond EAP staff without the employee's consent. If an adverse action is taken against an employee who was given a written offer of EAP assistance and who subsequently denied having received it, the written referral may become part of the adverse action file as the supervisor's record of compliance.[11]

SUPERVISOR'S BILL OF RIGHTS

The supervisor's Bill of Rights is needed to combat the cover-up process in which many supervisors participate. This denial that a problem exists prevents the problem from being constructively addressed. The rationales for the cover-up might include: "I know he doesn't have a problem because . . ."

- He/she doesn't drink any more than I do (and I *know* I don't have a problem).
- He/she is the best person I've got (when he/she is here).

- I've known him/her for years (and I'd lose his/her loyalty if I turned him/her in).
- He/she has never missed a day of work (of course, with his/her usual hangover, he/she doesn't produce as much as he/she should).
- When we find a drunk, we fire him/her (but I don't want to be responsible for a person losing his/her job, so I'll ignore it as long as I can; maybe he/she will change).
- He/she is a fine individual. I know his/her spouse and family (and if I turned him/her in, everybody would hate me).[12]

By covering up, the supervisor is wasting an inordinate amount of time trying to deal with a complex problem that he or she is not equipped to handle. This iron curtain of ignorance can be lifted through supervisory training sessions, education, awareness, and management programs.

Arthur Purvis, a private consultant in employee assistance, developed the following Bill of Rights to help supervisors ask for help and to clarify what they have a right to expect once that help is sought.

Article I

When I ask my agency counseling program for advice, it:

(1) Is not a cop-out or admission of any failure on my part as manager/supervisor. On the contrary, it's good management. When I need a specialist—whether it's to fix a typewriter, program a computer, or paint a wall—I should get one. Helping a troubled employee is one of those times. Letting professionals do their job is part of my job.

(2) Doesn't commit me to anything. The decision(s) whether to confront an employee, to refer that person, or to take action against an individual remains mine. The advice I receive will be just that—advice, but it will be professional advice.

(3) Is confidential. What I say will not be passed on to my employee, my manager/supervisor, or anyone else.

Article II

As a supervisor I'm entitled to the following services from my agency counseling program:

53

(1) A patient, understanding, and professional hearing of my problems with and feelings about the employees whom I supervise.

(2) Assistance in working out those problems and feelings in a productive way, so my employees can do their jobs and I can do mine.

(3) Guidance and support in confronting my employees about their performance and behavior problems, where this is necessary.

(4) Competent and professional handling (counseling and/or referral) of employees I send for help.

(5) Follow-up with treatment resources to determine whether employees are receiving the services promised and whether they are following the prescribed treatment programs.

(6) Follow-up with me, to the extent permitted by confidentiality regulations.

(7) Continued assistance, as necessary, to the employee and to me in readjusting to a productive work relationship.[13]

ROLE OF LABOR

In November 1979, the AFL–CIO adopted a resolution favoring programs that are supported jointly by labor and management. The resolution pointed out that "negotiated union–management programs have proven to be the most effective method of bringing the many community services to our people who are afflicted with alcohol and drug problems."[14] Lane Kirkland, president of the AFL–CIO, later stated,

> American trade unions have a fundamental concern with the well being of their members and their families. Moreover, the labor movement has for some time adopted its policies and principles under the doctrine of improving the quality of life for the total community. We are also concerned about the cost of alcoholism to industry. . . . The AFL–CIO, therefore, has urged its affiliated unions to negotiate alcohol and drug abuse programs at the bargaining table so as to include this subject in their agreements.[15]

Although both sides—union and management—are in agreement on the goals of the alcoholism program, the broad-based assistance programs that deal with a variety of behavioral problems are viewed by many union officials as extending management's option to deal with mental health, an area of traditional union suspicion.[16] Such programs can be viewed as a device for management control of practically any form of dissent. There is also a concern that these programs may compete with similar services already provided by most major unions to their membership. Finally, these programs may lead to new and difficult collective bargaining and grievance problems, especially in such areas as the definition of impaired work performance.[17] Because of the diverse organizational makeup of American unions and their adherence to central AFL–CIO policy, there is a variety of union reactions to the broad-based EAP; some are vigorously opposed, some supportive, and some indifferent.

Thomas A. Murphy, chairman of the General Motors (GM) Corporation, offered encouraging words about the joint corporation-wide alcoholism recovery program of GM and the United Auto Workers (UAW):

> The spirit of cooperation was really essential to the program's success. Neither local management nor the local union working alone can always provide the level of motivation required for the alcoholic to help himself or herself. In fact, both GM and the unions saw case after case in the past where the alcoholic employees used both parties, playing one against the other, to perpetuate his or her drinking. So the distinct advantage of a unified approach was apparent.[18]

In a similar vein of support, the Texas AFL–CIO, co-sponsor of the Texas Employee Assistance Program (EAP) Symposium, voiced its desire that labor and management learn to work together for mutual benefits and humanistic solutions to the impact on the work site of drug and alcohol abuse. Jim Stinson, president of the Texas State Association of Painters and Allied Trades, expressed a strong need for the program as an effective alternative to current methods of dealing with personal problems that affect job performance. International union support was expressed by Guy Leber, general vice-president and head of the Department of Human Resources for the union. He indicated that such a program is overdue in the construction trades industry and that the international union strongly endorses establishing these programs.[19]

Unions exercise a strong influence on the formation and implementation of company personnel policy. The union can affect the formal organization, its climate, its efficiency, and its communication effectiveness with employees. It can approve or oppose company policies on such issues as job content, selection, and placement; job evaluation; performance ratings; and training.[20] The historical thrust of unions in the United States has been the emphasis on "shop rights" in an effort to prevent "wrongful discipline of employees by management."[21] Since job performance and productivity criteria usually are more easily applied to those in bargaining unit jobs, labor has naturally been suspicious of management programs that may be a guise for antiemployee practices. Perhaps this was why Leo Perlis, of the AFL–CIO, stressed that "while the effects of alcoholism in production and profits must be always a concern, labor feels that an industrial alcoholism program should aim at achieving a well adjusted human being not as a means to increased production, higher profits, and lower absenteeism rates, but as an end in itself."[22]

Yet despite these fears, there has been a substantial willingness on the part of labor to cooperate with the overall confrontation strategy that is the core of the EAP. The NCA has issued a series of bulletins and pamphlets prominently featuring well-known AFL–CIO officials who call for joint, cooperative programs. The policy recommendations are based "strictly on unsatisfactory job performance from which an apparent medical or behavioral problem, regardless of its nature, arises."[23] Whenever a union is involved, however, refusal of an employee to take advantage of the constructive offer of help must be managed within existing contractual agreements relative to job performance.

Labor's receptivity is also documented by the Smithers Foundation:

> Supervisors, shop stewards and union counselors play the key role in any company alcoholism program because they not only must serve to identify the problem drinker, but also must precipitate the job crisis by confronting the employee with the evidence of his deviant and unsatisfactory job performance.[24]

Bureaucratic methods of dealing with employee alcoholism must be replaced by the formation of a triad in which problem drinkers, union spokespeople, and management representatives relate closely. As labor starts to play a more integral role in the EAP, the need for such a triad becomes even more evident if a truly constructive approach to the problem is to evolve.

EMPLOYEE EDUCATION AND ORIENTATION

A necessary and vital component of any effective EAP is to ensure that employees are acquainted with its policies and procedures. The distribution of policy statements and procedures is the primary means of disseminating information about the program. Placing an article in the company newspaper is also an effective means of introducing the program and its staff to the employees. Posters displayed in the workplace may help publicize the EAP. Some companies even mail letters to the home of employees to describe the new program. This last method is often seen as beneficial in helping to break the alcoholic's denial.

The education segment provides an opportunity for employees to receive updated information about such topics as stress, alcoholism, drug abuse, obesity, and hypertension, which may be sources of difficulties for them on and off the job. Group presentations, slide shows, on-site workshops, and flyers are some of the many methods that may bring such information to the employee.

The orientation segment introduces the EAP to the employee; the goals and directives, the policy and procedures, and the specifics of the program are addressed, and the employee is given an opportunity to raise questions and concerns, either at the orientation session or in a confidential meeting or phone call. An orientation program can also introduce the company policy to the employee, as well as discuss such issues as confidentiality, release of forms, and availability of community programs. In addition, it allows the employees an opportunity to raise questions, receive additional information, or speak confidentially at a different time and location. Examples of methods used for employee education, either during this orientation or at a later date, are brochures, pamphlets, posters, videotapes, alcohol awareness weeks, films, speakers, and newspaper articles.* This combination of education and outreach is designed to encour-

* Marilyn Montgomery, ECS regional administrator in Atlanta, is currently developing a series of videotapes on (1) the definition and components of ECS; (2) self-test for alcohol; (3) health promotion; and (4) Valium. My film "Alcohol and the Working Woman" uses examples from my experience as the director of several EAPs in Boston to reveal the problems and solutions for working women with alcohol problems. My latest film, "The Marathon Woman," produced by Shepphard Pratt, Division of Professional and Public Education, focuses on the diverse stress experiences that most working women encounter.

age employees to refer themselves to the EAP department of the organization if they are experiencing problems. This is often the preferred alternative of many who wish to avoid a supervisory confrontation and possible disciplinary action.

CONCLUSION

The success of the EAP depends in part on the person who is in the role of the supervisor. The elements of self-awareness, confidentiality, documentation of work performance, intervention, and confrontation are fundamental to the supervisory training, which focuses on identifying the troubled employee through poor job performance. The supervisory responsibilities are extensive and diverse and are outlined in the comprehensive DHHS ECS supervisory training package. Management consultation must be available to ensure that the supervisor has an outlet to vent his or her emotions, problems, and difficulties relating to the troubled employee. Such consultation alerts the supervisor to expect an employee response of denial and allows him or her to plan for the confrontation that focuses on the employee's deteriorating level of work performance, rather than moralizing or becoming overly involved in the employee's personal life. This confrontation culminates with the written memo that documents the interaction between the supervisor and the employee and represents the company's acknowledgment of the problem and willingness to provide assistance.

REFERENCES

1. Peter F. Drucker, *Management: Tasks, Responsibilities, Practices* (New York: Harper & Row, 1973), pp. 5–6.
2. Cited in Richard M. Weiss, *Dealing with Alcoholism in the Workplace* (New York: The Conference Board, 1980), p. 14.
3. Cited in ibid., p. 15.
4. Adapted from citation in ibid., pp. 14–17.
5. Allen R. Martin, "An Approach to Supervisory Training for N.C. Occupational Program's EAPs" (Paper prepared for the N.C. Department of Human Resources, Division of Mental Health Services, Alcohol, and Drug Abuse Services, March 1976), pp. 11–12.

6. DHHS, "Employee Counseling Services (ECS) Program: Supervisory Training," *Trainer's Manual* (Prepared by Management Concepts, Washington, D.C., December 1981), pp. 1-6.

7. OPM, *Manager's Handbook* (Washington, D.C.: Government Printing Office, Spring 1981), p. 139.

8. DHHS, *Trainer's Manual*, handout #6, p. 3-6.

9. Anthea Stewart, "Increase Utilization and Development Skills . . . Through EAP Training," *EAP Digest*, July/August 1982, p. 31.

10. Karen Annette Lewis, "Employee Assistance Programs: The State of the Art of Mental Health Services in Government and Industry" (Ph.D. diss., Northwestern University, 1981), pp. 47-48.

11. DHHS ECS, "ECS Policy Guidelines," DHHS Instruction 792-2, *Personnel Manual*, DHHS Transmittal 82.16, August 13, 1982, pp. 4-5.

12. Doyle Lindley, "A Philosophical Approach to Cost Reduction in Industry" (Unpublished paper for Rechtel Corporation, San Francisco, 1970), pp. 1-2.

13. Arthur J. Purvis, "Getting Rid of the Lone Ranger Syndrome in Supervisors," *The Labor-Management Alcoholism Journal*, Vol. 9, No. 1 (July–August 1979), p. 25. Reprinted, with permission, from *The Labor-Management Alcoholism Journal*, © 1979, by the National Council on Alcoholism, Inc.

14. 13th Constitutional Convention of the AFL–CIO (Washington, D.C., November 1979).

15. Lane Kirkland, Statement from the *Proceedings of The Tenth ALMACA Annual Meeting and Exhibits* (San Diego, November 17–20, 1981), p. 73.

16. Hyman Weiner, "Labor-Management Relations and Mental Health," in *To Work is Human*, Alan McLean, ed. (New York: Macmillan, 1967), pp. 193–202.

17. Joseph Morris, "The Unions Look at Alcohol and Drug Dependency," *International Labor Review*, Vol. 106 (1972), pp. 355–366.

18. Thomas A. Murphy, Remarks delivered at the Association of Labor-Management Administrators and Consultants on Alcoholism (Detroit, October 5, 1979), p. 3.

19. Cited in Workers Assistance Program of Texas, "Delegates Voice Support for Workers Assistance Programs," *Health in the Workplace* (suppl. to Texas AFL–CIO *Labor News*), July 1983, p. 1.

20. Marvin Sutermeister, *People and Productivity* (New York: McGraw-Hill, 1963), p. 48.

21. Jack Bartosh, *American Unions: Structure, Government, and Politics* (New York: Random House, 1967), p. 46.

22. Leo Perlis, "The Human Equation: An Interview with Leo Perlis," *Alcohol, Health and Research World,* Fall 1973, pp. 17–21.

23. National Council on Alcoholism, *Labor-Management Approach to Employee Alcoholism Programs* (1973), p. 13.

24. Smithers Foundation, *The Key Role of Labor in Employee Alcoholism Programs* (New York: Plenum Press, 1970), p. 15.

Chapter 4

Consortiums

An EAP consortium is a cooperative agreement among companies and agencies that do not have enough employees to warrant their own EAP. Instead, they pool their resources and develop a collaborative program to maximize the individual resources of each company. Consortiums work best for companies with fewer than 2,000 employees; larger ones do better to set up their own EAPs.

With the majority of workers in the United States employed by small companies, the consortium represents a unique vehicle for the organization and delivery of EAPs. Although the government has set a good example in the development and implementation of consortium programs, it is in private industry, where the majority of persons are employed, that the consortiums have the greatest potential. The relatively recent development of such industrial alliances signals the need to examine various delivery models, their effectiveness, and the issues and problems pertaining to consortiums. The use of consortiums has grown tremendously in recent years, particularly within the federal government.

This chapter will discuss my own role in the development of consortiums in the private and public sectors, including the development and implementation of the first industrial and the first federal consortiums and the roles of OPM and DHHS. The discussion will also focus on the technicalities of running a consortium, including funding, use of advisory committees, the organization itself, evaluation, fee structure, and the counseling site.

CONSORTIUMS IN THE PUBLIC SECTOR

The Role of OPM

As stated previously, the Hughes Act of 1970 mandated that OPM serve as the lead agency in the development of EAPs in the federal sector. As part of this responsibility, OPM periodically releases Federal Personnel Manual System (FPM) Letters, on various areas of concern to the EAP development. FPM Letter 792–12, dated May 20, 1980, discussed the cooperative (used synonymously with consortium) employee counseling service program and includes a set of guidelines for developing interagency EAP programs. The guidelines are purposely broad, suggesting several alternative approaches. This is to encourage the development—in various workforces and geographic locations—of programs most likely to provide effective rehabilitation opportunities for emotional and behavioral problems.

The topics covered in the FPM letter include the cooperative program model and the development and administration of a federal agency consortium with contract capability (including preaward and postaward functions). The guidelines also include a sample memorandum of agreement, sample materials for a proposal request, and the responsibilities of the contracting officer's representative.

OPM further states that the

> development of consortiums first requires a survey of interest in participation among Federal installations located in close proximity in a given geographic area. The Federal Executive Association, if present, is a natural vehicle for initiating this. Department and agency heads are also encouraged to conduct such a survey and to establish appropriate cooperative programs for employees in their location.[1]

OPM was not always so involved in the establishment of federal consortiums. In the early 1970s, at the suggestion of William Pitochelli, OPM consultant in Boston at the time, I wrote to Alan Campbell, former commissioner of civil service. I urged the adoption of a position that would allow OPM to assume the role of the lead agency in the development and implementation of consortium programs, a role that had not previously been authorized. The commissioners granted the authorization, and OPM became the lead agency in Boston, with Boston College providing the services. Thus, the first federal consortium was conceived in 1974.

Then in 1977 the General Accounting Office (GAO) spoke favorably of this consortium and joint agency counseling programs in their report to the Congress:

> Boston College is conducting broad-based employee assistance programs at five locations in the Boston area—one is located in the John

F. Kennedy Federal Building. Although the program is being conducted under a NIAAA training grant, it offers the full range of services, including training supervisors and educating nonsupervisory personnel, training coordinators, counseling employees with problems, and referring these employees to community-based treatment facilities. In total, some 4,000 employees from 14 agencies located in the John F. Kennedy Federal Building are covered by the program. Based on information obtained from the program, the program appears to be moderately successful in getting alcohol abusers into treatment. Cooperative programs appear to benefit groups of smaller agencies located in the same building or geographic area. These programs are valuable because agencies can jointly utilize qualified staff to train supervisors and educate employees, to offer counseling services, and to maintain liaison with community-based treatment facilities. Further, these programs can often provide a neutral counseling environment outside the agency, thus reducing employee reluctance to seek assistance. We recommend that CSC and OMB support the development of consolidated employee assistance programs through Federal Executive Boards.[2]

The Role of DHHS

In 1979, the OPM Letter of Agreement stated that DHHS, when appropriate and when OPM is unable, may take the lead in the development of consortiums throughout the United States.[3] Since the writing of the letter, DHHS has initiated and is the lead agency in the following consortiums:

- The ECS consortium in Dallas/Ft. Worth, which services 3,400 employees in 25 agencies.
- The ECS consortium in New Jersey, which services 1,270 employees in 3 agencies.
- The ECS consortium in Atlanta, which services 3,000 employees in 2 agencies.
- The ECS consortium in Philadelphia, which services 9,864 employees in 26 agencies, both federal and nonfederal.
- The ECS consortium in Queens, New York, serving 3,000 employees in 3 agencies.[4]
- The ECS consortiums being developed in Hartford, Puerto Rico/Virgin Islands, Kansas City, and San Francisco.
- The expansion of the DHHS ECS consortiums in Dallas and Puerto Rico to include services to private industry.

Before an agency gets involved in developing an ECS consortium, two questions must be answered:

1. Is the consortium model best suited for the agency's ECS needs and resources?
2. How much money should the agency spend for an ECS program?

The DHHS standards for ECS consortiums provide the following information as a guide to the advantages, disadvantages, costs, committees, and agency agreements of the consortium model.[5] Briefly the advantages are:

1. The consortium decreases costs for small or medium-size employers.
2. Confidentiality is easier to maintain.
3. Often there is better identification of and communication with community resources.
4. The range of employees served is increased.
5. Usually the ECS staff has greater diversity and better credentials.

The disadvantages are:

1. Some supervisory and management staff are reluctant to deal with outsiders.
2. The service provider usually knows little about the participating organizations.
3. Consortiums are more complex because they include several companies.
4. There is some communication difficulty concerning role definition.
5. Participating agencies may disagree about the services needed and the apportionment of costs.
6. Some counselors find it difficult to become a part of the formal and informal work site networks.

Once a group of agencies decides that the consortium approach best suits its ECS needs and resources, a written commitment of funding must be obtained. ECS consortium development cannot proceed without it. There are several ways to structure cost:

Consortiums

1. Per capita assessments for member agencies. Agencies with a larger number of employees pay more than smaller agencies.
2. Flat fee for all participating agencies. Smaller agencies pay the same as larger agencies, on the theory that the time and cost to deliver such services as supervisory training and employee education are the same, regardless of the number of employees.
3. Fee for service. The cost of the services billed is tied to the volume of services delivered. There are two possibilities with this method: (1) each type of service is given a price tag; or (2) such basic services as educational/outreach efforts and training are billed by item to those who elect to receive them. The costs for other services, such as diagnostic and referral counseling, are included in the up-front per unit cost of service assessed to each consortium member.[6]

FPM Letter 792 states that the per capita cost for services provided by a contractor is based on total employee population covered, agency employee population covered, and total cost of the contract. In other words:

$$\text{Agency's cost} = \frac{\text{Total contract cost}}{\text{Total number of employees covered by contract}} \times \text{total number of agency's employees}$$

For example,

$$\$7,500 = \frac{\$75,000}{5,000} \times 500, \text{ or } \$15 \text{ per capita cost}$$

In some cases, an initiation fee may be included as part of the setup cost.[7]

In addition to cost, the key elements of committees and inter-agency agreements are essential to effective ECS consortiums. Each participating agency should designate a representative to be part of a steering committee for the planning, implementation, and maintenance stages of ECS consortium development. The goal of such a committee is to establish among the participating agencies a vested interest in the program's success. This committee should meet at least once during the program's planning phase and again before program implementation. Thereafter, the committee should convene at least twice yearly. In addition, one agency must be designated to serve as the principal or lead contracting agent for all the participating agencies. The participating agencies are then committed to the contract through a memorandum of agreement with the lead agency.

For example, when DHHS serves as the lead agency, a contractor must comply with the DHHS policy guidelines[8] (discussed in Chapter 2 of this book under "Development of a Policy Statement"). These include the five basic features of the ECS program: (1) administrative issues; (2) policy and procedure; (3) professional counseling services; (4) supervisory training; and (5) educational activities.

The administrative issues are the foundation for operating an ECS consortium and focus on staffing qualifications, accessibility, insurance, program evaluation, and billing and payment.

The professional counseling services require that providers be able to ensure services, which include diagnostic and referral counseling, community resources development, management consultation, and record keeping. The supervisory training component is designed to help key management officials understand their responsibilities and their critical roles in ECS program utilization. Training should always encourage the self-sufficiency of the participants, not their dependency on the trainer. The last feature, educational activities, includes program visibility and credibility, and employee awareness of health promotion issues.[9]

The DHHS consortium model complies with departmental policy and operates effectively within a limited budget. The consortium stems from a framework that is responsive to the diverse levels of needs, expectations, and resources, and represents one of the best ways of meeting the challenges that an ECS administrator must face.

CONSORTIUMS IN THE PRIVATE SECTOR

Taunton-Brockton Industrial Consortium

The City of Taunton, Massachusetts, 50 miles southeast of Boston, is essentially an industrial community with a residential population of 44,000. Taunton has a highly diversified industrial base characterized by small manufacturing, with the largest company employing 900 workers. A growing concern about alcoholism among the employee population was shared by three key persons in the community: the president of the Greater Taunton Council on Alcoholism, the administrator of the Substance Abuse Commission, and the executive director of the Taunton Chamber of Commerce. The Chamber of Commerce agreed to promote a meeting of industrial representatives to discuss alcoholism and employment.

At the time, I was project director of occupational training at Boston College Graduate School of Social Work and was invited to a special meeting of the Taunton Chamber of Commerce to explore the formation of a consortium similar to one I was starting with the federal agencies. I presented information about occupational EAPs, and an agreement was reached between ten Taunton companies and the Boston College unit. The ten companies would form a consortium, and the college would contract to staff the industrial alcoholism program for three years.

In September 1974, the first Boston College intern was assigned and began the process of planning and organizing the Taunton Area Employee Assistance Program (TAEAP), the first industrial consortium. The chief executive of each of the participating ten companies appointed a representative to the consortium committee, whose first meeting was held on October 15, 1974. This group immediately incorporated into a not-for-profit organization, which was legally separate from the chamber yet remained under its sponsorship. It defined the Taunton EAP as "a broad program" designed to bring resources and assistance to personnel in business and industry to deal with social problems affecting job performance.

The committee then identified the key elements of such a program:

- Assessment of the needs of Taunton and of individual companies.
- Formulation of consortium and individual company policies.
- Training of supervisors to identify and refer workers on the basis of deteriorating job performance.
- Development of an information and referral system.
- Development of materials for alcoholism information dissemination.

The committee continued to act as a board of directors and assumed responsibility for the program. They met monthly, and their enthusiasm and dedication were a major source of the success of the consortium. A division of responsibilities was agreed upon:

- The consortium committee would evaluate the program on a continuing basis.

- Individual members would be liaisons between their companies and the consortium.
- These members would implement program policy and encourage participation in their individual company's program.

Boston College staff would:

- Undertake general coordination, technical assistance, and implementation of consortium plans.
- Assist in policy development, training, and education programs in individual companies.
- Create and maintain a referral system with treatment agencies for use by participating employees.
- Provide intake, diagnosis, referral, and ongoing counseling to appropriate cases.
- Maintain a liaison with local community agencies.

Among the original ten companies in the program were a variety of Taunton employers, including Reed & Barton Silversmiths, Bay State Gas Company, Rand McNally Company, and two local banks. Employee population ranged from 40 to 875. Then in 1978 the city of Brockton joined with six companies, including Shaw Food Markets and Brookfield Engineering Labs. At this time the name of the consortium was changed to Employee Assistance Program, Inc. (EAP, Inc.). The employee range then increased to 1,500 for one company, and the total number of employees being served reached 7,834. Separate offices were maintained in each city.

Although this consortium developed as a result of a complex series of events and actions, certain factors are critical to the broad acceptance and heavy utilization of the program by participating companies. These key contributors are (1) the role of the executive director of the Taunton consortium committee; (2) program staffing; (3) supervisory training; (4) flexible treatment; and (5) cost-effectiveness.

The executive director of the consortium committee, Charles Volkman, provides the credibility needed to give the staff and the locally untested program an opportunity to prove themselves. He also effectively functions as a liaison between the industrial participants and the developing service, often communicating program needs, statistics, and issues to the board of directors of the consortium committee. Staffing expertise is ensured by the combination of

Boston College's knowledge and specialty in occupational alcoholism treatment and the EAP staff's community organization skill. The community organizers emphasize that the program was the creation of the community, not the college.

The goal of the supervisory training is to teach the supervisors how to recognize problems and increase sensitivity to and awareness of employee needs, and to educate them about alcohol, drug problems, and the referral process. Training, as well as employee education, takes place in each company separately. The flexible treatment stems from a careful assessment of each case and the establishment of the most appropriate treatment plan. This focus on the needs of the individual and the ability to treat within the program, or to refer to the appropriate community treatment resources, permits the achievement of an effective treatment plan and contributes to the high regard in which the program is held by employees and management. Individual monthly reports of program use are furnished to each company. However, careful measures were devised by the advisory committee to avoid revealing the identity of any employee.

In September 1984 the Taunton–Brockton consortium celebrates its tenth anniversary. This is a landmark event for industrial consortiums. The Taunton–Brockton consortium now employs two social workers full time and three half time, as well as several social work interns.

The Malden–Medford Consortium Plan

Another design I negotiated, in the spring of 1979, was for the Malden–Medford (two industrial cities in the Boston area) consortium. Nancy Kaufman, former executive director of the Tri-City Community Action Program (Tri-Cap) and a former student of mine from Boston College School of Social Work, first voiced concern about the high incidence of alcohol-related problems in the Medford community work sites. Kaufman was the vital inside advocate who possessed the necessary knowledge of the inner mechanics of the two communities. The planning group comprised five interns who were recruited to develop a feasible EAP model for the Malden–Medford business community.* All the interns were second-year

* When I left to join the DHHS in August 1979, Mary H. Cahill, my first occupational student, assumed the faculty role from the Boston College Graduate School of Social Work and supervised the activities of the intern planning group.

social work students at Boston College who had been placed in an EAP during their first year. Funding for the project was made available through the Malden and Medford chambers of commerce.

A needs assessment survey was administered to the business community in September 1979, and approximately 71 percent of the businesses surveyed expressed an interest in participating in an EAP. The interested businesses varied widely in terms of size, geographic location, function, and skill level of employees. But the majority had small employee populations and were therefore unable economically to support in-house EAPs of their own. Therefore, it was determined that a consortium EAP would feasibly accommodate the needs of these businesses.

Together the components of an EAP consortium should reflect a truly comprehensive and well-developed EAP. However, many consortiums choose to support a program that comprises only those components they can financially support or those that best reflect the specific needs of a particular business community. The components for the Malden–Medford consortium are:

1. Information and referral
2. Intervention (referral and treatment process)
3. Aftercare
4. Training and outreach
5. Prevention
6. Evaluation (of information and referral intervention)[10]

The evaluation, one of the most important components, measures the cost-effectiveness and success of the program. It represents a vital and authoritative source that assesses the capabilities of the consortium while revealing areas for further consideration.

CONCLUSION

It is significant that more than half of the workers in the United States are employed by small companies. Consortiums provide a creative solution to the problems faced by these companies and their employees. This special type of program design succeeds because it is able to assess and deliver services according to the unique needs of individual companies whose small employee populations prevent them from establishing independent programs of their own. The use of consortiums increases efficiency and economy without hampering program effectiveness or the essential internal administration of the agency, and confidentiality is also easier to maintain with this kind of EAP. In addition, consortiums offer the opportunity for several companies to share the cost of hiring an EAP staff that is diverse and very well qualified.

Because of these advantages, the use of consortiums has become increasingly widespread since the mid-1970s, both in the federal government and in the private sector. The number of consortium programs such as the Taunton–Brockton and the Malden–Medford plans continues to grow. And in the fall of 1983, ALMACA made the development of consortiums its highest priority.

Companies considering establishing or participating in a consortium should, however, bear in mind that there are certain disadvantages as well as advantages to this type of EAP. Some supervisors and managers are reluctant to deal with outsiders and may therefore hesitate to refer employees to the program. Also, the administration of a consortium requires a highly skilled staff who can relate to many diverse companies. This responsibility is not for neophytes in the EAP field. Consortiums can certainly be highly successful, but they require an inside advocate as well as an experienced professional contractor if they are to function smoothly.

REFERENCES

1. OPM, FPM Letter 792-12, "Cooperative Employee Counseling Services Program," May 20, 1980.

2. General Accounting Office, "Most Agency Programs for Employees with Alcohol-Related Problems Still Ineffective," Report to the U.S. Congress, September 7, 1977, pp. 61–63.

3. OPM, FPM Letter 792-12.

4. DHHS, "Summary Report on the Employee Counseling Services Program," Washington, D.C., August 1979–March 1983, p. 4.

5. Robert Mazzochi, "Standards for ECS Consortia Programs When DHHS Serves as the Lead Agency" (Unpublished paper prepared for DHHS, June 1983), p. 2. Mr. Mazzochi is the regional ECS administrator in New York.

6. Keith McClellan, "The Consortium Approach to EAP Services," *EAP Digest*, January/February 1982, p. 34.

7. Mazzochi, "Standards for ECS Consortia Programs," pp. 2–5.

8. DHHS ECS, "ECS Policy Guidelines," DHHS Instruction 792-2, *Personnel Manual*, DHHS Transmittal 82.16, August 13, 1982.

9. Ibid., pp. 5–6.

10. William C. Sproule et al., "Malden–Medford EAP: A Plan" (Unpublished paper submitted for graduate-level course, 1979).

Chapter 5

Alcoholism in Industry

According to the NCA, alcoholism is the nation's most untreated treatable illness, ranking third behind cancer and heart disease in total fatalities.[1] The most significant characteristics of the disease are that it is primary, progressive, chronic, and fatal. It is primary in the sense that it effectively blocks treatment of any other medical or emotional problem. It is always progressive—it never plateaus but always worsens, and when it is left unchecked, the disease is impossible to survive.

Alcoholism is defined as a chronic illness or disorder characterized by some loss of control over drinking, with habituation or addiction to alcohol, or causing interference in any major life function—for example, health, job, family, friends, or the law. George E. Vaillant in *The Natural History of Alcoholism* states that alcoholism, like coronary heart disease, must be regarded as both a disease and a behavior disorder.[2] He maintains that the number and frequency rather than the specificity of alcohol-related problems best define the clinical phenomenon known as alcoholism; no single set of traits can invariably do so. Similarly, there is no single, best, or only treatment for alcoholism; a combination of treatments (group therapy and vocational rehabilitation, for example) must be employed for maximum effectiveness.

The loss of control involved in alcoholism need not be total—loss of consistent control is sufficient for diagnosis. Dependence can be either psychological (habituation) or physiological (addiction). The interference with normal functioning must be notable or habitual— when the alcohol means more to a person than the problem it causes.[3] Problem drinkers, however, are often regarded as those who have had a single incident around alcohol, such as a teenager arrested for drunken driving. No matter which term is chosen, if alcohol interferes with any major life area, then there is a serious problem that demands immediate attention.

73

This chapter will discuss the scope of the problem, the disease concept, the addiction experience, the patterns and types of alcoholism, its stages, alcoholism in industry, women and alcohol, and the spouse and family of the alcoholic.

SCOPE OF THE ALCOHOL PROBLEM

In the country as a whole, there are at least 13 million alcoholics and problem drinkers. Of them, 3 million are teenagers who misuse alcohol. Figures for New York State are close to the national average in alcohol consumption per person, since New York ranks twenty-third among the states. Of the 14 million New Yorkers over the age of 13, about 1.4 million are alcoholics or problem drinkers.[4]

If, as estimated by Royce,[5] each alcoholic or problem drinker affects the lives of four or five other people—spouse, children, employer, employee, innocent victim of accident—then the 13 million alcoholics and problem drinkers have an impact on 65 million others for a total of almost 80 million citizens. Alcohol causes more than alcoholism. Numerous reports indicate that about 67 percent of child beating cases, 40 percent of forcible rapes, and 51 percent of felonies are alcohol related.[6] Studies also show that in 69 percent of beatings, 72 percent of stabbings, and 64 percent of homicides, either the attacker or the victim or both had been drinking.

Perhaps the most startling statistic is that automobile accidents in the United States kill more people each year than the 46,500 U.S. soldiers killed in the entire dozen years of the Vietnam War. Including the drinking pedestrian, alcohol is involved in about 52 percent of these fatalities.[7] It is impossible to measure, in dollars or otherwise, the value of lost human lives, wrecked families, deteriorated personalities, and human misery that stems from alcohol abuse in our country.

The high incidence of alcoholism is also revealed in the statistics of the health care industry. Americans in 1981 spent some $250 billion for health care. By the middle of the 1980s, health care expenditures will top 10 percent of our gross national product.[8] While the explosion of health care costs has received great notoriety, little attention has been paid to the role of alcohol as a key contributor. Many of our general hospitals are overwhelmed by patients with alcohol-related problems who are not formally identified as alcoholics or problem drinkers. The gap between hospital reports and research findings is wide in the emergency room: A 1979 Manhattan hospital study found that some 38 percent of the patients seen in the emergency room were alcoholics but that attending physicians had made no such diagnosis in more than two-thirds of the cases uncovered by the investigators.[9] Other studies show similar patterns: In 1977, interviews with 162 emergency room patients at Kings County Hospital in Brooklyn revealed that 25 percent were alcoholics. Yet only 40 percent of the patients identified as alcoholics by the interviewers were diagnosed as such by attending physicians.[10]

Beyond the emergency room, the proportion of alcoholic inpatients is also extremely high. At St. Vincent's Hospital and Medical Center in New York City, 53 percent of the male medical–surgical ward patients were found to suffer from alcoholism. Max Cleland, former head of the Veterans Administration, reported that 25 percent of the patients in VA hospitals were there because they drank too much.[11]

The inordinately high rate of admissions of alcoholics to both general and emergency treatment may be attributed to several factors. The physiological consequences of excessive drinking are numerous and include cirrhosis of the liver, hypertension, gastritis, pancreatitis, and cancer of the mouth, tongue, throat, esophagus, liver, pancreas, and bowel. In addition to these diseases, accidental injuries bring many alcoholics to the hospital. Although automobile accidents comprise the majority of these admissions, suicide and on-the-job accidents are also frequent. Up to 64 percent of attempted suicides—and 80 percent of those that succeed—involve alcohol. Estimates of alcohol's involvement in injuries on the job range as high as 47 percent.

The tremendous scope of the alcohol problem costs us billions of dollars in higher insurance premiums and higher taxes to fund Medicare, Medicaid, and many other federal, state, and local health care programs. By some estimates, employers pay nearly one-half of all health care costs, which are then passed on to consumers in the form of higher prices for goods and services. The health care price tag for an alcoholic or problem drinker exceeds $2,000 each year over and above the health care expenditures of the average nonalcoholic. If we could successfully treat just one-quarter of New York City's 500,000 alcoholics, the savings in health care costs would be $250 million each year.[12] If half the alcoholics employed by the federal government were successfully treated, the annual savings to tax-payers would be almost one billion dollars, according to the estimating formulas described earlier in this book.

THE DISEASE CONCEPT OF ALCOHOLISM

The philosophy and goals of prevention and treatment, length of recovery period, and attitudes regarding return to life in a drinking society all depend on a person's conception of the nature of alcoholism. The disease concept replaced the view of alcoholism as a crime and a sign of moral depravity or weakness of the will, with the view that it is an illness to be understood and treated rather than punished. Alcoholism became the respectable object of scientific research, as it gained acceptance by various professional organizations and as E. M. Jellinek's book *The Disease Concept of Alcoholism*[13] also won approval. The AMA's acceptance in 1956 of alcoholism as a disease was important in obtaining medical insurance coverage for alcoholism treatment, and in the acceptance of occupational alcoholism programs for employees. The acceptance of the term by the World Health Organization (WHO) in the early 1970s helped the alcoholic admit the need for help and removed the stigma of moral degeneracy associated with earlier theories. The disease concept replaced guilt with self-respect and dispelled the folklore surrounding the myths of alcoholism and its victims.

Popular arguments against the disease concept include:

1. The disease concept is incompatible with many treatment approaches.
2. Alcoholism cannot be a disease because it is self-inflicted.
3. Alcoholism is not just physical, hence it cannot be called a disease.

Yet each of the preceding assertions is fallacious. Treatment approaches, from aversive conditioning to the spiritual approach of AA, often allow people to accept the disease concept, since many treatment programs are based on its acceptance. A person chooses to drink, not to be an alcoholic, and a person never gives up alcoholism any more than a person gives up diabetes. It is a disease that cannot be cured, but can be controlled.

No one word can adequately describe the cycle of repeated promises, relapses, remorse, resolutions, renewed efforts, and broken families that alcoholism engenders. *Sickness* usually connotes mental disorder; *behavior disorder* implies a purely learned reaction and does not account for psychological or physiological addiction; *illness* is often construed as a primary physical disorder; and *disease* connotes bacteria and is often rendered unacceptable. Although none of these terms matches precisely the nature of alcoholism, this cannot be used to invalidate the disease concept.[14]

Other arguments against the disease model cannot so easily be dismissed. For instance, can an alcoholic be excused from all responsibility for debts incurred on the grounds that he or she is sick? Can an alcoholic be excused for crimes committed while intoxicated, and can a drunk driver be excused for causing injury or death to others? The disease model also creates guilt feelings for the person who vowed to keep his or her spouse "in sickness and in health." Lastly, the disease concept implies full acceptance of the medical model, yet surveys reveal that the average American physician is still both reluctant to treat alcoholics and often ignorant about alcoholism, and the average medical student's education today does not include a required course on addiction.

The alcohol field as it stands today is divided, as the holistic view of pathological drinking gains renewed acceptance. The view considers alcoholism as a pathology in its own right, not merely a symptom of something else. It takes into account the multifaceted aspects of alcoholism—heredity, the environment, and medical and psychological factors, including addiction and learned behavior. The AMA's interpretation of alcoholism as a disease states that "the treatment primarily involves merely not taking a drink . . . most alcoholics cannot break the cycle alone."[15]

The disease concept points to physiological differences as a reason why 1 in 7 drinkers becomes an alcoholic, a focus that has important implications for long-term recovery. The view of alcoholism as a chronic disease prompted studies that concluded that it may take years for the alcoholic body to return to normal, if ever, and that the drop in tolerance to alcohol common in late-stage alcoholics seems to be irreversible. Even after years of sobriety, a relapse would place the alcoholic at the stage where he or she quit, not at the start of social drinking. Although one drink may not trigger a relapse, if continued, the drinking may get out of control. The alcoholic must learn to accept the fact that he or she has an enduring disposition to alcohol at all times—even when the person is not drinking. Hence, the statement "I *am* an alcoholic" rather than "I *was* an alcoholic" more adequately represents the case of the "recovered" alcoholic who now controls the disease but has not been cured.[16]

THE ADDICTION EXPERIENCE

Stanton Peele debunks the myth of a single biochemical source for addiction. In its place he develops a complex social, psychological, and physiological model of addiction based on the role filled in a person's life by the experience with a given drug. "Addiction," he maintains,

> is not caused by a drug or its chemical properties. Addiction has to do with the effect a drug produces for a given person in given circumstances—a welcomed effect which relieves anxiety, and which (paradoxically) decreases capability so that those things in life which cause anxiety grow more severe. What we are addicted to is the experience the drug creates for us.[17]

Peele believes that the cycle of addiction begins as the person retreats to the drug to avoid coping. Soon those things with which he or she must cope become less manageable and more frightening to contemplate. The negative self-image and low self-esteem on which the surrender to the drug is based are key points in the descent into addiction.

Peele maintains that the disease theory of alcoholism is designed to convey the helplessness of the victims and to offer an explanation that removes the primary responsibility from them and places it somehow on their bodies. His theory, on the other hand, focuses on the strength of our culture's orientation toward individual accomplishment and responsibility in which many people feel trapped by feelings of inadequacy. The loss of control that we experience in an increasingly institutionalized society further aggravates the problem. Addiction, in Peele's view, is not a chemical reaction to one drug or another. Rather, it is an organic outgrowth of a person's relationship to the world. He states, "Addiction is a lifestyle, a way of coping with the world and ourselves, a way of interpreting our experience. It is the way the person interprets and responds to the impact of a drug which is at the core of addiction."[18]

PATTERNS AND TYPES OF ALCOHOLISM

Alcoholism is not a single disease entity any more than cancer is; it is a multiple illness, which justifies the growing trend toward use of the term *alcoholisms*. The best-known classification is that presented by the late E. M. Jellinek, who deliberately identified his various types of alcoholics by the letters of the Greek alphabet to avoid names that might imply theories of cause or nature.[19] These types—alpha, beta, gamma, delta, and epsilon—do not represent stages of progression.

Alpha: This is purely a psychological dependence on alcohol that is marked by poor frustration tolerance or inability to cope with tensions. Alcohol is used to boost morale, block out reality, bolster self-confidence, or relieve emotional or bodily pains. There is little or no progression and a lack of physical addiction or withdrawal symptoms, although some nutritional deficiences of alcoholism can occur.

Beta: This is a social dependence on alcohol, without either psychological or physical dependence. The cause of drinking is largely sociocultural or situational and is common in occupations where "everybody" gets drunk every weekend. This heavy social dependence is one of the major obstacles in long-term rehabilitation of chronic alcoholics.

Gamma: This is the chronic, progressive type of alcoholism, most commonly seen in American males. Psychological dependence progresses to physical dependence. Control over how much one drinks is lost, and a person's tolerance to alcohol is increased. This is the classic instance of habitual addiction. The gamma type is the most responsive to the AA approach.

Delta: This is often called the "maintenance drinker," the alcoholic who has lost control over when rather than how much he or she drinks. Inability to abstain, rather than inability to stop once they start, is the characteristic. Increased tolerance and severe withdrawal symptoms (delirium tremens, or DTs) are common. Deterioration is gradual, and, because the drinking rarely precipitates a crisis, this is not a very visible group. A delta type may never have been drunk in his or her life.

Epsilon: This is the periodic or binge drinker who abstains without difficulty for long periods but, once started, drinks heavily until passing out. He or she may experience no craving or struggle to maintain sobriety and may keep liquor at home without being tempted to indulge. The physical and psychological dependence leads to a loss of control and possibly more severe organic damage than the previous four types.

Some have added a sixth type—the *Zeta* alcoholic (akin to pathological intoxication) who gets violent when he or she drinks. There are also numerous subdivisions of alcoholics, who are distinguished by their drinking patterns and their reactions to alcohol.

The common characteristics shared by the various types of alcoholics include confusion, the search for magic, negative feelings, and assorted coping devices. Confusion arises because the alcoholic is able to recall periods of normal social drinking that did not have unpleasant effects. Many even have happy memories of boisterous good times from early drinking experiences. This incongruity between images from the past and present misery adds to the confusion. The search for magic represents the unfounded hope that if one searches hard enough and long enough, one can find a way to control and enjoy drinking. The negative feelings that the alcoholic experiences range from remorse, guilt, shame, and self-hatred to depression and feelings of hopelessness, futility, loneliness, and alienation.[20]

Ironically, many of these feelings are augmented by alcohol. The alcoholic develops elaborate defense mechanisms or coping devices to escape from these feelings. For example, rationalization is used to find a reason why one should have a drink—to relax, to go to sleep, to avoid offending someone, to celebrate, and so on. Another device is projection of blame onto the spouse, the boss, the parents, the police, or the system. This draws others into the delusional system of the alcoholic and often becomes the excuse for drinking. Denial, like rationalization, allows the alcoholic to kid him- or herself into believing that no problem exists. Such denial is often reinforced by others refusing to accept that a loved one, co-worker, or friend may have a serious drinking problem. Even professionals are often involved in the denial system. In one study, 91 percent of the clergy saw a need for alcohol programs in the nation, but only 40 percent saw a need in their own congregations.[21]

High-Risk Groups

It is helpful to be aware that certain groups have a high statistical probability of becoming alcoholics. In *Alcohol Problems and Alcoholism*, Royce includes the following factors as indicators of high risk:

- A family history of alcoholism, including parents, siblings, grandparents, uncles, and aunts. This does not necessarily mean that alcoholism is a result of heredity. It could mean that the environment in which a person grew up condoned heavy drinking and alcoholism, and the child saw this as normal behavior. Just as children of smokers have a much higher chance of being smokers, the same holds for alcoholics. The parents as role models are a powerful force that is difficult to counter.
- A history of total abstinence in the family, particularly where strong moral overtones were present and, most particularly, where the social environment of the person has changed to one in which drinking is encouraged or required.
- A history of alcoholism or teetotalism in the spouse or in the family of the spouse.
- A broken home or a home with much parental disorder, particularly where the father was absent or rejecting but not punitive.
- A lack of leisure activities that do not involve drinking; most activities focus on meeting friends for a drink or discussing business over cocktails.
- Membership in a cultural group having a high incidence of alcoholism (for example, the Irish, Native Americans, the French, or Scandinavians).
- A history of more than one generation of female relatives, who have had a high incidence of recurrent depressions.
- The incidence of heavy smoking; heavy drinking is often associated with heavy smoking, but the reverse need not be true.
- A tendency to use other psychoactive drugs.
- Confused and inconsistent attitudes about one's own drinking, even with no conflict about drinking by others.[22]

STAGES OF ALCOHOLISM

It is easy to diagnose alcoholism in the last deteriorative stages. The challenge is to recognize the early signs that are important in allowing intervention to prevent the disease. Studies have shown that alcohol addiction progresses through early, middle, and late stages, and that each stage has characteristic symptoms.

The early stage is characterized by increased tolerance to alcohol, drinking to relieve tension, occasional memory lapses, preoccupation with alcohol, and lying about how much and how often one is drinking. Gradually, this progressive loss of control leads to the middle stage, which is characterized by increased rationalization devices and difficulty in coping with one's job and family. Unreasonable resentments, suspiciousness, irritability, self-pity, and remorse are common in the middle stage. The alcoholic begins to hide liquor and neglect food, and often encounters legal and financial trouble. Physical signs, which become apparent in the middle to late stage, may include acid stomach, insomnia, morning cough, sweating, and elevated blood pressure and pulse.

Binge drinking, coupled with loss of tolerance for alcohol, can culminate in the late stage of alcoholism. In this final stage drinking becomes an obsession. Impaired thinking, tremors, dry heaves, and hospitalization are common. By this time the alcoholic has usually run out of alibis.[23]

ALCOHOLISM IN INDUSTRY

According to one study, 60 out of every 1,000 American workers must have a continuous level of alcohol in their bloodstreams in order to perform their daily jobs.[24] These late-stage alcoholics hide liquor supplies in lunch pails, thermos bottles, and pocket flasks; stow it in lockers and desk drawers; and mask it in coffee mugs and styrofoam cups. Middle-stage alcoholism in the workplace is even more common. Less than a decade ago, alcoholism was labeled industry's "$1 billion hangover." Since then, estimates of cost to industry have risen to more than $20.6 billion each year, while published estimates of the losses to society as a whole are pushing the $45 billion mark.[25] This increasing loss to American businesses is the product of the epidemic growth of alcoholism in our society. The country's 13 million alcoholics are men and an increasing number of women, most of whom are between the ages of 35 and 50 and, despite their illness, hold full-time jobs. Of the 6.5 million employed alcoholics, 25 percent are white collar workers, 30 percent blue collar workers, and 45 percent professionals and managers.[26] A study to assess the frequency of alcohol problems among male and female employees in selected federal agencies and manufacturing companies with ongoing occupational alcoholism or EAP programs surveyed randomly selected employees about their alcohol-related behavior as well as about demographic and occupational characteristics. Results indicated the incidence of alcohol problems to range from 9.2 percent to 17.5 percent for women and from 20.0 percent to 29.9 percent for men.[27]

The growing national concern for the high incidence of alcoholism, coupled with the increasing loss to business, paved the way for the development of alcoholism programs in industry. The tools with which such programs were built evolved over several decades. The first was the formation of AA in the 1930s, which provided a social-psychological group treatment method that can be applied almost universally to all social levels and ethnic groups. The second was the recognition of alcoholism as a disease by the AMA in 1956, which removed the moral stigma and allowed the alcoholic to be regarded and treated as an ill person, not as an outcast of society. It also opened the way to health insurance coverage for alcoholism.

In the 1970s, stimulated by the success of the early programs, managers of businesses came to recognize that a similar activity in their plants not only had the potential for rehabilitating employees who were alcoholics but also could achieve major financial savings by improving attendance and work performance. Also, the necessity of costly training of new employees as replacements for dismissed alcoholics could be avoided. As a result, these managers provided the third and fourth tools, money and official support, for the development of effective rehabilitation units. The last tool was the evolution of the now familiar technique of confronting an employee suspected of having an alcohol problem and offering a choice of accepting help through a rehabilitation program or facing disciplinary action, possibly dismissal.

By the time the work problems of the alcoholic are apparent, multiple social problems have developed, including financial difficulties, threat of divorce or actual separation, and disturbed children. The threat of job and income loss seems to mean more to many alcoholics than any other consideration—the average alcoholic gives up his family seven years before he gives up his or her job.[28] The importance of a job is perhaps related to social recognition, personal self-worth, identity, security, and stability.

Confrontation is the most effective technique that can be used with executives, according to James Kemper, chairman of the Kemper Group and a recovered alcoholic. He states, "The last thing that an alcoholic voluntarily gives up is his right to drink." It is the importance to the alcoholic of holding a job that grants the employer the necessary leverage to intervene and confront the alcoholic employee. It prompted former secretary of health, education, and welfare Joseph Califano to publicly launch his special initiative to control alcoholism and concentrate on the workplace as the most effective arena in which to control the problem. The threat of job loss is perhaps the most powerful tool that can be used to increase worker productivity and morale, an increase that results from a successful referral to an EAP.

WOMEN AND ALCOHOL

The relationship between women and alcohol remains one of the most neglected areas of research in the field of alcoholism. Although data on this subject are often scattered and deficient, certain conclusions are expressed frequently: Women usually turn to drinking because of a specific life situation; women most often follow a pattern of drinking alone; women drinkers prove more harmful to themselves and others than do men; and women in treatment show poorer results than do men.[29] Studies reveal that women who drink heavily are more likely than male social drinkers to be "escapist drinkers"[30] and that female alcoholics are more frequently found to have been deprived of one or more parents at an early age than are male alcoholics.[31] Sheila Blume, former commissioner of alcoholism for the State of New York, identified several other facts about women and alcohol:

- Women alcoholics are more likely to attempt suicide than men alcoholics.
- Women are often misdiagnosed as having a history of psychiatric illness rather than alcohol abuse.
- Women are more dependent on secondary drugs than are men.
- Women do not experience blackouts and DTs as much as men do.
- Women start drinking alone later than men do; however, since the effects of alcohol accelerate faster in women, men and women tend to enter treatment at the same age.
- For women, alcohol is primary and depression is secondary; for men, alcohol is primary and psychopathic behavior is secondary.
- Pregnant women often experience the fetal alcohol syndrome (FAS); excessive and continued alcoholic intake by pregnant women is the third largest cause of retardation in children.[32]

Alcoholism in Industry

Although differences in drinking patterns may be noted, the scope of alcoholism among women is not known with certainty. Over the last few decades, problem drinking and alcoholism surveys have reported male–female ratios ranging from 8 to 1 to 4 to 1. But these statistics, like many, are low because of inherent male bias in most alcoholism surveys. Nearly all these surveys measure problem drinking partially on the basis of how much alcohol a person consumes; however, the same consumption level is used for both men and women, even though women weigh 40 pounds less than men on the average and are thus likely to become drunk on substantially less alcohol. Further, in responding to survey questions, women may be more likely than men to minimize alcohol-related problems because of more intense guilt and shame. Consequently, when women's advocates demand more treatment programs and related services for women, budget directors of alcoholism agencies point to the low survey statistics and ask: Why should we spend money on women when women aren't having the problems? And the available money is used for yet another program for skid row men, or for an outreach program for a male-intensive industry, or for a study of male drinking patterns in working class taverns.[33]

Although recent surveys show that the American public understands the effects of alcohol better than it did in the past, these same surveys underscore the lack of change in attitude toward alcoholism. Since women have always been perceived as upholding and perpetuating the moral standards of society, their nonconformity to these standards are, indeed, judged harshly. The deviation of a woman from society's moral standards quite clearly seems to result in a differential perception of her behavior. Alcoholic women, like all women, have internalized this differential perception. As stated by Eileen M. Corrigan, a professor at the Graduate School of Social Work at Rutgers University, "Change may occur when both women and men equally share in responsibility for societal standards and when the perception of alcoholism is moved out of the moral domain and into the mainstream of the dependencies."[34]

Working Women and EAPs

The statistical picture of working women in general reveals further insights. According to occupational program practitioners, female alcoholic workers do not frequently use existing company programs for help with their problems. Moreover, little attention has

85

been paid to the strategies of identifying and referring female employees to company programs, or to the possible differences in approach that might be needed for women versus men. Existing models for identification are based on job criteria developed for men. Labor and management studies are increasingly concerned with the effects of female employees on male supervisory personnel; frequently, traditional sex role stereotypes are at the base of supervisory attitudes. In this sense, management's expectations of female employees are different from its expectations of male employees—generally, less is expected of women—and it may be that women are able to get by with less than satisfactory job performance. While female and male alcoholism may be manifested in a similar way in the workplace, outreach techniques may need to be changed to allow women equal entry into treatment.

Congressional legislation directed the NIAAA to support efforts to assess and meet the needs of the female alcoholic in the workplace. On September 1, 1978, the Occupational Program Branch of the NIAAA contracted with several evaluation teams, including the Planners Studio (PS), to conduct a demonstration project for women in the field of occupational alcoholism. The objectives of the three-year contract awarded to the Planners Studio were fourfold:

1. To describe alcoholism in selected work settings in terms of frequency of occurrence among female employees, male-female differences, and special needs among the female workforce, as well as the success of the existing alcoholism program.
2. To design components for an existing EAP that would address the needs of a targeted female employee group.
3. To measure changes in effects within the existing program by adding a special component designed for female employees.
4. To establish parameters by which future project efforts involving women as a target population can be evaluated and improved.[35]

The Planner's Studio study revealed that fewer female clients compared to male clients stated their problems as alcohol related on entry to the EAP. In addition, fewer women had a chance of being referred to inpatient alcohol treatment, even though they might have indicated binge drinking or problem use of alcohol to a counselor. Lack of child-care coverage, as well as lower average incomes, made a 28-day treatment impractical for some women. The researchers contend that, in addition to the changes in management training, some changes in the focus and content of nonmanagement employee education might result in more self-referrals, especially among female workers, for the specific problem of alcoholism. Educational sessions that emphasize that alcoholism is a disease with the associated risk factors of family history of drinking problems, marital status, and economic status would prove useful in lessening the stigma associated with alcoholism. All employee health education efforts must also include information on alternative sources of help, since it is possible that some females, because of the stigma attached to female alcoholism, will not use a company program under any circumstances.[36]

THE SPOUSE AND FAMILY OF THE ALCOHOLIC

Studies show that 50 percent of alcoholics have an alcoholic parent and that another 30 percent marry alcoholics.[37] Claudia Black, author of *It Will Never Happen to Me*, recognizes that children of alcoholics have a high risk of developing alcoholism and would seem likely targets for prevention programs. Yet very little work is being done in the area of prevention. Black notes that family alcoholism treatment programs typically have their main emphasis on the alcoholic person. Whatever encouragement is made to the children—to see films on alcoholism, for example—is often made via one of the parents. Black's philosophy focuses on children's groups, art therapy, and various other techniques to prevent alcoholism and the psychological predisposition to be alcoholic or to marry an alcoholic.[38]

By working with children in a variety of settings, Black grew to believe that the child who is from an alcoholic home and who has behavioral problems is in the minority. In her groups, Black finds that children of alcoholics are above average in intelligence and often admired as a result of the role(s) they have adopted. The three roles that appear to allow children to survive in alcoholic homes are (1) the responsible one; (2) the adjuster; and (3) the placater. The children may adopt one role or any combination of the three to maintain a sense of balance. When the family is viewed as an operational system, then the change in one family member's function is automatically followed by a compensatory change in that of another member. To each action there is an equal and positive opposite reaction in the family.[39]

The role most typical for an only or an eldest child is one of being responsible—for him- or herself and for others in the family, including siblings and parents. The responsible role is an attempt to provide a sense of order and stability to an inconsistent setting. The role of the adjuster is assumed by the child who easily follows directions and does not feel the great sense of responsibility that the elder child often feels. The child adapts to whatever is called for on a given day and often bounces from one extreme to another through both emotional and physical fluctuations. The placating child finds a great need to smooth over conflicting situations and, as the sociable one, helps others adjust and feel comfortable. In all these roles, children in alcoholic homes struggle to survive by bringing peace to the chaotic, denying family in which they live.[40]

The children whose roles have allowed them to survive do not change roles just because they leave the alcoholic environment; these roles become patterns they carry into adulthood. It is often after they have settled into life as an adult that they realize the old methods of coping no longer provide a sense of meaningfulness to their lives. Depression, loneliness, and difficulty in maintaining intimate relationships often evolve. Children who had the responsible role find their need to be in control leads to difficulty in relationships at work and socially; the adjusters often continue to allow themselves to be manipulated by others as their self-esteem diminishes; and the placaters continue to seek a situation where they can take care and meet the needs of others. Although these negative consequences often do not becomes apparent until adulthood, Black believes that the pattern begins to develop at a very young age. Therefore, she opens her groups to all children of alcoholics, no matter what their age.[41]

THE KEMPER INSURANCE EAP
FOR FAMILIES OF ALCOHOLICS

Although alcoholism professionals acknowledge that alcoholism is a family disease, the most neglected employees in the occupational alcoholism field are the working family members of alcoholics. One EAP that is attempting to fill this void is the Personal Assistance Program for the Kemper Insurance Companies. Since 1962, Kemper has had an alcoholism program for its employees. Supervisory referrals were made to the rehabilitation director and, in 1969, a behavioral–medical approach was instituted in which managers and supervisors were trained to refer employees with job problems to informal volunteer coordinators, usually recovered alcoholics, who reported to the director of rehabilitation. Yet very few employees who had an alcoholic family member were referred. In 1975, the Family Development Program was initiated and introduced additional trained staff persons to address a growing caseload of employees, including family members of alcoholics, who were experiencing marital, family, and job conflicts.

The philosophy of the Kemper program is to assist family members by teaching them the dynamics of the illness, their role in it, how and where to get help, and, finally, how to intervene. The family member is not viewed primarily as a treatment tool for the alcoholic, as he or she often is by treatment programs. Instead, the aim of the Kemper program is to help the family member before he or she is able to intervene with the alcoholic. Clients are referred to Al-Anon and to counseling at alcoholism treatment and counseling centers, in addition to being encouraged to read a variety of books, such as Vernon Johnson's *I'll Quit Tomorrow* and Reverend Joseph L. Kellerman's *Guide for the Alcoholic.*[42]

The following observations were made in 1978 about the clients seen in the Kemper Family Development Program:

- 48 (70 percent) had job problems or health problems affecting their jobs, including absenteeism, moodiness, and poor interpersonal relationships and attitudes.
- 17 (25 percent) of the 69 clients were battered women.
- Many of these women were regular visitors to the medical department for headaches, colitis, and gastric problems.
- Many of the clients were excellent compulsive workers whose workday was an escape from their chaotic home lives.
- Many clients in their late teens and early twenties were abusing alcohol or drugs themselves. Such female clients were often in emotional relationships with men who were alcoholic or drug addicted, and were usually being physically abused.
- The average age of family member clients was 32.6 years compared with 39.2 years for alcoholic clients.[43]

The high percentage of job performance problems among alcoholics' family members demonstrated the need for business, industry, and government to devote time, energy, staff, and money through their occupational alcoholism programs to deal with the employees who have alcoholics in their families. Issues that need closer scrutiny include (1) how to motivate male employees to seek help when they have a female alcoholic family member; and (2) how to help the battered woman who works.

CONCLUSION

Meeting the alcoholism service needs of hard-to-reach workers poses a challenge to the human services field. The change in the public's attitude toward alcoholism, concurrent with the AMA pronouncement of alcoholism as a disease in 1956, has altered the public's stereotyped image of the alcoholic as a skid row derelict. This change in public attitude has extended to industry, as numerous alcoholism programs and EAPs provide assistance for alcoholic employees. Yet no one readily admits to being an alcoholic; in fact, it is characteristic of alcoholics to deny the illness until there is no other alternative but to recognize its existence. The EAP focuses on the early identification and referral for treatment of middle-stage alcoholics and confronts the massive denial that accompanies the disease. In this vein, it represents a viable, humane, and cost-effective approach to addressing the employee's alcoholism, which also affects co-workers and family members.

REFERENCES

1. National Council on Alcoholism, "A Joint Labor-Management Approach to Alcoholism Recovery Programs," NCA pamphlet, 1976.

2. George E. Vaillant, *The Natural History of Alcoholism* (Cambridge, Mass.: Harvard University Press, 1983), pp. 306, 309.

3. James E. Royce, *Alcohol Problems and Alcoholism: A Comprehensive Survey* (New York: Free Press, 1981), pp. 10–11.

4. Joseph A. Califano, Jr., "The 1982 Report of Drug Abuse and Alcoholism" (Report to Governor Hugh L. Carey, State of New York, June 1982), p. 48.

5. Royce, *Alcohol Problems and Alcoholism*, p. 29.

6. Cited in Richard T. Rada, "Alcoholism and Forcible Rape," *American Journal of Psychiatry*, Vol. 132 (1975), pp. 444–446.

7. Royce, *Alcohol Problems and Alcoholism*, pp. 24–25.

8. L. Paringer et al., *Economic Costs of Illness: Fiscal Year 1975* (Washington, D.C.: Georgetown University, Public Services Laboratory, 1977).

9. Royce, *Alcohol Problems and Alcoholism*, pp. 152–156, 291–302.

10. S. Zimberg, "Alcoholism: Prevalence in General Hospital and Emergency Room and Walk-In Clinic," *New York State Journal of Medicine*, Vol. 79 (1979).

11. J. Zuska, "Wound Without Cause," *Bulletin, American College of Surgeons*, October 1981.

12. General Accounting Office, "Projections on Economic Impact of Alcoholism" (Washington, D.C., 1981).

13. E. M. Jellinek, *The Disease Concept of Alcoholism* (New Haven, Conn.: College & University Press, 1960).

14. Royce, *Alcohol Problems and Alcoholism*, pp.159–162.

15. Dr. Manin Block, "American Medical Association Committee Study" (Washington, D.C., 1976).

16. "AA Guidelines," 1977 (rev.), p. 5.

17. Stanton Peele, "The Addiction Experience," *Addictions*, Vol. 24, No. 2 (1977), p. 26.

18. Peele, "The Addiction Experience," p. 22.

19. Jellinek, *The Disease Concept of Alcoholism*, pp. 36–41.

20. Royce, *Alcohol Problems and Alcoholism*, pp. 91–94.

21. Ephraim T. Lisansky, "Alcoholism—The Avoided Diagnosis," *The Bulletin of the American College of Physicians*, Vol. 15 (1974), pp. 18–24.

22. Royce, *Alcohol Problems and Alcoholism*, p. 96.

23. M. M. Glatt, *The Alcoholic and the Help He Needs*, 2nd ed. (Lancaster, England: M&P Co., Ltd., 1972).

24. Peg Palisano, "Alcoholism: Industry's $15 Billion Hangover," *Occupational Hazards*, September 1980, p. 55.

25. Kenneth A. Randall, President, The Conference Board, Foreword to *Dealing with Alcoholism in the Workplace* by Richard M. Weiss (New York: The Conference Board, 1980), p. vii.

26. Palisano, "Alcoholism: Industry's $15 Billion Hangover," p. 55.

27. Mary H. Cahill and B. J. Volicer, "Male and Female Differences in Severity of Problems with Alcohol at the Workplace," *Drug and Alcohol Dependence*, Vol. 8, No. 2 (1981), pp. 143–156.

28. Dale A. Masi and George E. Spencer, "Alcoholism and Employee Assistance Programs in Industry: A New Frontier for Social Work," *Social Thought*, Winter 1977, pp. 21–22.

29. Eileen M. Corrigan, *Alcoholic Women in Treatment* (New York: Oxford University Press, 1980), p. 3.

30. G. Knupfer, *California Drinking Practices Study*, Report No. 6 (State of California, Department of Public Health, April 1963).

31. J. E. deLint, "Alcoholism, Birth Rank and Parental Deprivation," *American Journal of Psychiatry*, Vol. 120 (1964), pp. 1062–1065.

32. Sheila Blume, "Women and Alcohol" (Lecture delivered at Virgin Islands School of Alcohol Studies, June 8, 1983).

33. Marian Sandmaier, *The Invisible Alcoholics* (New York: McGraw-Hill, 1980), pp. 72–73.

34. Corrigan, *Alcoholic Women in Treatment*, p. 166.

35. Mary H. Cahill et al., "Evaluation of a Women's Occupational Alcoholism Demonstration Project" (Paper prepared for the NIAAA, DHHS, May 1982), pp. 1.2–1.5.

36. Mary H. Cahill, "Tailoring EAP Service to Organizational Needs," *EAP Digest*, May/June 1983, p. 34.

37. J. Sauer, "The Neglected Majority" (Lecture delivered at NCA annual meeting, Milwaukee, May 1975).

38. Claudia Black, *It Will Never Happen to Me* (Denver: M.A.C. Printing and Publications Division, 1981), pp. 4–5.

39. M. Bowen, "Alcohol and the Family System," *The Family*, Vol. 1, No. 1 (1973), pp. 20–25.

40. Black, *It Will Never Happen to Me*, pp. 53–55.

41. Ibid., pp. 55–60.

42. John J. Lavino, "Family Members of Alcoholics: The Forgotten People of Occupational Alcoholism Programs" (Paper prepared for the National Council on Alcoholism, Labor-Management Section, St. Louis, May 1, 1978), pp. 4–5.

43. Ibid., pp. 6–7.

Chapter 6

Drug Abuse Counseling in Industry

Nonalcoholic drug abuse in industry has not received the attention that alcoholism has. As previous chapters explained, the EAP has its very roots in the alcoholism field. However, many self-referrals and emotional cases that do not have an addiction etiology are now coming to the attention of the EAPs. The increase in mental health cases, which has been attributed to the influx of mental health professionals in the EAP field, is not surprising. A familiarity with mental health problems enables these programs to provide outreach services to their clients. Expertise with drug abuse in the workplace, on the other hand, is virtually unknown. The literature is minuscule, and solid research efforts are nonexistent. The symptoms of drug abuse in the workplace and the most effective methods for reaching and successfully treating drug-abusing employees are all in the speculative stages. People like Lee Dogoloff (formerly President Carter's chief advisor on drug abuse), Robert Du Pont (former director of the National Institute on Drug Abuse), and Peter Bensinger (former Drug Enforcement Agency director) have made important contributions to this field and are now actively involved in preventing drug abuse in the private sector. Their efforts must be pulled together.

This chapter discusses the current status of the field and is presented with the qualifier that the novelty of this area demands the attention of the entire field. An open mind is needed to new ways of structuring programs, as well as to new company policies, to solve the problem.

DEFINITIONS AND CLASSIFICATION OF DRUGS

The drug business is flourishing. Attorney General William French Smith reported that drug sales nationwide approached $79 billion in

93

1980—"about equal to the combined profits of America's 500 largest corporations."[1] In 1981, the Research Triangle Institute completed a five-year study of drug use for the federal government and revealed many startling statistics:

- 60 percent of high-school seniors (in 1981) used marijuana.
- Daily amphetamine use tripled from 1976 to 1981, with the steepest rise between 1980 and 1981.
- Cocaine use in the month preceding the end of the survey was nearly triple the use for the same month in 1976.
- One out of every six drivers responsible for accidents in which somebody was killed was high on marijuana when the accident took place, according to a Massachusetts study.[2]

The majority of people surveyed by the Research Triangle Institute were currently in the workforce, which reveals the fact that drugs are having a national impact on businesses and workplaces in this country. Michael Beaubrun, a psychiatrist and president of the National Council on Alcoholism of Trinidad/Tobago, classifies drugs as narcotics, sedatives, stimulants, and hallucinogens according to the levels of psychological and physical dependence they cause. Common narcotics include opium, heroin, codeine, and methadone; sedatives include alcohol, Valium, Librium, and barbiturates. Stimulants include amphetamines, caffeine, nicotine, and cocaine; hallucinogens include LSD, mescaline, and phenacyclidine (PCP). Cannabis (marijuana) is unique because it is classified as a sedative, stimulant, and hallucinogen. All these drugs, whether prescription or nonprescription, alter the human consciousness and have both short-term and long-term physical and psychological effects.

Drug abuse was defined in the early 1970s as the use of mind- or mood-altering substances (with the exception of alcohol) for purposes other than medical. Yet the terms *abuse* and *dependence* do not have the same meaning, and a misunderstanding arises from the incorrect use of these terms. The following definitions will help prevent these misunderstandings:

Drug: A chemical substance that has an effect upon the body or mind. (The terms *substance abuse* and *substance dependence* are frequently used instead of *drug abuse* and *drug dependence* because many forms of abuse and

	dependence—for example, glue sniffing—deal with substances not usually considered drugs.)
Psychoactive drug:	A mind-altering drug.
Abuse:	The excessive or inappropriate use of a drug or substance so as to cause behavior that adversely affects the person's social or occupational functioning—in other words, use that damages the user by adversely interfering with either work, domestic life, or social behavior.
Dependence:	A state of psychological and/or physical need that results from constant or periodic use.
Psychological dependence:	A psychological need that results from the repeated use of a drug to relieve tension or other emotional states.
Physical dependence:	A craving for the drug that comes about through the body's attempt to adapt to the drug. Physical dependence depends on tolerance and withdrawal.
Tolerance:	Larger and larger amounts of the drug are required to achieve the same effect.
Withdrawal:	Very unpleasant sensations, such as shaking, sweating, fright, and even hallucinations, occur if the drug is suddenly reduced or stopped. Some drugs have a much greater tendency than others to produce withdrawal and tolerance and are therefore more prone to cause dependence. The drugs that most rapidly produce physical dependence are narcotics.
Addiction:	A combination of both physical and psychological dependence.
Cross-tolerance:	The tendency for tolerance built up for one drug to be transferred to other drugs of the same class. For example, alcohol, barbiturates, and minor tranquilizers are all depressant drugs of the sedative class. An alcoholic who has developed high tolerance levels for alcohol will also require high

levels of barbiturates or tranquilizers. If this person breaks a leg in a traffic accident, two or three times the normal amount of anesthetic may be required to set the fracture.[3]

HISTORICAL PERSPECTIVE

Although drug use for recreational purposes can be documented as far back as the beginning of recorded history, the development of drug use as a major social issue began only recently. It has only been since the turn of the century that drug use has warranted government intervention. Prior to such intervention, drug use was often tolerated and no social stigma was attached. The shift in popular attitudes toward drug use followed from its increased association with crime and other socially deviant behavior. Drug users turned to illegal sources to support their previously tolerated habits, and the association of drug use with criminality led to increased penalties and to the definition of drug use, on moral and legal grounds, as an evil.[4]

The passage of the Pure Food and Drug Act in 1906 represented the initial intervention of the government. The passage of the Harrison Act in the early 1960s demonstrated the government's position that drug use was a major social problem that required criminal sanctions.[5] The stringent government regulations placed the drug user in the extremely difficult position of having to choose between entering treatment or withdrawal or turning to illegal sources.[6] Many drug users chose the latter because of the ineffectiveness of treatment at that time.

In the early 1960s government policies concerning the strict enforcement of laws pertaining to the importation, manufacture, sale, and possession of drugs were ineffective. Subsequently, however, a deemphasis on criminal sanctions led to a focus on the treatment and rehabilitation of the individual drug user.[7] Ironically, the principal mode of treatment adopted by the government was the maintenance of drug users—the very approach that the government had rendered illegal 50 years earlier.[8]

In 1970, Congress passed the Compehensive Drug Abuse Prevention Act (P.L. 91–513), which granted new federal authority to attack the drug trafficker and pusher. All federal first-offense cases for narcotics users were lowered from felonies to misdemeanors. However, stronger penalties were implemented to restrict the manufacture and sale of dangerous drugs. Two years later, the Congress passed the Drug Abuse Office and Treatment Act of 1972 (P.L. 92–255). At the time of the act's passage, Congress was conscious of the adverse impact of drub abuse on individuals, families, and communities. Section 413 of the act specifically addressed the issues of drug abuse in the workplace. The Civil Service Commission (now the Office of Personnel Management) in cooperation with the National Institute on Drug Abuse (NIDA) and other federal agencies, was given the responsibility for developing and maintaining appropriate prevention, treatment, and rehabilitation services for drug abuse among federal civilian employees.[9] Since drug abuse is pervasive in all levels of society, it is essential to look at its impact in the workplace. The federal effort in the early 1970s represented a major turning point in which the government recognized the urgency of addressing the escalating problem of drugs in industry.[10]

ILLEGAL DRUG ABUSE: MARIJUANA AND COCAINE

Today a sizable portion of the population has moved to a less restrictive position that sanctions recreational or social drug use or self-medication as acceptable behavior. Although drug abuse encompasses a wide variety of both legal and illegal drugs, including LSD, Quaalude, heroin, and Valium, the discussion in this section will focus on the use of marijuana and cocaine, and the effect of such use in the workplace.

The flower children of the 1960s are now in their midthirties and working. As their parents continued their habit of drinking alcohol from their youthful years in the 1940s and 1950s, so did the 1960s generation continue its use of drugs. Because of the present respectability of recreational drug use, changes in drug laws, and the existence of a highly profitable drug paraphernalia industry, drug abuse has increased dramatically in recent years. Findings in the sports and entertainment industries, as well as in the business and political communities, reveal the increasing prevalence of drugs, especially marijuana and cocaine, in the workplace.

In 1962, only 4 percent of adults aged 18–25 had smoked marijuana; by 1982, that figure had risen to 64 percent. Among the 182.5 million Americans aged 12 or older, more than 57 million, or 31.3 percent, had tried marijuana.[11] The startling increase in marijuana use stems from a change in attitude based on the comfortable illusion that marijuana is a relatively benign substance. However, evidence shows that marijuana is at least as threatening to physical health as tobacco or alcohol, and recent studies reveal that marijuana is potentially more damaging to the respiratory system than tobacco and a significant threat to the reproductive system.[12] In addition, and even more dangerous than the physical effects of marijuana, is its impact on behavior—the impairment of judgment, memory or learning disability, the loss of motivation, and a lack of coordination or motor skills.[13]

Marijuana use is in the process of being replaced by the current crisis of cocaine. When used recreationally, cocaine represents the ultimate symbol of status and prestige. In the 1960s, only a small fraction of the populace had encountered cocaine, let alone used it. By 1982, some 2 million people had done so. Among adults 26 and older, about 1.5 million had tried cocaine, according to government figures in April 1983.[14]

Nationally, the cocaine industry is estimated at between $26.8 billion and $32.2 billion a year.[15] One-half ounce of the drug sells for as much as $1,400. Selling coke is, in the words of one U.S. drug official, "the most lucrative of all underworld ventures."[16] It seems unlikely that its social acceptability and elite image alone could account for the tremendous growth of the cocaine industry; however, scientists have not yet been able to determine the exact effects of cocaine on the brain or what leads to compulsive use. Some theorize that cocaine stimulates the action of the neurotransmitters (chemicals that facilitate the electrochemical workings of the brain) in that portion of the brain that controls emotional pleasure and depression.[17] In any event, it cannot be denied that cocaine has profound physical and psychological effects that include short-term memory loss, nausea, paranoia, hallucinations, and, upon prolonged and frequent use, delusions of grandeur and cerebral aneurysm.[18] Despite these ill effects, the fact remains that cocaine is being used and abused in epidemic proportions in this country by people of varying racial and socioeconomic backgrounds.

It is easy to see how any of the drugs previously mentioned can interfere with an employee's job performance. Although the physical manifestations of drug abuse often remain undetected, such abuse will inevitably be recognized in a deteriorating level of work productivity. This recognition is crucial in detecting a drug problem in the workplace and in restoring the employee to full productivity.

LEGAL DRUGS AND WOMEN

The issues surrounding drug abuse and addiction among women have generated a great deal of discussion, but little has been done to determine the factors leading to these problems and few substantive solutions have been suggested.

Research indicates that women differ from men in the amount, kind, source, and pattern of drug use. It is fairly clear that, at least in reference to licit drugs, women's involvement is much heavier. Women use a wider spectrum of psychotropic chemicals[19]—60 percent of all psychotropic drugs, 70 percent of all antidepressants, and 80 percent of all amphetamines are used by women.[20] The National Institute on Drug Abuse (NIDA) estimates the following figures regarding the use of prescription drugs in the United States:

- 32 million, or 42 percent, of adult females as compared to 16 million, or 21 percent, of adult males have taken tranquilizers.
- 16 million, or 21 percent, of women have taken some kind of sedative, whereas only 12 million, or 16 percent, of men have.
- 12 million, or 16 percent, of women have used stimulant medication (for weight control or physical/emotional fatigue), whereas only 5 million, or 8 percent, of men have ever used prescription amphetamines.

The factors associated with the massive use of mood-altering chemicals by American women are complex. Drug companies align themselves with the theories and ideologies of the medical profession regarding women and their health. Screening drug industry advertisements and approaches to marketing shows that, not only were women targeted early as major drug consumers, but the drug industry capitalized on and even generated negative stereotypes.[21]

The predominantly male-dominated medical profession, as well as the drug industry, often depicts women as hyperactive shrews or as weeping, depressive, and helpless. The message is clear: The solution lies in the drug—"Librium rather than liberate; instead of new vistas, Luminal."[22] The American Medical Association (AMA) is aware of the strong, sometimes subversive, advertising practices of the drug industry, but it has taken few steps toward preventing the rise of advertising pushing mood-altering drugs for women:

The AMA's board of trustees admits that it leaves much of what is advertised in their periodicals to the discretion of the manufacturers.

Advertisements of drugs are fully accepted even though the claims made for them do not conform to the findings of its own monographs and AMA Drug Evaluation: even *Good Housekeeping* and *Parent* magazines do better in protecting their readers-consumers.[23]

These advertising practices of the drug industry are aimed at developing physicians as agents for drug distribution. Physicians are the main sources of drugs for women, especially drugs with abuse potential, such as the psychotropics. Some 80 percent of prescriptions for psychotropic drugs are written by obstetricians/gynecologists, internists, and general practitioners. Not only are these the physicians women see most often, they are also the physicians with the least amount of training in pharmacology.[24] There is also a double standard held by physicians in treating women and men; they are far more likely to prescribe drugs for women: "Physicians with more pessimistic attitudes toward treatment outcome are more likely to prescribe tranquilizers for women, because they feel women need not be as mentally alert as men, because they hold the same pessimistic view about women's role in this culture."[25]

Part of the problem of women and drug abuse lies in the huge gaps in knowledge about the problem, its causes, the women at risk, and the signs and symptoms of women in trouble. Women's treatment needs to go far beyond crisis hotlines, emergency room care, and detoxification. Additional appropriate treatment facilities must be provided to instruct women on the dangers of drug use. In addition, federal agencies and the medical profession need to become more involved—the Federal Trade Commission, the Food and Drug Administration, and the American Medical Association all need to strengthen guidelines and regulations to prevent false and misleading advertising and to assist in a massive national educational effort to stop this continued drugging of women.[26]

DRUGS IN INDUSTRY

The presence of a drug problem in the workplace will manifest itself in many forms, including security, safety, quality control, productivity, first-line supervisory, medical, personnel, and general management problems. Common examples include frequent employee theft, embezzlement, and accidents (both on and off the work premises); a decrease in the quality of work produced; extended coffee breaks; a rise in lateness and absenteeism rates (particularly on Monday); and an increase in grievances, personality changes (aggression), and disciplinary problems.[27] The need to provide a comprehensive program in response to these problems is apparent, yet any such effort will face many difficulties, including:

1. Estimating the actual size of the drug problem and its cost to employees.
2. Ascertaining the specific effects of drug use on job performance.
3. Identifying the problem individual.
4. Identifying and referring him or her to an appropriate treatment resource.
5. Being bound to the legal and regulatory procedures that protect the employee.[28]

Reaching the drug-dependent employee has become increasingly difficult, as have the efforts to ascertain the extent of drug use and misuse among employed people. In 1978, Kenneth R. MacNulty, while a student at Boston College, completed study in Washington, D.C., under my supervision. It was one of the first studies done of EAPs and drugs and was funded by NIDA. He found that few federal agencies were differentiating between alcohol and drugs. The Government Printing Office, St. Elizabeth's Hospital, and the Department of Defense were the clear exceptions. None were giving attention to drug abusers unless alcohol was the primary drug.

Because of the stigma associated with drug problems, it is often difficult to identify the troubled employee. A lack of documentation clouds the effects of drug abuse on job performance, yet an awareness of such indicators is crucial to the referral of persons who need treatment. Special education and outreach efforts are needed to encourage the identification of problems rather than driving them further underground.[29]

Once the employees with drug-related problems have been identified, the problem of identifying appropriate treatment resources still remains. National efforts in drug treatment programming have focused on users of illegal drugs, who are usually unemployed. There is not yet an established network of treatment programs for the employed person, whose drug problem is often related to the misuse of legal drugs. Special expertise is needed to ascertain the philosophies of the various treatment agencies and to help evaluate a specific agency's appropriateness as a referral resource. All supervisory–employee relations are covered by some regulation or company procedure. The federal government, for example, must carry out its personnel management functions according to regulations that cover such issues as performance, appraisal, equal employment opportunity, and reasonable accommodation of the handicapped. The cases of drug abuse invoke even more regulations because of the law enforcement and confidentiality issues; hence, supervisors are particularly reluctant to deal with employees who are experiencing problems due to drug abuse.[30]

These are just some examples of the numerous problems that complicate the issue of drugs in industry. Clearly any program that attempts to address the prevalence of drug use in the workplace, whether it be in the government or in private industry, must recognize these problems and aim to find solutions.

THE PUBLIC SAFETY

The element of public safety includes corporate theft, accidents (on and off the work site), and criminal offenses due to drug use and abuse.

I recently heard of an employee who sold confidential corporate information to foreign agents in order to support a costly drug habit. Drugs are also at the root of cases of corporate theft in which funds are embezzled or data are leaked to secure the necessary financial support for the employee's drug use. In addition, an alarming increase in the number of accidents, both on and off the company premises, is linked to drug use:

- A Houston production worker who had just given himself a fix decided that he could fly. He jumped from a third-floor balcony; miraculously he survived.[31]
- At an automobile plant near Detroit, a female employee directing trains in a switching yard was crushed by one of the trains; her senses reportedly were dulled by prescription drugs.[32]
- Six of the 14 sailors and Marines killed in the crash aboard the aircraft carrier Nimitz in 1981 had marijuana in their systems.[33]

Criminal offenses are also common occurrences when drug abuse is prevalent:

- At a TRW, Inc., plant in Houston, several workers broke into the plant during a Christmas holiday and stole several hundred thousand dollars worth of expensive carbide cutting tool materials used in making oil well drill bits. When apprehended at their homes the following day, they admitted pulling the theft to get money for drugs.[34]
- At a Georgia furniture plant, a group of employees admitted to purposely damaging more than $100,000 worth of furniture so that they could buy it at a discount and resell it to support their drug habits.[35]
- One employee started taking a gram of cocaine a day while working at a lumber company outside Aspen, Colorado, then embezzled more than $7,000 to pay for it.[36]
- A Beverly Hills lawyer took $75,000 from one of his actor clients, half of which he used to pay for the cocaine that was destroying his practice.[37]

The severe health and legal consequences need to be addressed through the implementation of systematic prevention strategies, in addition to legal sanctions, as a discouragement of drug use both on and off the job.

The term *public safety* also applies to those people who are employed in positions that carry responsibility for the safety and welfare of the general public—for example, police officers, fire fighters, nuclear plant workers, and federal and military personnel with sensitive clearances. However, when we consider public safety, do we include surgeons, school bus drivers, and airline mechanics? It is very difficult to draw the line, and companies are becoming increasingly vulnerable to relevant legal issues. Each of these special populations must be addressed by the EAP in order to ensure an effective and comprehensive program.

Drug use by individuals empowered with positions of public safety represents a unique problem. A 1983 New York *Daily News* investigation revealed that "some NYC police officers smoke pot, snort cocaine and inject themselves with heroin while on patrol." Commissioner John Guido, commander of the Inspectional Services Bureau, which investigates police misconduct and corruption, added "We don't recruit from a monastery. . . . Drugs are proliferating everywhere. Cops just reflect society."[38]

The U.S. Nuclear Regulatory Commission (NRC) is currently addressing this crucial element of public safety. It is proposing a rule that would require utilities to ensure that workers with access to protected areas of nuclear power plants are not under the influence of drugs or alcohol or otherwise unfit for duty. The agency, responding to substantial increases in drug and alcohol abuse at the plants, believes the rule would prevent those workers from adversely affecting the health and safety of the public.

Similarly, military and federal personnel with sensitive clearances are a highly vulnerable population. Federal program policy mandates that people with sensitive clearances be automatically fired upon detection of drug use and made ineligible for assistance programs. An office in the Department of Defense is notified of all such cases concerning sensitive clearance personnel, yet no recourse other than prompt dismissal is available. What is needed is a specialized program, staffed with social workers, psychiatrists, and psychologists who have sensitive clearances, to assist the employees who are suffering from drug problems. This population merits special attention, and EAPs must accommodate the unique circumstances of the high-level security position.

DETECTING THE DRUG-ABUSING EMPLOYEE

A history of drug use has been regarded as prima facie evidence of unsuitability for employment. The physical and behavioral effects, in addition to the legal liabilities, often disqualified the person.[39] The moral stigma attached to drug use, especially in the 1960s, further complicated the issue, as did such factors as a criminal record and lack of education or work skills, which often characterized a person with a history of drug use. Today, however, use of both legal and illegal drugs is so prevalent that industry no longer has the option of not employing any drug users. It must find a way to accommodate persons with a drug abuse history into the employment pool.

One choice an employer has is to do nothing about an employee's drug problem. Signs of drug use are often ignored, neglected, and denied. Poor work quality and low productivity are accepted, accidents happen, employees are fired, and grievances are fought in arbitration. But as Lee I. Dogoloff, who presently serves as executive director of the American Council for Drug Education, states:

> It is sinful not to do anything . . . work and drug use do not mix. You can say to your employees, "If you have a problem here, we will try to

help. But we will not tolerate drug use. Not because we don't want people to have fun. But because this a matter of health—your health and of course the health of the company that employs you. There isn't a moral–legal argument here. This is a health problem."[40]

Robert T. Angarola, Washington attorney and former general counsel to the Office of Drug Abuse Policy in the White House, outlines the following three basic reasons for confronting an employee with a drug problem: (1) public trust; (2) public safety; and (3) fitness for duty. It is important, Angarola maintains, to seek input from several sources—legal counsel, security experts, medical authorities, and drug abuse experts—after the warning signs of drug abuse are detected, but before steps are taken against the employee.[41]

Peter Bensinger, of Bensinger, Dupont and Associates, reveals further reasons for instituting a drug abuse program.

The employer has the biggest stick there is for alcoholics and drug abusers. Employers have leverage—discipline, loss of job, etc. There is not just the bottom line to consider here, but social responsibility. Nobody else has the leverage to do this. . . . And the glory of it is that when an employer helps the employee with alcohol and drug problems, the employer helps itself to higher profit margins as well.[42]

THE EAP AND THE DRUG-ABUSING EMPLOYEE

In addition to using the job performance model and confrontation already described in a previous chapter, the EAP must use new approaches to reach and treat drug-abusing employees; programs are now dealing with illegal activity. This component alone introduces a new element into EAPs, since it requires working closely with a company lawyer. Administrators and counselors must be sure of what their responsibilities are toward both the employee and the company. For instance, the implications of taking drugs on the company premises are different from those of selling drugs. The article "Pushers on the Payroll" clearly shows the problem an employee faces with such a situation.[43]

EAPs must ensure that companies have a clear policy regarding drug abuse. The company must state unequivocally that taking illegal drugs on company premises will not be tolerated. It must spell out what the result will be if an employee is found taking drugs and what steps will be taken. Hopefully, the EAP will be regarded as an alternative to punitive actions.

EAPs must be willing to work closely with medical units in the administration of urinalyses. A written company policy statement should state that such tests will be administered and clarify the usage of test results.

All EAP intake interviews should include questions regarding drug-taking habits regardless of the presenting problems. Because employees will probably lie if they feel they are being cross-examined, the counselor should ask these questions casually and intersperse them with other kinds of questions, to avoid making the employee defensive. A skilled counselor will often be able to discern hesitation or uneasiness even if the employee is trying to deny using drugs.

The following questions are suggested as a guide:[44]

1. Do you sometimes need medications to stay calm (for example, Valium, Compoz, Quaalude, Librium), or to sleep well (for example, Sleep-Eze, phenobarbitol, or Seconal)?
   a) If yes, how often do you take these?
2. Do you use or have you ever used marijuana or hashish?
   a) If yes, how often?
3. Do you use or have you ever used cocaine?
   a) If yes, how often?
4. Do you use or have you ever used heroin or any other narcotics (morphine, codeine, dilaudid, etc.)?
   a) If yes, how often?
5. Do you use or have you ever used any street (nonprescribed) drugs not already mentioned, such as (1) hallucinogens (PCP, LSD, mescaline, peyote, psilocybin); (2) inhalants (glue, paint, gasoline); (3) stimulants (amphetamines, speed)?
   a) If yes, how often?
6. Have any of these drugs presented a problem for you at work?
7. Have you missed work, had an accident, or become ill because of the drug(s)?
   a) Has your drug use ever resulted in poor performance at work, in terms of a suspension, adverse action, or any similar action taken against you?
   b) Have you ever been fired from a job because of drug use?
   c) Are you often irritable at work and find yourself arguing with your co-workers?

Finding appropriate treatment resources for drug-taking employees is difficult. Traditional drug treatment facilities have been geared to the younger, unemployed street abuser. Finding facilities for the Valium-addicted middle-class employee or the cocaine-dependent executive represents a challenge. As a result of the DHHS project, the report "Treatment Guidelines for Drug-Abusing Employees for EAPs" was developed. This report was used by DHHS regional counselors to determine by telephone interviews the appropriateness of treatment centers that could not be visited. On a more fundamental level, it provided guidelines for detecting drug abusers in the workplace, documenting their presence through job performance history, and developing an effective approach for treating them. These guidelines focused on the referral and diagnosis of the employee, the function of the treatment center, and the applicable type of aftercare. In addition, they served as a liaison between the treatment center, the counselor, and the workplace.

The company's code of conduct will have to be examined in relation to drug abuse. One employer fired a group of employees who were taking illegal drugs at a public cocktail lounge off work premises. The code must clearly delineate what behavior is expected off company grounds.

The union must be closely involved in developing these procedures, to protect employee rights as well as employer responsibilities. The role of public safety is also crucial. The EAP counselor must be sensitive to the issues previously discussed.

DETECTING THE DRUG PROBLEM IN INDUSTRY

The state of the art of identifying employees with drug abuse problems affecting their jobs is in its infancy. Because case reporting is low thus far, data to help employers develop appropriate methodology for reaching such employees are speculative. EAP figures have to be examined in light of problem definition; it is shocking that many EAPs today still do not separate alcohol- from drug-related problems in their reporting. What is most critical is the need for program administrators, personnel directors, and physicians to begin to communicate with each other, to share each other's experiences, and to begin to help both the employee and the company with this growing problem.

The first clues that someone may be a drug user are prolonged absences from the office during the day, wandering, a tendency to fall asleep on the job, appearing not to be giving full attention to work, constant trips to the rest room, loss of weight, or financial problems so obvious that they even show up at work. However, the only legitimate symptom that may be used to confront the employee is poor job performance. Signs of poor performance include the need for extensive overtime work (without a substantial increase in workload), an increase in rates of rejected work, an increase in absenteeism, an inability to relate to co-workers, and frequent job-related accidents. Such evidence of declining job performance is sufficient reason to refer the employee to the EAP; the supervisor, who is not trained as a diagnostician, does not usually need to prove that drugs are at the root of the problem. But if such proof is necessary, there are three alternatives:

1. The employee may volunteer the fact that he or she has a drug problem.
2. The employer may require a urine test to detect the trace of drugs.
3. The employer may use a counseling program, including confrontation therapy, to determine whether the employee is using drugs.[45]

Denial is especially strong in the case of drug users and must be overcome at the beginning of a therapy program if substantial progress is to be expected. It is only when the employee is confronted and realizes that he or she has a drug problem that the employee may become motivated and actively work toward solving the problem. Documentation of declining work performance can serve as a basis for confronting the employee with specific measures of deteriorating productivity and for referring him or her to the EAP at the workplace. If the employee denies having any such problems, the EAP counselor may bring in people who work closely with the employee for a group discussion of the employee's on-the-job behavior. Like a confrontation with an alcoholic, such a meeting should clearly stay away from labeling the employee as a drug abuser. It is always important to avoid a moralizing or accusatory stance when confronting an employee, but with drug abuse the situation is even more sensitive. Drug abuse, unlike alcoholism, is actually illegal, so great care must be taken to avoid accusing an employee.

USE OF URINALYSIS

The decision to perform a urinalysis, although surrounded by legal issues, is not solely a legal concern. The test represents a verifiable and authoritative means of detecting the use of drugs, and enables the employer to intervene and refer the troubled employee for counseling and treatment, if deemed necessary. Although drug testing is appropriate in certain government and industrial settings, I believe that random, nondiscriminatory testing can be justified only when public safety is at stake. Although the test can be used to verify drug use in other settings, serious ethical and legal questions arise.

When appropriate, drug tests, administered on a routine, nondiscriminatory basis, may be used as an early identification system, especially if these tests are used in conjunction with an effective EAP. Test results may be used to refer employees to rehabilitation programs before disciplinary actions or termination proceedings become necessary.[46] Some claim that the benefits of this approach are enormous for industry and employees. Employees can effectively deal with their drug problems and are restored to full productivity, which represents a profitable outcome for the business or industry. Employee conduct, especially that which affects job performance, has never enjoyed protection from legitimate employer inquiries. In this sense, the positive results of a urinalysis, verified by a second test, may provide the necessary documentation to account for poor job performance and to warrant confrontation and intervention.

The urine test aims to shatter the denial of people with drug problems, yet it is surrounded by ethical and legal ramifications. Urine samples may be tested in a medical laboratory or in a work site urine-testing program. The most widely used system is the EMIT-ST, manufactured by the Syva Company in Palo Alto, California. The EMIT systems can test for the presence of marijuana, cocaine, PCP, barbiturates, amphetamines, methaqualone (Quaalude), tranquilizers (Valium, Librium), ethyl alcohol, methadone, and opiates. The presence of drugs in the urine can be detected with a 95–99 percent accuracy, depending on the drug in question.[47] Upon a positive test result, it is advisable to use a second test, such as the Gas Chromatograph/Mass Spectrometer (GC/MS) Test, of the same urine sample to provide additional verification. In order to ensure verification, however, the procedure for such testing, including the urination itself, must be witnessed. This requirement challenges employee's privacy rights, which are protected on the work premises.

All previous challenges to urine testing for illicit drug use have been based on the employer's failure to follow certain procedures in the administration of the tests. The major bases of legal challenge include: (1) violation of a private employment contract or a collective bargaining agreement; (2) unconfirmed test results or improperly performed tests that resulted in a negligence action; and (3) violation of an employee's right to privacy. This last basis for legal challenge is extremely important.[48] Although in 1971 the U.S. Supreme Court held that the employer–employee relationship is not one in which employees have a reasonable expectation of privacy,[49] this issue is still being debated. Protection of privacy may apply more to government employees than to their private sector counterparts. Such concepts as violation of search-and-seizure protections and due process apply only to government action, although the constitutional right to privacy has never been extended to include illegal conduct.

Further legal issues arise concerning the use of test results. If the employee with a positive test result is to be referred to an EAP, the legal ramifications are substantially reduced. Since no punitive action is taken and since the records of such counseling remain confidential and do not go into the personnel files, any possible error would be uncovered in the counseling sessions without recrimination. The legality of the urinalysis is usually challenged when an employee is discharged or suspended from work because of positive test result.

Robert Angarola, former general counsel to the Office of Drug Abuse Policy, advises employers to warn employees before starting any systematic testing program. Angarola also believes that the private employer can substantially limit his or her potential liability by following certain procedures:

1. Inform all applicants and employees that urine tests will be performed. A written company policy should state how the test results will be used and include any disciplinary actions that might be invoked.
2. If the workers are union members, review the collective bargaining agreement and renegotiate, if necessary. Include the right to conduct drug detection tests in employee contracts.
3. Obtain employees' and job applicants' consent to such tests.

4. Ascertain and document the need for the information provided by the tests by demonstrating a relation between drug use and job performance or safety.
5. Ensure (by contract or direct supervision) that the device manufacturer's instructions are strictly followed. Confirm positive test results by a second test, using alternative measures.
6. Notify employees of positive test results and give them an opportunity to contest disciplinary actions based on the results.
7. Consider referring employees to medical units or EAPs before taking punitive action.[50]

THE DHHS RESPONSE

A special demonstration project, entitled "Employee Counseling Services Special Initiative: Reaching the HHS Employee with Drug-Related Problems," was designed to address major issues regarding the provision of ECS to DHHS and other federal agencies. The project was a cooperative effort by the assistant secretary for personnel administration, the Region V personnel office, and NIDA, which provided the funding. Activities occurred between October 1, 1981 and July 31, 1982.

The purpose of this demonstration project was to develop and implement a variety of new programs and strategies for reaching DHHS employees with drug-related problems. Program elements included (1) developing education and outreach strategies for reaching the employee with a drug problem; (2) developing guidelines regarding treatment issues; (3) designing a booklet as a guide for supervisors and managers; (4) designing an evaluation component to measure program impact and to assess the strengths and weaknesses of program strategies in generating ECS referrals; and (5) developing the training component of the project, which emphasizes the importance of specialized drug abuse training for the ECS counselor.

An analysis of the ECS special initiative resulted in recommendations for further research. Areas targeted included (1) an exploration of the nature and extent of substance abuse within different types of work sites; (2) the sensitivity of the drug issue as a criminal activity, which had an impact on self-referral; (3) the emphasis on the job performance model as the basis for supervisory referrals to identify work problems arising from drug abuse; and (4) an exploration of the capacity of various education and outreach strategies that encourage participation in ECS programs by both self-referral and supervisory referral.[51]

CONCLUSION

Drug use and abuse among employees represents a serious and complex problem facing many companies in the United States. The EAP has emerged as a viable means of addressing the high incidence of drug use at the work site and of providing the necessary counseling to discourage such use. The problems involved are numerous and range from the identification of drug users and the avoidance of stereotypes to the legal ramifications of urine testing. No clear-cut answer is available for all the difficulties related to the applicability of the EAP to the drug-using employee population.

The use of deteriorating job performance as a basis for referring employees to the EAP is hampered by the variety of indicators of drug use, the use of denial among drug users (which is even stronger than among alcoholics), the narrow stereotype of the drug user, and the legal concerns that regulate the employer's intervention. The use of illegal drugs poses an additional concern. When illegal acts are committed on the work premises, it is essential for the manager or supervisor to call the authorities rather than to attempt to take on the problem single-handedly. Management must publicize the fact that illegal drug use and drug abuse are unacceptable in the work setting and will not be tolerated. The traditional EAP must adapt itself to the increasing problem of drugs in the workplace. The company has a responsibility not only to itself but to its employees and to the public.

REFERENCES

1. Nicholas Pileggi, "There's No Business Like Drug Business," *New York Magazine*, December 13, 1982, p. 38.

2. Research Triangle Institute, "Study of Drug Abuse for the Federal Government," 1981.

3. Michael H. Beaubrun, *Drug Education Manual* (West Indies: Trinidad and Tobago National Council on Alcoholism, 1981), p. 5.

4. Troy Duster, *The Legislation of Morality: Law, Drugs and Moral Judgment* (New York: Free Press, 1970), pp. 9–10.

5. Ibid., pp. 14–23.

6. Bertram S. Brown, "The Treatment and Rehabilitation of Narcotic Addicts in the United States," in *Drug Use in America: Problem in Perspective and Report of National Commission on Marijuana and Drug Abuse*, Vol. IV, Shafer, ed. (Edison, N.J.: Mss Information Corp., 1975), pp. 128–129.

7. Task Force on Narcotics and Drug Abuse, "Task Force Report: Annotations and Consultants' Papers" (Washington, D.C.: Government Printing Office, 1967), p. 1.

8. "Drug Use and Employment in Perspective," in *Drug Use and Public Employment: A Personnel Manual*, p. 10.

9. DHHS, "Employee Counseling Services Special Initiative: Reaching the DHHS Employee with Drug Related Problems," Final Report (Washington, D.C., 1982).

10. Carol Kurtis, "Drug Abuse as a Business Problem" (New York: New York Chamber of Commerce, April 1971), pp. 52–53.

11. Kevin McEnearney, "Social Drug Use: Causes and Implications" (DHHS, NIE, June 26, 1980), p. 1.

12. Ibid.

13. DHHS, National Institute on Drug Abuse, "National Survey on Drug Abuse: Main Findings" (Prepared by Response Analysis Corporation, under contract No. 271-28-3508, Princeton, N.J., 1979).

14. "How Drugs Sap the Nation's Strength," *U.S. News & World Report*, May 16, 1983, p. 55.

15. Emily Freeman, "After the Party: When Cocaine Becomes Your Only Friend," *D Magazine*, March 1983, p. 78.

16. "Crashing on Cocaine," *Time*, April 11, 1983, p. 23.

17. Freeman, "After the Party," p. 82.

18. DHHS, NIDA, "National Survey on Drug Abuse."

19. DHEW, "Drugs, Alcohol and Women's Health" (Prepared by An Alliance of Regional Coalitions, National Research and Communications Associates, under contract No. 271-77-1280, Washington, D.C., 1978), p. 37.

20. Linda S. Lidell, "Psychiatric Drug Use by Women: Health, Attitudinal, Personality and Demographic Correlates" (Paper presented at meeting of the American Psychological Association, San Francisco, August 28, 1977), pp. 1–2.

21. Dale A. Masi, *Organizing for Women* (Lexington, Mass.: Lexington Books, 1981), p. 121.

22. Robert Seidenberg, "Images of Health, Illness and Women in Drug Advertising," *Journal of Drug Issues*, 1974, pp. 264–266.

23. Robert Seidenberg, "Advertising and Drug Acculturation" (Statement made before the Subcommittee on Monopoly, Senate Small Business Committee, July 23, 1971), p. 19.

24. DHEW, "Drugs, Alcohol and Women's Health," p. 37.

25. Linda Lidell, "Put Her Down on Drugs: Prescribed Drug Usage in Women" (Paper presented at meeting of the Western Psychological Association, Anaheim, Calif., April 12, 1973), p. 72.

26. Masi, *Organizing for Women*, pp. 124–125.

27. "Employee Relations and Human Resources Bulletin," Employee Resources Bulletin Report No. 1540, Section III (Waterford, Conn.: Bureau of Business Practice, March 21, 1983), pp. 3–4.

28. DHHS, "Employee Counseling Services Special Initiative," p. 1.

29. National Institute on Drug Abuse, "Drug Use in Industry" (DHHS Publication ADM 81-811, 1979).

30. National Institute on Drug Abuse, "Guidelines for Establishing Occupational Drug Abuse Programs," 1976.

31. Thomas M. Rohan, "Pushers on the Payroll," *Industry Work*, February 8, 1982, p. 82.

32. Ibid.

33. "Taking Drugs on the Job," *Newsweek*, August 22, 1983, p. 57.

34. Rohan, "Pushers on the Payroll," p. 8.

35. Ibid.

36. "Taking Drugs on the Job," p. 56.

37. Ibid., p. 57.

38. New York *Daily News*, March 13, 1983.

39. "Public Employment Strategies and Issues" (Washington, D.C.: National Civil Service League, 1972), pp. 42–70.

40. Cited in "Employee Relations and Human Resources Bulletin," p. 17.

41. Robert T. Angarola, "Drug Detection in Industry: Legal Issues" (Unpublished paper, Fall 1982), pp. 10–12.

42. Cited in "Employee Relations and Human Resources Bulletin," p. 17.

43. Rohan, "Pushers on the Payroll."

44. Dale A. Masi et al., "DHHS Recommended Intake Questions" (Washington, D.C., 1981).

45. "Employee Relations and Human Resources Bulletin," pp. 14–17.

46. Patti Scheimer, "The Use of Biochemical Testing for Alcohol and Drug

Detection in Industry" (Unpublished paper submitted for class seminar, November 19, 1982), p. 13.

47. "Employee Relations and Human Resources Bulletin," pp. 16–17.

48. Angarola, "Drug Detection in Industry," pp. 2–6.

49. *Donaldson* v. *U.S.*, 400 U.S. 517, 1971.

50. Angarola, "Drug Detection in Industry," pp. 6–14.

51. DHHS, "Employee Counseling Services Special Initiative," pp. 3–4.

Chapter 7

Mental Health Counseling in the Workplace

The report of the President's Commission on Mental Health stated that America's mental health problems cannot be defined only in terms of disabling mental illnesses and identified psychiatric disorders. They must also include conditions that involve emotional or psychological distress that do not fit conventional classifications. Documenting the incidence and types of mental health problems, the methods of treatment, and the associated financial costs is difficult because of varying diagnostic criteria, misleading or inaccurate data, and the strong stigma associated with mental illness.

The most commonly used estimate of the past few years is that anywhere from 10 percent to 15 percent of the U.S. population needs some form of mental health services. As much as 25 percent of the population is estimated to be suffering at any given time from mild to moderate depression, anxiety, and other emotional disorders. In addition, it is estimated that 25 percent of the working population—not merely 10 to 15 percent—has some type of mental, emotional, or personality problem. On-the-job manifestations of mental illness range from preoccupation with details, poor work habits, inefficiency, chronic indecisiveness, and job dissatisfaction to friction with fellow employees and customers, increased frequency of illnesses and accidents, and increased absenteeism.[1]

There is a profound need for mental health services for the working population. The workplace is an ideal location, since many deterrents to the employees' seeking help (cost, transportation, time off) are eliminated.[2] This chapter includes an introduction to the subject area, a discussion of the differences between mental health counseling in the workplace and in the community, an exploration of specific areas of counseling—mental health, occupational stress, counseling for victims of crime and sexual harassment—and the DHHS proposal to develop an ECS model for executive stress.

MENTAL HEALTH SERVICES AT WORK

The term *mental health counseling* refers to (1) a relationship established between the trained counselor and the employee; (2) thoughtful and candid discussion of the personal problems experienced by the employee; (3) an appropriate referral that secures the necessary assistance; and (4) the provision of short-term counseling, when a referral is not necessary, to alleviate a temporary crisis. Mental health counseling does not imply that an employee is "crazy." No one is immune from experiencing emotional problems.

Mental health counseling in the workplace represents a relatively new area in the field of social and mental health care services. Although the incidence of mental health problems in the workplace is extremely high, the existence of pertinent data is disproportionately low. The information that is available, however, suggests that employees often do not use existing mental health counseling services, possibly because of the stigma of being labeled "mentally ill." Bertram Brown, the former director of NIMH, reports that emotionally troubled auto workers do not use psychiatrists and mental health centers even though the cost of treatment is covered by the union's insurance. Instead they rely on themselves, family, and friends. The implication is that the provision of health insurance coverage does not invariably lead to the use of mental health services. A survey done in Michigan discovered that only 13 percent of the UAW members knew about the mental health coverage in their company insurance plan and that only 1 percent were using the benefits. The majority of workers thought that the family doctor was an appropriate source of help for workers with mental health problems.[3]

Many workers use the physician or nurse at the workplace, who becomes a key referral source for the EAP. One study found that not one of the 500 employees interviewed in the work setting had ever seen an outside psychiatrist, psychologist, or social worker. The employees trusted social workers in the workplace because they were employed by the organization.[4]

Assuming that the need for mental health services was established, a team of researchers studied whether the workplace was the appropriate environment for the delivery of such counseling services to the working population.[5] They performed a demonstration project in the New York garment industry that confirmed their impression that even men and women with severe emotional problems are able to function on the job. The group of employees studied was found to have mainly neurotic disorders, although a small portion were diagnosed as psychotic. Although it is generally believed that psychotic people are unable to work, the fact that most of these men and women continued to work throughout the project represented a significant finding—that a job may be within the capabilities of an emotionally ill person.

In my experience, the following types of mental health and emotional cases are most common in EAPs:

- Individual adjustment problems (neurosis to psychosis).
- External factors such as battering, incest, rape, or crime.
- Sexual problems, including impotence and sexual preference.
- Divorce and marital problems.
- Inability to cope with stress.
- Depression and suicide attempts.
- Difficulties with family or children.
- Sexual harassment in the workplace.
- Trouble adjusting to upcoming retirement.
- Legal and financial problems. These can be symptomatic of other problems or can be separate.

A MODEL FOR MENTAL HEALTH COUNSELING IN THE WORKPLACE

Mental health counseling in the workplace is different from mental health counseling in the community. Too many mental health professionals think they are interchangeable. They falsely assume that community mental health skills are comparable to industrial mental health skills. To help clarify, I have developed a model for the delivery of mental health services in the workplace. Its unique characteristics are:

1. Counseling in the workplace is short term. Long-term therapy is appropriate in the community.
2. There are logistical as well as legal problems when families

are included. Although EAP programs often offer services to families, they are based on self-referral.

3. The manager or supervisor is the key person in the client's work life. The work associates are similar to family members. The counselor should learn their configuration and how it operates on the employee.

4. The counselor assumes the role of a "broker" or go-between for the employee between the supervisor and the therapist in the community.

5. The counselor should have skills in management consultation, that is, meeting with supervisors to determine whether they have a problem employee, advising them on a course of action, and supporting them through the referral and after-care process.

6. The need for crisis counseling (to deal with emergency episodes such as suicide attempts) is present in the workplace.

7. The counselor must have special skills in confrontation to break the denial of the employee appropriately, especially the addicted person.

8. Confidentiality is more of an issue in the workplace than in a community mental health clinic or social agency because of the uniqueness of the host setting. Competition for jobs, as well as an environment that does not necessarily understand employees' personal problems, mandate a clearly defined and enforced confidentiality policy.

9. Record-keeping procedures need to be carefully developed and delineated so that employees are assured of their privacy. This is not as necessary to explain to clients in a hospital or social agency; it is accepted in such situations. Employees worry about who will read their records (especially personnel officials). The Privacy Act and the Alcohol and Drug Regulations are guideposts that I recommend all EAPs follow, to be sure of protecting their employees.

10. Executive stress does not carry a stigma in the workplace and is a good subject for workshops that will reach managers in the workplace.

11. The counselor must also design and implement educational programs in the workplace.

12. There is little group counseling and interaction.

13. The counselor is a part of the same system as the client and must adapt to seeing him or her in other situations.

14. One goal of counseling is adjusting to the work situation.
15. The unique work system (personnel, company physicians) can be used to help the employee. The counselor needs to understand how these systems work.
16. Some clients may have more authority in the workplace and earn much higher salaries than the counselor.
17. Unions are extremely important in the workplace, and the counselor needs to work with them as appropriate.

For counseling purposes, I recommend that diagnosis be based on *Diagnostic and Statistical Manual of Mental Disorders* (DSM-III).[6] DSM-III incorporates several innovative features that represent major advances in the field of mental health assessment. One feature is the specification of five different areas of assessment that comprise the multiaxial evaluation system used for each person:

Axis I	(a) Clinical syndromes; (b) conditions that are not attributable to a mental disorder but are a focus of evaluation or treatment; and (c) additional codes.
Axis II	Personal disorders and conditions.
Axis III	Physical disorders and conditions.
Axis IV	Severity of psychosocial stressors.*
Axis V	Highest level of adaptive functioning in the past year.[7]

The incorporation of this multiaxial system is a significant advance and represents the American Psychiatric Association's acknowledgment of the importance of a holistic approach to mental illness. It provides EAP counselors and therapists with a common language and specifies criteria to ensure employees of appropriate diagnoses.

STRESS COUNSELING

Stress is a reaction by the body to an unpleasant stimulus; it is the behavior people exhibit when they can no longer meet the demands of their environment.[8] Symptoms of stress may include increased blood pressure, more intense and rapid breathing, increased alertness (insomnia), and increased strength due to a diversion of blood

---

* The term *stressor* is used to refer to any event, condition, or stimulus that is associated with the development or exacerbation of psychopathology.

supply to the muscles. Any one of numerous sources of tension may result in stress, anxiety, or depression: personal loss (death of a loved one, divorce); illness or injury; change in lifestyle; job changes (trouble at work, getting fired); financial problems; and retirement.[9] Joel Elkes, director of the behavioral medicine program at the University of Louisville, states, "Our mode of life itself, the way we live, is emerging as today's principal cause of illness."[10] A further study reveals that illness, both mental and physical, resulting from occupational stress costs American business an estimated $20 billion a year in the white collar job sector alone.[11]

We are beginning to learn more about stress, but it is still a new subject area. A study conducted in Canada discovered that workload was perceived to be the highest individual cause of stress in Canadian organizations. It found no relationship between stress and the person's age and education or the type of organization. This implies that the ability to cope with stress is related to such variables as social environment and personality configuration, and such extra-organizational stress-producing variables as marriage and finances. The basic problem is identifying the precipitators of the stress.[12] It can be multicausal, and this makes it difficult to identify the specific reasons for a given person's stress.

One method that addresses this problem is the life-crisis scale developed by Thomas Holmes and Richard Rahe, psychiatrists at the University of Washington Medical School.[13] The breakdown of life events and their corresponding mean values of stress are listed in Table 7-1. A life crisis is indicated by the accumulation of at least 150 points in a 12-month period; the body is at risk for the 24 months following the life crisis. Holmes and Rahe suggest thinking about the meaning of life events as they occur and identifying one's feelings in response to them, trying to anticipate life changes whenever possible and plan for them in advance, and taking one's time in arriving at decisions.

The federal government's National Institute for Occupational Safety and Health (NIOSH) has rated 140 occupations by the pressure they produce. The 12 jobs with the most stress are:

1. Laborer
2. Secretary
3. Inspector
4. Clinical lab technician
5. Office manager

Table 7-1.

The Social Readjustment Rating Scale.

Life Event	Mean Value	Life Event	Mean Value
1. Death of spouse	100	23. Son or daughter leaving home	29
2. Divorce	73		
3. Marital separation	65	24. Trouble with in-laws	29
4. Jail term	63	25. Outstanding personal achievement	28
5. Death of close family member	63		
		26. Spouse begins or stops work	26
6. Personal injury or illness	53		
		27. Begin or end school	26
7. Marriage	50	28. Change in living conditions	25
8. Fired at work	47		
9. Marital reconciliation	45	29. Revision of personal habits	24
10. Retirement	45	30. Trouble with boss	23
11. Change in health of family member	44	31. Change in work hours or conditions	20
12. Pregnancy	40	32. Change in residence	20
13. Sex difficulties	39	33. Change in schools	20
14. Gain of new family member	39	34. Change in recreation	19
		35. Change in church activities	19
15. Business readjustment	39		
		36. Change in social activities	18
16. Change in financial state	38		
		37. Mortgage or loan for lesser purchase (car, TV, etc.)	17
17. Death of close friend	37		
18. Change to different line of work	36		
		38. Change in sleeping habits	16
19. Change in number of arguments with spouse	35		
		39. Change in number of family get-togethers	15
20. Mortage or loan for major purchase (home, etc.)	31		
		40. Change in eating habits	15
21. Foreclosure of mortgage or loan	30	41. Vacation	13
		42. Christmas	12
22. Change in responsibilities at work	29	43. Minor violations of the law	11

SOURCE: T. H. Holmes and R. H. Rahe, "The Social Readjustment Rating Scale," *Journal of Psychosomatic Research,* Vol. 11, No. 23 (1967), p. 218. See this source for more complete wording of entries.

6. Foreman
7. Manager/administrator
8. Waitress/waiter
9. Machine operator
10. Farm owner
11. Miner
12. Painter

Other high-stress jobs include (in alphabetical order) bank teller, clergyman, computer programmer, dental assistant, electrician, firefighter, guard/watchman, hairdresser, health aide, health technician, machinist, meat cutter, mechanic, musician, nurse's aide, plumber, police officer, practical nurse, public relations person, railroad switchman, registered nurse, sales manager, sales representative, social worker, structural metal worker, teacher's aide, telephone operator, and warehouse worker.

M. J. Smith, M. J. Colligan, and J. J. Harrell, Jr., in a research paper they prepared for NIOSH, advise a person to follow the following four tips to cope better with stress:

1. Get plenty of exercise and maintain moderate habits.
2. Build a strong family life.
3. Have diverse interests.
4. Reengineer the work life.[14]

In addition, Hans Selye, world-renowned biologist who more than 40 years ago identified the stress syndrome in the human body, emphasizes that control, success, and satisfaction are the three qualities that may reduce job stress and provide the key to longevity.[15]

Since 1960, court decisions have forced 15 states to allow workers's compensation payments in cases of job-related anxiety, depression, and other disabling mental disorders. Such decisions have led to a sharp rise in the total cost of company payments for workers's compensation coverage, from $2.9 billion in 1965 to more than $20 billion in 1980. Many companies now offer their employees stress-reduction programs or psychological counseling by in-house experts or by outside firms. The overall quality of the work life and organizational climate is often regarded as a precipitating factor in cases of emotional illness for some people who are not as stress resistant as others. Yet many employers are reluctant to get involved in such programs since they regard them unwarranted intrusions into the private lives of the employees. However, if court decisions establish the employee's right to sue the employer for psychiatric injury by stress, then assuming responsibility for employee mental health may become a matter of legal obligation rather than an optional policy of management.[16] EAPs can be beneficial to both employer and employees. By producing stress-reducing programs and counseling, they can reach employees before long-term chronic problems result in workers's compensation claims or disability retirements.

THE ECS MODEL FOR SENIOR EXECUTIVE STRESS

Executives comprise a unique group in the workplace. Since they are located at the highest levels of the company, their problems are often not confronted and subsequently can be more serious. Senior executives are particularly vulnerable since they are not protected by unions and grievance proceedings as are other employees. In addition, executives have greater visibility in an organization, so their actions and attitudes draw more attention than those of people further down in the hierarchy. In terms of productivity, this group can be responsible for the company's greatest losses if problems go unattended.

Many studies have supported the presence of stress and stress-related problems among executives. Consider the following statistics:

- A study I conducted of the leave patterns of DHHS employees revealed that senior executives take almost no annual or sick leave. They are not getting away from the pressures of the job.
- Bertram Brown, president of Hanneman Medical College and former director of NIMH, estimates that as many as 20 percent of elected and appointed officials at high levels are suffering severe symptoms from the stress of problems in their lives.[17]
- In a study of *Fortune* 500 executives, 18 percent of those interviewed expressed concern about their own drinking.[18]

Although the work situation is believed to be the most effective environment for intervention, many barriers prevent EAPs from reaching the special population of troubled executives. First, the autonomy and isolation of executives make it difficult to identify problems through the traditional supervisor-based structure.[19] Because of the advanced nature of the executive's job, direct supervisory contact is usually minimal. Even when it is present, the usual signs of job performance deterioration are less noticeable, because no one monitors an executive's time. In addition, if the executive is able to give orders and delegate responsibility to lower-level executives, the work can still be done effectively—even at an increased profit level—while the executive's personal problems worsen and become a closely guarded secret.[20]

Second, the denial of problems is far greater by executives than by other employees. The pattern is reinforced by high motivation and success; the job becomes the foundation for the denial. Because the executive has more highly developed verbal and analytical skills, the denial system is further supported through intense and elaborate rationalization. Finally, colleagues and personal secretaries often create a protective barrier as does the pressure to maintain a good image.[21] Admitting a problem could reflect negatively on others.

The following model is currently being designed by DHHS to develop innovative methodologies to reach executives with problems where the traditional approaches of EAPs have not been successful. The model covers a 24-month period. This includes the development and study of strategies to implement educational outreach and referral methodologies. The strategies include:

1. Management consultation between the professional ECS staff member and the senior executive experiencing a problem or needing to confront a co-worker or employee.
2. Management training courses designed and conducted to help the executive identify and refer troubled employees and co-workers.
3. Educational conferences on topics linked to stress management, including anxiety and depression, burnout and boredom, drug and alcohol abuse, weight control, health promotion, managing aggression, stress management, and smoking cessation.

The DHHS ECS will assume responsibility for evaluating this research project. The program will be located in a facility separate from the ECS unit and the federal facility, such as the National Institutes of Health (NIH), that would be able to ensure adequate privacy.

Visits by the counselor to the executive's office will be encouraged to maintain anonymity.

SEXUAL HARASSMENT

Many men are still confused about the topic of sexual harassment. They believe that women in the workplace hope their physical appearance will encourage men to approach them and that, in some cases, the women want to be seduced. But regardless of what these men believe, the company cannot condone such harassment. Female employees are being harmed. They do not feel flattered; they feel intimidated and fear reprisals if they object, especially when the harasser is a manager or supervisor and the employee's job or promotion may be threatened.

Cases of sexual harassment usually affect at least two employees' job performances. Policies to deal with such situations should include automatic referral to the EAP for the victim and, when appropriate, for the harasser. Often victims do not report incidents because they do not want to pursue the legal route. In such cases, counseling provides a viable alternative for assistance and valuable support.

Sexual harassment is defined as any unwanted pressure involving a person's sexuality. It includes verbal innuendos and suggestive comments, unwanted physical contact, rape, and attempted rape. According to the results of a confidential survey of government employees conducted by the Merit Systems Protection Board, an estimated 9,000 women—about 1 percent of the federal government's female workforce—have been raped or sexually assaulted on the job by their co-workers or bosses. In addition, 15 percent of the men who answered the questionnaire reported that they had been subject to some form of sexual harassment in the period from 1978 to 1980.[22] In another study, conducted by the Illinois Task Force on Sexual Harassment and Sangamon State University, 63 percent of the 1,495 state female employees surveyed agreed that sexual harassment was a serious problem and 72 percent agreed that unwelcome male attention on the job was offensive.[23] The results of a study by the Working Women's United Institute in New York are equally disturbing. When asked their responses to unwanted male attention, 78 percent of the women surveyed reported feeling "angry," 48 percent "upset," 23 percent "frightened," 3 percent "indifferent," and 27 percent "alienated," "alone," and "helpless."[24] Although a systematic body of literature does not exist on the subject, the literature that does exist suggests that the relatively powerless positions occupied by female workers have contributed to their reluctance in exposing the issues.[25]

The widespread incidence of the sexual harassment of women in the armed services was reported by both top-ranking women officers and lower-ranking enlisted women of the Navy, Air Force, and Marines. Rear Admiral Frances McKee, the assistant deputy chief of naval operations for human resources management, said women would not be taken seriously in the military until they have access to "real" jobs, including combat positions. Several women testified that they felt they could not report specific incidences to superiors because they would be ignored or cast as troublemakers. The women said that men in the military police did not accept them as equals and that women felt they always had to prove themselves.[26]

These testimonies revealed the fact that women are often afraid to report cases of harassment because the entire process puts them in a precarious position. The victim, after filing a claim with the Equal Employment Opportunity Commission (EEOC), still continues to work under the accused supervisor. Diane Lenhoff, a staff attorney for the Women's Legal Defense Fund, states that hostile treatment of women who file sex-discrimination complaints against superiors is not unusual. "In fact," Lenhoff stated in a subcommittee investigation, "victims of sexual harassment often encounter the same problems as rape victims—ridicule from co-workers, embarrassment, hostile investigators, and ultimately, retaliation."[27]

Yet women are no longer covering up for the men who harass them as they frequently did in the past. "We are seeing an increasing number of complaints filed alleging sexual harassment because of the women's increased awareness that this is a prohibited act," said Carol Schiller, assistant chief of California's division of fair employment practices.[28] In 1980, sex discrimination accounted for nearly half the complaints filed with the EEOC, according to Daisy Voight, a spokeswoman in Washington, D.C. In contrast, 30,000 complaints were filed in 1978, with fewer than 1,300 in the category of "intimidations and reprisals," where most sexual harassment cases fall.[29] EAPs remain a largely untapped resource for harassed employees and should be available to them.

VICTIMS OF CRIME AS EAP CLIENTS

In 1982, President Reagan created a national Task Force on Victims of Crime to address the needs of the millions of Americans and their families who are victimized by crime each year and who often carry the scars into the years to come. He recognized that in the past these victims have needed help and that their wounds—personal, emotional, and financial—have too often been unattended. Through the establishment of the task force, the President committed himself to ending that neglect.

One of the areas of concern for the staff of the task force was ways in which victims could be helped at their workplace. The executive director of the task force contacted me at DHHS for recommendations in this area. A document was prepared in response to this request, and in December 1982, the task force completed its work and published a report outlining its recommendations to the President for addressing this problem.[30]

A number of recommendations were made by my staff and me encouraging expansion of EAPs to assist victims of crime. I feel that these are important recommendations and bring credibility to the EAP field. Here are some sections of the report that address EAPs.

- Legislation should be proposed and enacted to establish or expand employee assistance programs for victims of crime employed by the government.

Victims of crime and the problem that they face are so numerous that it requires the coordinated effort of many organizations and individuals, in both government and the private sector, to help them recover from the crime and contribute to a successful prosecution. Even an excellently staffed and operated victim/witness assistance unit depends on the cooperation and goodwill of other sources. Employee assistance programs are an excellent resource.

Examination of jurisdictions that have victim/witness assistance units has shown that many victims are unaware of the existence of such units. An individual is more likely to be aware of a service provided through his employment than he is of a unit associated with the criminal justice system.

Employee assistance programs can perform many services. Trained counselors can both advise the employee and explain his situation to his supervisor. They can maintain a list of mental health practitioners qualified to assist victims. They can help the victim with any difficulties that arise with creditors, and can refer them to needed social service and victim compensation programs. The existence of such a program conveys to the employee that his employer is concerned about his welfare and supports his willingness to assist the criminal justice system.

A number of states have also set up programs for their employees. The beneficial aspects of these governmental programs are twofold: first, their employees receive direct assistance at the work place, and second, they serve as a role model for organizations in the private sector. Federal, state, and local governments should fully support and expand employee assistance programs, with additional emphasis on assisting victims of crime.

• Business should establish employee assistance programs for victims of crime.

Every employer has to deal with personnel difficulties from time to time. In a small business, attention is usually given on a personal basis. Larger organizations, however, often have employee assistance programs to help their workers face problems such as illness, alcohol or drug abuse, and family difficulties. Many businesses have crime prevention programs for their employees, and some have programs specifically designed to assist employees who have been victims of crime. Both large and small businesses can profit by helping employees who have been victimized.[31]

CONCLUSION

According to the Washington Business Group on Health (WBGH), the American worker is being seriously hindered by many mental health problems, including legal, marital, and financial difficulties. The group maintains that employers will allocate more resources to mental health when the professional societies stop fighting over reimbursement and start working together for a truly comprehensive system.[32]

With the need for mental health services established, the workplace was determined to be the appropriate environment for the delivery of services to the working population:

At any given time, a portion of the labor force is experiencing difficulty maintaining employment because of emotional problems. The number of employees who can remain in the workplace on the job can be increased by having mental health professionals located in the hub of the network of the workplace. In order for the counseling service to begin a counseling program in the workplace and to be accepted and trusted by the employees and employers in the workplace, there will have to be a change in the service delivery and the clinical technology employed.[33]

Mental health counseling in the workplace can help employees maintain a productive role by addressing such problem areas as stress, anxiety, depression, and sexual harassment. They represent a viable response to the high incidence of emotional problems among employed people.

Studies have shown again and again that employers who take responsibility for mental health end up paying less in other medical claims. For example, a study by Blue Cross of 136 persons who utilized insured outpatient psychiatric benefits found that medical costs dropped by $9.41 per patient per month, from $16.47 before outpatient psychotherapy to $7.06 after contact.[34] Group Health Association (a Washington, D.C., health maintenance organization) reports that users of mental health counseling benefits reduced their non-psychiatric physician visits by 30.7 percent and lab/x-ray services by 29.8 percent.[35]

Clearly, mental health counseling in the workplace is not only a humane and much-needed service; it is highly cost-effective for the employer.

REFERENCES

1. The President's Commission on Mental Health, "Report to the President," Vol. I (Washington, D.C.: Government Printing Office, 1978), pp. 6–9.

2. Dale A. Masi, *Human Services in Industry* (Lexington, Mass.: Lexington Books, 1982), p. 49.

3. Bertram Brown, "Obstacles to Treatment for Blue-Collar Workers, New Dimensions in Mental Health" (Report from the director of NIMH, June 1976), pp. 3–4.

4. Cited by Carvel Taylor, in interview with Dale A. Masi, July 1978.

5. Hyman J. Weiner et al., *Mental Health Care in the World of Work* (New York: Associations Press, 1973), pp. 125–135.

6. American Psychiatric Association, *Diagnostic and Statistical Manual of Mental Disorders* (DSM-III), Washington, D.C., spring 1980.

7. Janet B. W. Williams, "DSM-III: A Comprehensive Approach to Diagnosis, 1981," *Social Work*, March 1981, p. 101.

8. Beric Wright, *Executive Ease and Disease* (London: Pan Books, 1975), p. 23.

9. "What Everyone Should Know About Stress" (A Scriptograhic booklet by Channing LiBete Co., Inc., South Deerfield, Mass., 1975), pp. 4–5.

10. Cited in "Stress: Can We Cope?" *Time*, June 6, 1983, p. 48.

11. Michael Roddy, "Overcoming Stress on the Job," *Business Magazine*, May 15, 1977, p. F-3.

12. Rolf E. Rogers, "Executive Stress," *Human Resource Management*, Fall 1975, p. 24.

13. T. H. Holmes and R. H. Rahe, "The Social Readjustment Rating Scale," *Journal of Psychosomatic Research*, Vol. 11, No. 23 (1967), pp. 213–218.

14. M. J. Smith, M. J. Colligan, and J. J. Harrell, Jr., "A Review of NIOSH Psychological Stress Research—1977" (Unpublished paper, Cincinnati, 1977).

15. Cited in Pam Proctor, "How to Survive Today's Stressful Jobs," *Parade*, June 17, 1979, p. 4.

16. Berkeley Rice, "Can Companies Kill?" *Psychology Today*, June 1981, pp. 81–85.

17. Bertram Brown, "Why So Many Public Officials Go Astray," *U.S. News & World Report*, February 16, 1981.

18. Paul Sherman, "Executive Case Management: A Specialized Approach for the Alcoholic Executive," *Labor-Management Alcoholism Journal*, Vol. 11, No. 5 (March/April 1982).

19. Paul Roman, "The Promise and Problems of Employee Alcoholism and Assistance Programs in Higher Education" (Paper presented at the Conference on Employee Assistance Programs in Higher Education, University of Missouri, Columbia, Mo., August 1976).

20. Linford Rees, "Executive Stress and Alcoholism" (Unpublished paper delivered to World Congress on Alcoholism, London, 1981).

21. Joseph Pursch, "The Alcoholic Executive," *The Corporate Director*, January/February 1981.

22. *The Washington Post*, September 26, 1980.

23. *The Washington Post*, March 2, 1980.

24. James C. Renick, "Sexual Harassment Threatens Job Security," *Public Administration Times*, June 15, 1980.

25. *The Washington Post*, March 2, 1980.

26. Cited in *The Washington Post*, Feb. 11, 1983.

27. Cited in Terri F. Shonerd, "Harassment Hearings: Badgered for Sex, but 'Defendant' Now," *Federal Times*, November 1, 1979, pp. 1, 6.

28. *The Washington Post*, March 2, 1980.

29. EEOC Guidelines, Section 1604.11, 1980.

30. "President's Task Force on Victims of Crime," Final Report, December 1982.

31. Lisa Teems and Dale A. Masi, "Victims of Crime as EAP Clients," *AL-MACAN*, Vol. 13, No. 10 (October 1983), pp. 20–21.

32. Cited in Willis B. Goldbeck, "Psychiatry and Industry: A Business View," *Psychiatric Hospital*, Vol. 13, No. 3 (1982), pp. 95–98.

33. Weiner et al., *Mental Health Care*, p. 143.

34. John Jameson, Larry I. Shuman, and Wanda W. Young, "The Effects of Outpatient Psychiatric Utilization on the Costs of Providing Third-Party Coverage," *Medical Care*, Vol. 16 (May 1978), pp. 383–400.

35. Cited by the Voluntary Effort to Contain Health Care Costs in *Voluntary Effort Quarterly*, Vol. 2, No. 4 (December 1980).

Chapter 8

Health Promotion in the Workplace

A comprehensive preventive approach to health care emerged in the late 1970s to replace the traditional disease model. This approach includes health promotion and maintenance, and is often referred to as a mental wellness program. Health promotion has been defined as "any combination of health education and related organizational, economical, or political interventions designed to facilitate behavioral and environmental changes conducive to health."[1] The definition often includes alcohol and drug abuse programs, and for this reason, it is extremely important to define the respective roles, as well as the similarities and differences, of the two types of programs. It is also important for the two programs to be properly coordinated in the work setting. Both have the same objective—improving the employee's health and ability to function.

The wellness program should not be viewed as being in opposition to the traditional medical care system, but as being part of the developing health system that is parallel to and supportive of the medical care system. There are programs in the schools and the community, as well as in the workplace. Health promotion in the workplace includes educational, organizational, and environmental supports for behavior conducive to the health of employees and their families. Program objectives include fewer absences, less frequent and less severe sickness, greater awareness of health matters, better knowledge, improved behavior, and less risk.[2]

The terms *health promotion* and *mental wellness* can be used interchangeably. In this chapter we will use *health promotion* (HP). The chapter discusses the development and growth of such programs in the workplace, the components of the programs (including evaluation), the important distinctions between HP and EAPs, the future

133

direction of the HP movement, and the necessity of a reconciliation between HP and EAPs in the workplace.

THE RISING COST OF HEALTH CARE

Between 1960 and 1980 there was an increase of approximately 700 percent in health care expenditures in the United States. It is projected that by the year 2000 the total annual cost of illness in this country will be in excess of $2 trillion. Heart disease, cancer, stroke, and accidents, many of which are aggravated by an unhealthy lifestyle, are expected to be responsible for roughly 40.2 percent of this amount.[3]

The HP movement, which grants each person significantly increased control of his or her future health status, was fueled by a growing understanding of the costs attributable to illness induced by unhealthy behavior or lifestyle. For example:

- A Pacific Mutual Life study showed that illness due to poor nutrition costs employers $30 million annually. The same study gave the average cost of replacing high-level corporate executives as $250,000–500,000.[4]
- Luce and Schweitzer estimated that in 1976 cigarette smoking cost this country $27.5 billion, of which 19 billion was attributed to lost production.[5] Estimates of the number of working days lost annually because of smoking range from 77 million in 1971[6] to 81 million in 1978.[7]

For employers, the medical costs are multiplied many times by the impact on absenteeism, productivity, disability insurance, workers' compensation, turnover, retraining, and reduced morale. The need is apparent for a comprehensive strategy to facilitate changes conducive to health. Victor Fuchs sums it up in his book *Who Shall Live?*:

> The greatest current potential for improving the health of the American people is to be found in what they do and don't do to and for themselves. Individual decisions about diet, exercise and smoking are of critical importance, and collective decisions affecting pollution and other aspects of the environment are also relevant.[8]

HP programs are not a fad. They are increasingly part of the American culture and have earned support from employers because they make sense, meet definable needs, and are good for business. Such programs provide educational, organizational, and environmental interventions to reduce the risks of chronic diseases linked to lifestyle, to moderate unhealthy behavior, to restrain increases in health care costs, and, in effect, to improve the nation's health.

The startling statistics lead one to regard the growth of HP programs as a viable and cost-effective alternative. The work site has been identified as an optimal location for such programs for two reasons:

1. People are generally willing to participate in health programs offered at the work site because they are both convenient and free to the employee.
2. The work site has other economic advantages—a sizable portion of the cost of health care is paid by employers who see their return in the form of lower absenteeism and disability, greater employee productivity, and ultimately reduced health care costs.

DEVELOPMENT OF HP PROGRAMS

A private labor–management group composed of major labor and business leaders established a health care task force in 1977 under the sponsorship of former Secretary of Labor John T. Dunlop. This task force developed a series of recommendations to be used by labor and business leaders in developing programs to reduce health care costs. The recommendations included:

- Review policies and programs with respect to the provision of exercise facilities, smoking cessation clinics, and low-fat and low-calorie alternative menus and vending machine products.
- Support programs that encourage wiser use of existing employee health benefits.
- Make health education programs available to all employees, retirees, and their dependents, wherever feasible.
- Explore methods of providing cost-effective health education as an integral part of all health insurance benefits and direct medical care programs.[9]

The DHHS, committed to fostering HP programs in the workplace, sponsored a Conference on Health Promotion Programs in

Occupational Settings in January 1979. This significant step harnessed the efforts of the public and private sectors to develop and implement HP programs at the work site. Representatives from industry, unions, insurance companies, and the scientific and academic communities were invited to discuss relevant program issues. The establishment of the Office of Disease Prevention and Health Promotion (under the assistant secretary for health) was further evidence of the government's interest in preventive health strategies.

As a result of this increasing interest in health and well-being, many firms initiated HP programs in an effort to reduce the costs of health benefits and to seek new approaches to improving and promoting the mental and physical well-being of their employees. The Chicago Heart Association (CHA), in collaboration with 84 industries, established a project that screened some 37,700 (55 percent) eligible employees for hypertension. The Texas operating division of the Dow Chemical Company instituted a smoking cessation program after it discovered that workdays lost by smokers cost the company an estimated $400,000 a year. This program used financial bonuses and prizes as incentives to promote both participation in the program and significant changes in smoking behavior. The Land O' Lakes Company in Minneapolis developed a program that used computer-aided instruction to create an awareness and interest in diet and exercise.[10]

PROGRAM COMPONENTS

Typical HP activities range from low-cost information dissemination to comprehensive programs involving screening, treatment (clinically and/or educationally), and follow-up procedures. During the January 1979 DHHS conference, specific program components were discussed, which included: (1) nutrition and weight control; (2) high blood pressure control; (3) alcohol and drug abuse education; (4) stress management; (5) smoking cessation; and (6) fitness and exercise. Strategies, techniques, and approaches to combat health problems in these areas were also discussed.

Nutrition and Weight Control

Malnutrition, including both underconsumption and overconsumption of food, has become a major health problem in the United

States. Coronary disease, hypertension, obesity, diabetes, and even some forms of cancer, as well as other conditions related to the foods we eat, account for over one-half of all deaths each year. Strategies for weight control aim at teaching people not only what to eat but how to use behavior modification techniques to stick to a recommended diet. Dietary changes, including a decrease in calorie consumption, saturated fats, and cholesterol, require substantial changes in eating behavior. Techniques to modify a person's behavior include self-monitoring, stimulus control, and reward.

High Blood Pressure Control

Hyptertension (high blood pressure) is one of the major causes of cardiovascular disease (stroke), which is the leading cause of death and disability in the United States. Efforts to promote blood pressure control at the work site include comprehensive programs that include detection, referral for treatment, and follow-up. Results have been encouraging; a study conducted by the University of Michigan concluded that 88 percent of hypertensives identified in a work site hypertension control program followed through with a physician consultation. After two years, 80 percent of the referred employees maintained satisfactory blood pressure control.[11]

Alcohol and Drug Abuse Education

HP programs often include alcohol and drug abuse programs; however, HP and EAPs maintain distinct roles. Drug and alcohol programs under the HP strategy are designed to educate and increase the employee awareness about alcoholism and drug problems, to identify the risk factors, and to motivate employees to accept the program option for risk reduction and improved health. The program itself is an intervention designed to prevent the development of the problem.

Stress Management

The workplace may be a primary determinant of stress that results in personality, cognitive, and behavior changes. Studies reveal that such classic psychosomatic disorders as hypertension, gastrointestinal problems, and asthma may be influenced by psychosocial stress. In addition, susceptibility to and recovery from infectious disorders are determined, at least in part, by stress in the environment and the person's style of coping with it. Stress management training causes people to change their lifestyles and reduces absenteeism and medical costs while it increases productivity. Common stress-reduction procedures include assertiveness training, relaxation techniques, meditation, biofeedback, and guided imagery.

Smoking Cessation

Smoking is considered to be the primary cause of 40 percent of respiratory disease and 20 to 25 percent of deaths due to all forms of cancer and cardiovascular diseases.[12] The business community, recognizing the dangerous health consequences of smoking, now offers special programs to encourage employees to quit. Typical work site programs include: (1) physician counseling; (2) sponsorship of outside consultant groups such as SmokEnders; and (3) in-house incentive programs, support groups to help smokers quit, and educational programs about the effects of smoking.

Fitness and Exercise

Physical fitness and exercise are integral components of HP programs at the work site. Activities range from exercise and education groups to YMCA/YWCA membership and the assignment of part-time physical fitness leaders; such activities are designed to save money by reducing employee illness and increasing productivity. Motivational factors influencing a person's decision to exercise include knowledgeable and enthusiastic leadership, convenience, and adequate instruction, peer support, and the establishment of appropriate short-term and long-range goals. These factors are crucial to the success of any in-house program aimed at the achievement of mental and physical fitness.[13]

FUNDING

Research and informally gathered data suggest that HP programs are relatively inexpensive and cost-effective, yet companies still question how they will pay for such services. The funding of health promotion programs varies with the organization. There are three basic alternatives: to provide programs and materials to employees and their families (1) on a tuition-reimbursement basis; (2) on a cost-sharing basis; and (3) at cost to participants. In the first alternative, costs can be limited to incremental costs, costs can be fixed, or costs can be offered on a tuition refund basis. The third alternative requires rules for the setting of fees and the employee's payment in advance. The funding of the program also changes according to which option is chosen.

EVALUATION

A comprehensive evaluation system is a fundamental component of HP programs. Two crucial questions must be asked:

1. What evidence is there that HP programs will improve employee health?
2. What evidence is there that workplace HP programs are cost-effective?

A range of evaluation methods and designs is available to industry, depending on the specific program objectives set (increased awareness, behavioral change, risk factor reduction), the type of comparisons desired (changes over time, changes between groups, changes compared to mandated standards) and the resources available to conduct the evaluation (simple record keeping, sophisticated statistical techniques, epidemiological assessments).

Evaluation of HP programs has traditionally focused on two levels of measurement—process and outcome evaluation. Process evaluation focuses on the manner in which program activities are conducted and the methods of assessing the quality and appropriateness of the program. Outcome evaluation measures the consequences that are attributable to program activities, such as changes in knowledge, attitudes, behavior, risk factor profile, morbidity, and mortality. Expected short-term outcomes of HP programs include decreased rate of cigarette smoking, increased compliance with high blood pressure regimens, increase of regular aerobic exercise, and increased belief in the prevention of chronic disease. Long-range effects include increased productivity, decreased absenteeism, and reduced health care claims. The evaluation system, regardless of what particular method for measurement is chosen, represents a vital structure in the overall effectiveness of the HP program.[14]

DISTINCTIONS BETWEEN HPs AND EAPs

Ruth Behrens, the former senior advisor on work site health promotion in the Office of Disease Prevention and Health Promotion (ODPHP) at DHHS, spells out some of the differences between HP programs and EAPs:[15]

HP	EAP
Strictly voluntary.	Uses coercion and threat of job loss as stimuli for seeking assistance.
Deals with healthy employees.	Deals with employees with personal problems.
Aimed at all employees and often deals with employees in groups.	Focuses on individual employees.
Concentrates on alcohol and drug abuse education, along with other lifestyle topics.	Involved with diagnosis and treatment of alcohol- and drug-addicted employees.
Emphasis on health.	Emphasis on job performance.

Businesses may become confused unless they are aware of the distinct roles of the HP program and the EAP. The waters can become muddied for businesses if HP programs try to offer alcohol and drug programs beyond education; EAPs on the other hand are not prepared to deliver a full HP program. Evaluation of the two programs must also be done separately. Each program must generate its own data to justify its continuance. Using data without clearly differentiating source and methodology will further confuse an already hazy picture. It is imperative that the trained professionals in the HP and EAP fields be directly involved in designing and implementing evaluations of their programs.

CONSIDERATIONS FOR THE FUTURE

Corporate involvement in health affairs has been on the rise since the 1970s in an effort to curb escalating health care costs. Many firms have made aggressive commitments to contain these costs and to improve the health of their employees, yet there still remains uncertainty about which programs are effective and how such effectiveness is manifested. Efforts in HP have proven successful since their development in the 1970s, and efforts to update strategies continue. Although industry is generally supportive of a government commitment to encourage private sector initiatives and remove burdensome regulations, some aspects of the Reagan administration's proposals cause concern:

- A cap on Medicaid, reductions in Medicare, and major cuts in other federal programs will shift more responsibility for health care financing to the private sector. Firms already feel hard pressed and are very reluctant to take on additional burdens in this area.
- Several health care bills now before Congress will put heavy emphasis on consumer choice. There is a widespread feeling that business, as the aggregate consumer, can be more effective than individuals in controlling health care costs on the national level. Furthermore, whether individual consumers will develop the sophistication, or even the interest, to acquire the knowledge needed to make wise health care decisions is questionable.
- A cap on the employer's contribution for health care may dampen active business interest in cost-containment efforts. Such a limit could result in a loss of some innovative health programs now included in benefits packages, specifically those relating to HP and disease prevention.
- Business is worried about the additional administrative costs involved in offering multiple-choice plans on an annual basis. Some have suggested that firms be given a tax credit to offset some of these expenditures.[16]

The preceding proposals of the Reagan administration are of vital concern to business and industry and must be recognized in the development and implementation of an HP program as a cost-effective alternative to promote employee health.

CONCLUSION

The concept of HP hinges on the notion of self-responsibility. Most people have a vastly exaggerated view of what medical science can do to restore their health when it is lost. In addition, many still believe that somehow they are immune from illness caused by behaviors known to make everyone else who engages in them ill. The neglect of personal accountability for one's own health is a major factor in the increasing amount of productivity that U.S. industry loses to sick days taken for mental and physical health problems.

Accepting responsibility for one's own health does not guarantee well-being, but it is the fundamental notion upon which a healthy lifestyle rests. A high level of health, a sense of well-being far beyond the simple absence of illness, is the true "normal" standard, the expectation to which men and women are entitled.[17] Unfortunately, the country has not yet made a commitment to health. Employers, through the type of reimbursement provided by health insurance policies, have fostered a dependence on the medical system.

The HP concept provides an opportunity for employers to make cost-effective resource allocations and to express a growing awareness that health care problems can be addressed by the direct education and participation of well-informed employees. Although HP programs and EAPs differ in philosophy and administration, it is essential that the two exist harmoniously in the workplace. Both the health and personnel departments must cooperate in developing an effective and systematic method for the administration and staffing of the two programs. However, this joint effort must allow the EAP to retain its unique emphasis on the job performance model, which is under the jurisdiction of the personnel department. Both programs come under the common umbrella of preventing illness and the expense it causes for the employer.

REFERENCES

1. Lawrence W. Green, "Guidelines for Health Promotion Programs in the Worksetting" (DHHS, Office of Health Information, Health Promotion, Physical Fitness and Sports Medicine, November 28, 1980), p. 49. Dr. Green is director of the Center for Health Promotion Research and Development at Houston's Health Science Center.

2. Ibid., pp. 49–50.

3. Blue Cross/Blue Shield, "The National Health Promotion Media Campaign: An Action Plan for the Washington Metropolitan Area" (Washington, D.C.: Group Hospitalization, Inc., 1980), p. 3.

4. Cited by The Voluntary Effort to Contain Health Care Costs, in *Voluntary Effort Quarterly*, Vol. 2, No. 4 (December 1980), pp. 1–2.

5. R. B. Luce and S. D. Schweitzer, "Smoking and Alcohol Abuse: A Comparison of Their Economic Consequences," *New England Journal of Medicine*, Vol. 298 (1978), pp. 569–571.

6. L. T. Terry, "The Future of an Illusion," *American Journal of Public Health*, Vol. 61 (1971), pp. 233–240.

7. American Cancer Society, "A National Dilemma: Cigarette Smoking or Health of Americans" (Report of the National Commission on Smoking and Public Policy, New York, 1978).

8. Cited in Blue Cross/Blue Shield, "The National Health Promotion Media Campaign," pp. 4–5.

9. The Labor Management Group, "Labor Management Group Position Papers on Health Costs" (1978), p. vii.

10. *Public Health Reports*, official journal of the U.S. Public Health Service (Washington, D.C.: U.S. Government Printing Office), Vol. 95, No. 2 (March/April 1980), pp. 133–162.

11. A. Foote and J. Erfurt, "A Model System for High Blood Pressure Control in the Work Setting," *High Blood Pressure Control in the Work Setting* (National High Blood Pressure Education Program, 1976).

12. *The Reporter* (Newsletter of Federal Employee Health and Alcoholism/Drug Abuse Programs), Vol. 12, No. 9 (September 1981).

13. *Public Health Reports*, Vol. 95, No. 2, pp. 109–149.

14. Green, "Guidelines for Health Promotion Programs in the Worksetting," p. 49.

15. Ruth Behrens, "The Distinction Between Health Promotion Programs and Employee Assistance Programs" (Lecture to DHHS EAP administrators, in Employee Counseling Services Units Directors' Workshops, Washington, D.C., February 14, 1983).

16. Newsletter of the National Health Policy Forum held at The George Washington University, June 1981, pp. 7–8.

17. Donald B. Ardell, "The Nature and Implications of High Level Wellness, or Why 'Normal Health' Is Rather a State of Existence," *Health Values*, Vol. 3, No. 1 (January/February 1979), pp. 17–24.

Chapter 9

Working Women

Women in the workplace represent a unique population that is growing each day. Inflation has made working an economic necessity for women, whether or not they are married. Fewer and fewer women are remaining in the traditional roles of housewife and mother:

> Think for a moment of the nuclear family . . . husband working, wife not working outside the home and at least one child under college age living with parents. What percentage of American families do you think this comprises? . . . only 17%![1]

This chapter demonstrates the economic importance of work to women and discusses the relevant issues in the workplace. By understanding the particular stresses on women and the unique situation that women face, EAPs can better meet the needs of this large group of employees. Women have been entering the EAP field, but usually in the role of counselor, not policymaker. Because the vast majority of EAP administrators are men, it is of paramount importance that they be sensitive to the working woman and adapt their programs to her.

There has been and will continue to be a steady influx of women into the labor force. In recent years, public media and popular literature have been filled with stories of working women. Articles concerned with the new women managers, executives, and professionals have surfaced at nearly every newsstand. At face value, America's women seem to be making progress in the business world; however, deeper investigation into the statistics and facts reveals that this progress is not as great as it first seems. For example, in 1980, the median salary for fully employed white women was $11,197 for the year, compared with $18,612 for men; in other words, women earned 60.2 percent of the amount earned by their male counterparts.[2] This wage gap of approximately 40 percent is primarily due to occupational segregation (which is discussed later in this chapter).[3]

WOMEN IN THE WORKPLACE

Since the period immediately preceding World War II, the number of working women has more than tripled.[4] In the 1980s, more women have worked outside the home than at any time in our nation's history. In 1982 there were 47 million women in the labor force. They comprised 43 percent of the total workforce. Of these working women, 24 million were married and living with their husbands, 11 million were never married, and 12 million were separated, widowed, or divorced.[5]

There are many reasons for the steady increase in female labor force participation over the last decade: delayed marriage and motherhood, increasing numbers of divorces and separations, inflation, recession, the women's rights movement, and a growing belief in the opportunities for women in the marketplace. Regardless of the particular reason, women are entering the labor force in ever-increasing numbers, are staying in that labor force until retirement age, and are taking their careers and economic pursuits seriously. Most women enter the labor force before they begin their families and tend to stay in their jobs during pregnancy and return after their children are born.

Since the early 1970s, the fastest growing demographic category has been the female-headed household. These households, which usually include at least one dependent child, have grown at ten times the rate of two-parent households. From all indications, this group of single mothers will continue to grow in the future. One explanation for the increase is that remarriage rates are not keeping up with divorce rates. The Bureau of Labor Statistics reported that by 1978 in every socioeconomic group one out of every six children under age 18 lived in a family headed by a woman, and that by 1979, 55 percent of all mothers with children under 18 years (16.6 million) were in the labor force. The 6.0 million working mothers with preschool children in 1979 had 7.2 million childen under age 6, compared with 5.1 million working mothers with 6.1 million children under age 6 in 1974.[6] The statistics for 1982 are even more startling: almost 50 percent of women with preschool children are working or looking for work, as compared with only 20 percent as recently as 1960.[7]

Certainly the fact that women are now major bread earners for families deflates the argument that they do not take their jobs seriously or that they are merely supplemental wage earners. It has been estimated that two out of every three American women will enter the labor market during the 1980s and that a large percentage of these women will be single heads of households. The stereotype of a wife as someone who stays home and looks after the children will fit only one-quarter of American mothers.[8] By the year 2000, women are expected to constitute the majority of the labor force in the United States.[9]

The fact that women are working is nothing new. The fact that wives and mothers of small children are working is also not new. What is new is their numbers, the extent of their participation, and the mounting pressures and responsibilities they face. To deal with these pressures and responsibilities, working women need to develop new strategies for full and equal participation in the workplace.

OCCUPATIONAL SEGREGATION: ECONOMIC IMPLICATIONS

Although more and more women are working, their general well-being, both economic and social, has not greatly improved. Women's economic issues are still characterized by dependency, poverty, low wages, tax and social security disincentives, and credit discrimination.[10]

In 1956, the median earnings of a full-time working woman were only 63 percent of those of a full-time working man. At the beginning of the 1970s, the same woman earned 59 percent as much as her fully employed male counterpart. With the reemergence of the women's movement, women began to demand equal pay for equal work, and the media publicized the great developments in equal rights for women through affirmative action and social awareness. By 1974, 11 years after the passage of the Equal Pay Act and 2 years after the establishment of the Equal Employment Opportunity Commission, women were earning 57 percent of men's wages;[11] in 1978 the figure was 59.4 percent. The figure has held fairly steady despite the fact that more than half of the nation's adult women (43 million, which is more than two-fifths of all workers) were in the labor force in 1980, compared with only one-fifth of adult women at the turn of the century.[12] Even with our nation's enlightenment and the women's rights movement, women's economic condition has still been losing ground. It is important for EAPs to realize that many women—even those employed full time—live close to the poverty line.

Even when women function as heads of their households, the wage discrepancy gap persists. The greatest myth about this discrepancy of income is that women earn less than men because they are less educated. In fact, the average female worker is as well educated as the average male worker; both have completed a median of 12.6 years of schooling. Women are comprising more than half of college enrollments, and their enrollment has risen ninefold in law school and fourfold in medical school since 1970. Women for the first time are gaining half of the undergraduate degrees and almost one-third of the doctorates.[13]

The more education a woman has, the greater the likelihood that she will seek paid employment. Among women with four or more years of college, approximately two out of three were in the labor force in 1979.[14] However, 1981 statistics indicate that a female college graduate can expect to earn roughly 60 percent of the earnings of a male college graduate of the same age. Average income for a female high-school graduate was $11,498, whereas a male high-school graduate earned an average income of $19,126. The median income for a woman who has completed four years of college was $16,599, whereas her male counterpart earned $26,422. One reason for this discrepancy could be that 20 percent of women who graduated from college became employed in clerical positions, which as a class are notoriously underpaid and economically devalued.[15] The U.S. Census Bureau reports in 1983 that the average lifetime earning for women with bachelor degrees is $523,000; for men it is $1,190,000. Women high-school graduates will earn $381,000 in their lifetime, while male high-school graduates can expect to earn $861,000.[16] The median annual income for a female college graduate is less than the median annual income for a male who has graduated only from high school.

This gap in income is primarily due to the occupational segregation that has become particularly prevalent since the turn of the century. The U.S. labor force is in fact polarized by gender. In 1900, one-third of all working women were employed in domestic service jobs. Valerie Kincade Oppenheimer concluded that, between 1900 and 1960, fully one-half of all working women were employed in occupations in which at least two-thirds of the labor market were women.[17] Today, this is still true. In 1978, Louise Kapp Howe wrote: "The more detailed your analysis of a particular occupation becomes by specific types of work, by industry, by firm, by department within the firm, and by level of advancement achieved—the higher the rate of occupational segregation becomes."[18]

In the 1970s, two-thirds of working women were employed in white collar sales or clerical positions. So vivid is occupational segregation that traditionally female professions have come to be known as "pink collar" professions. Whenever a particular occupation has a female population of 80 percent, it qualifies as a pink collar profession. Nursing is a pink collar profession since 97 percent of nurses are women. In addition, 95 percent of sewers and stitchers are women, as are 99 percent of secretaries.[19]

As Stellman wrote, "Occupational opportunity and achievements of men are much more diversified than those of women."[20] The 57 occupations employing the most male workers employ 52 percent of the entire male labor force. In contrast, most professional women in the labor force work in only *four* job categories. Even within their own professions, women are not able to penetrate the higher levels of management that are accompanied by higher-pay scales. In social work and teaching, which are female-dominated professions, males hold most top management positions. The rise of corporate power and industrialization has placed the greatest labor demands in the traditionally female labor markets (for example, the clerical and service professions), which also happen to be some of the most stressful positions. Stress studies (as described in Chapter 7) reveal that secretaries are in the second most stressful occupation. Low autonomy, lack of upward mobility, and responsibility without authority characterize the stressful occupations. Since almost all workplaces use secretarial skills in one capacity or another, and since, as mentioned earlier, 99 percent of secretaries are women, EAPs need to incorporate this awareness and seek to accommodate the special needs of women.

The forces that govern occupational segregation are subtle, elusive, and based on social, psychological, and economic factors. Many pink collar professions involve giving some form of help or support to others. The secretary takes care of her boss and the nurse attends the sick. Many female professions are simply extensions of the traditional female roles of homemaker and mother. Women gravitate

toward these professions because they are consistent with the socialization imposed on them during their education. Occupational segregation will change only when this socialization process changes
and women are encouraged to pursue the traditionally male-
dominated professions, something that is just now beginning to
occur.

BLUE COLLAR WORKERS

Female blue collar workers come from various cultural backgrounds
that have strong sexual stereotypes. One expectation is that women
cook, clean, and care for the children whether they are employed or
not. In addition, the blue collar woman is usually the wife of a manual laborer; she lives with her family in an ethnic-oriented community in an urban center. Although she is frequently aware that her
wage is substantially less than the blue collar male's she can rationalize this on the basis of the differences in the jobs that men and
women hold. This form of occupational segregation can be seen by a
simple walk through a factory. Men operate the heavier machinery,
while women do the more intricate and detailed wiring work on the
assembly line. Heavy machinery jobs pay more than the detailed assembly line work, even though there is some question as to which
requires more skill.

If the blue collar wife were to push for increased wages and benefits, she would be more likely to do so for her husband rather than
for herself. Blue collar women have indicated that their husbands
become more restless as their wives' wages increase, resulting in
more domestic quarrels. Such husbands tend to regard the growing
social and economic independence of their wives as a threat. To
push for women's rights might fuel an already inflammatory home
situation. The situation has been summarized this way:

> Breaking into jobs traditionally held by men is not all it's cracked up
> to be. Women in telephone companies and auto industries talk not
> only of sexism but of sex on the assembly line, jealous husbands who
> don't want their wives to work with men, male coworkers hostile
> about a woman taking over a male job, male against female battles
> over seniority, and the strong blue collar male attitude that women
> should stay at home.[21]

Women who challenge the status quo by entering male blue collar jobs may do so at considerable cost. They are in a dual stress position—at home and at work.

WOMEN IN UNIONS

EAPs have taken a strong position on including union participation in support of programs. It is important, however, for EAPs to recognize that, by including unions, women may not always be equally represented. It behooves ALMACA and EAPs in general to ensure adequate representation of women, who comprise close to 50 percent of the workforce. On the other hand, unions have acted as valuable allies on some women's issues. For example, when I was on the national board of ALMACA, the board's representative from the AFL–CIO joined me in pressuring ALMACA not to hold its 1978 annual conference in Illinois, a non-ERA state. By myself I would not have had enough influence to sway the board, but when the AFL–CIO threatened to boycott the conference, ALMACA agreed to hold its annual conference in California instead.

Women have been members of labor unions for nearly a century. The early unionization efforts of the mill workers of New England were almost all organized by women working in the textile mills and living in company quarters. Yet several problems have persisted between women and organized labor groups. First, women have not participated in organizing efforts in numbers great enough to influence their own work conditions and wages. Second, women who have participated in these efforts over the years have not learned much from their more successful organizing brothers, who have become skilled and effective in winning benefits for male workers.

As members of unions, women are theoretically entitled to equal pay for equal work, but even organized women are concentrated in the female-dominated occupational categories in much the same way as their nonorganized sisters. These sex-specific job categories are characterized by low wages and unequal benefits packages. In addition, many blue collar women are not members of unions. Most of these women workers are concentrated in industries that are not organized and have not been known for aggressive organizing efforts. The trend of minimal participation by women workers has been present since the efforts of the mill workers in the late 1800s.

As a result of this trend, women have achieved little through unions in the way of benefits and wage increases. During the nineteenth century, 98 percent of all working women were not represented by any union. At the turn of the century, 1.5 percent of full-time working women belonged to unions.[22] By the early 1980s, union membership by women had increased only to 10.5 percent (by contrast, 27 percent of the male labor force is unionized). To put it another way, approximately six out of seven women who work are not represented by organized labor. Occupational segregation is partly responsible for this trend.

It was not until the formation of the Coalition of Labor Union Women (CLUW) in 1974 that women united to address the particular economic issues and unique needs and problems of blue collar women in the marketplace. The failure of industry and union representatives to resolve the inequities in pay between male and female blue collar workers is symptomatic of the slow progress of unionized women. Organizational efforts, such as formation of the CLUW, symbolize the direction women in unions must take to obtain inclusion at the collective bargaining tables and in all phases of labor–management negotiations. Because women meet overt and often subversive resistance in their personal and work lives, the process of organizing may remain painful and slow.

DIVORCED WOMEN

There are more than 5 million divorced women in the United States. These women form a new group of economically disadvantaged. Whereas the average man experiences a 75 percent increase in income after divorce, the average divorced woman experiences a 47 percent decrease.[23] Only one woman in seven is ever awarded alimony, and fewer than 50 percent receive any form of child support. Yet most divorced women are responsible for the care of their children,[24] so they must work.

If a woman has been out of the workforce during her marriage or has worked only part time, she is at a disadvantage following a divorce. Her earning power remains low. In addition, her standard of living is lower at a time when her resources may be depleted. Any children she has will compound her depressed status. In contrast, most men have fewer increases in their expenses as a result of divorce and no change in employment capacity. The divorce courts in America tend not to take this state of affairs into account, so divorced women often suffer financially and professionally for reasons that actually have nothing to do with their capacity to work. EAPs need to be aware of this unique pressure on divorced working women.

IMPLICATIONS FOR EAPs

The EAP must address the unique role of women in the workplace and the additional stresses they may face, such as the responsibility of being a single parent, securing adequate day-care facilities for their children, receiving an inequitable salary in relation to their male counterparts, and working in some of the most stressful jobs, including secretarial and clerical work. Many women suffer psychological and economic pressure because child-related constraints make it very difficult for them to develop their careers. The working mother performs her job at the workplace during the day and goes home to other responsibilities in the evening, leaving little time for much else.

The EAP must be sensitive to the special needs of women. If possible, an EAP should have at least one female counselor, since some women employees (whether rightly or wrongly) feel that another woman will understand their problems better than a man. The EAP can run special programs like support groups for women and workshops to help them develop their skills and plan their careers. It can also provide referrals for those who need day care. In addition, the EAP can serve a very valuable function by making higher corporate management more aware of the special problems of working women. It can recommend—and provide documentary evidence to encourage—personnel policies that accommodate the needs of working parents, such as adequate maternity leave, flexible work hours and leave time, and day-care reimbursement policies.

Because the EAP is a relative newcomer to the human services field, few EAPs have evolved far enough to develop comprehensive programs for women, and little research has yet been done to document the effectiveness of such programs. I am confident that, as the EAP field continues to grow and to gain respect, it will be increasingly recognized as a viable system to address the needs of working women (as well as those of the working population in general). The final section of Chapter 13, Barbara Feuer's case study of the EAP run by the Association of Flight Attendants, describes the best-known example so far of a highly successful EAP designed primarily for women.

CONCLUSION

It is critical for the EAP to address the unique role of working women with respect to income differentials and stressful family situations by accommodating the need of this special population for upward mobility and training. Management must be alerted to the potential problems of the working woman. In addition, EAP staff need to relate these issues to a particular company. If too many of these conditions converge on the working woman, she may become depressed or turn to alcohol or drugs. Rather than waiting for women employees to become less productive and less effective, EAP workers may intervene at an earlier stage. They can encourage companies to develop strategies that alleviate these stresses and save countless numbers of employees from developing personal problems.

REFERENCES

1. Sarah Weddington, special assistant to the President (Lecture delivered at Radcliffe College, Fall 1979).
2. "Quick Quotes from the National Commission on Working Women," U.S. Bureau of Labor Statistics (Washington, D.C., 1983).
3. Janet Norwood of the U.S. Bureau of Labor Statistics (Lecture delivered at the Clearinghouse of Women's Issues, Washington, D.C., January 25, 1983).
4. "20 Facts on Women Workers," U.S. Department of Labor (Washington, D.C., 1980).
5. Ibid.
6. Janet Norwood (Lecture delivered at the Clearinghouse of Women's Issues).
7. *The Baltimore Sun*, May 11, 1983.
8. Ralph Smith, ed., *The Subtle Revolution*, cited in *The Washington Post*, October 1979.
9. Addie Wyatt, "What's Happening to Working Women in America?" in *The Church and the Wage Earner* (1974), pp. 26–32.

10. Jane Roberts Chapman, *Economic Independence for Women: The Foundation for Equal Rights* (Beverly Hills, Calif.: Sage Publications, 1976).

11. Louise Kapp Howe, *Pink Collar Workers: Inside the World of Women's Work* (New York: Avon, 1978), p. 1.

12. "20 Facts on Women Workers."

13. *The Baltimore Sun*, May 11, 1983.

14. "20 Facts on Women Workers."

15. "Women in the Economy: Preferential Mistreatment. A Report to the 1977 Working Women's Conference," in *Employed Women* (Chicago, 1977).

16. Cited in *Parade*, July 24, 1983.

17. Valerie Kincade Oppenheimer, *The Female Labor Force in the United States: Factors Governing Its Growth and Changing Composition* (University of California, Institute of International Studies: Population Monograph Series, No. 5, 1970).

18. Howe, *Pink Collar Workers*, pp. 5-10.

19. "Quick Quotes from the NCWW."

20. Jeanne Mager Stellman, *Women's Work, Women's Health: Myths and Realities* (New York: Pantheon, 1977), pp. 56-57.

21. *The Washington Post*, June 19, 1977.

22. Judith Papachristou, *Women Together: A History in Documents of the Women's Movement in the United States* (New York: Knopf, 1976), Chapter 8.

23. *The Washington Post*, June 16, 1983.

24. Alice Lake, "Divorces: The New Poor," *McCall's*, Vol. 103 (1976), p. 12.

Chapter 10

Counseling Minorities and Handicapped in the Workplace

Several populations, including minorities and the mentally and physically handicapped, have special needs that must be addressed by any effective EAP. Although minority and handicapped groups comprise a sizable portion of the workforce, little attention has been focused on the development of EAPs to reach these target groups. The present scarcity of information on this subject is comparable to the lack of available resources concerning women in the workplace ten years ago. As Joseph A. Califano, Jr., stated in his 1982 Report on Drug Abuse and Alcoholism,

> To assess the (minority alcohol) situation requires more penetrating and comprehensive research than anyone has yet conducted. The goal is not simply to identify the unique characteristics of alcoholism for each minority group. . . . It is . . . important to know in what ways two alcoholics, drawn from different cultures and communities, are alike. Treatment design and planning for prevention and intervention may depend on an understanding of both the differences and the similarities.[1]

It is the responsibility of the EAP administrator to reach all employees; it is also this person's responsibility to develop innovative methods for this.[2] This chapter will discuss the cultural characteristics of blacks, Hispanics, and Native Americans, as well as strategies for reaching the problem employees within each group. In addition, the mentally and physically handicapped will be discussed as a special population that merits the attention and accommodation of EAPs.

It is not possible to cover the subjects of alcoholism, drug addiction, and mental health for each group; rather, the focus will be on the group's relationship to EAPs, and individual examples will be cited. The need for research and services for each of the minority groups is great in all these areas. The purpose of this chapter is to highlight the relationship of these problems to the workplace. My failure to mention all appropriate problems for these different populations must not be construed as an implication that the area is adequately covered.

BLACKS

Incidence of Alcohol and Drug Abuse

Alcohol and drug abuse are serious problems that have been ignored in the black community. Among many blacks, the combination of psychological stress, racial problems, poverty, unstable employment, poor health care, and lack of education interacts with heavy drinking and drug taking to cause explosive and detrimental consequences. Alcohol abuse has been cited as the number one health, mental health, and social problem in black America. It may also be the number one problem that is most ignored by black Americans.[3] Alcohol has been linked to over 50 percent of homicides among blacks, especially young black men. But alcohol has been a part of the black community and its social functions for so long that it is often overlooked in relation to its impact, role, and prevalence. As a result, a level of tolerance is generated.

Cultural Differences

The etiological theories of why Americans drink are primarily based on the drinking patterns of white Americans. Black Americans often differ in their drinking habits because their history, culture, behaviors, and economic status differ from those of traditional white America. There is often a tendency among blacks either to drink heavily or to not drink at all. Heavy drinking is especially prominent among black urban communities, among black men, among poor blacks, and among various rural black communities where alcohol is easily available.[4] Yet there seems to be no significant research available that tests the major hypotheses about the size of the black alcoholic population.

Prejudice and Racism

The element of racism similarly distorts the picture of mental health problems among black employees. As stated by one black employee, "Do you succeed, really succeed, by imitating white men, or by being yourself and waiting for the white men to become comfortable with who you really are?" Perhaps he most adequately reveals the plight of the black employee when he states, "If Henry Kissinger can make it in America, why do I have to speak like Walter Cronkite to be trusted by the inner circle?"[5]

Preston Wilcox, author of "Positive Mental Health in the Black Community," states that the mental health of blacks is largely a reaction or an adaptation to the conditions of white institutional racism. To accept white definitions of the black condition is to rehabilitate blacks into a state of "psychological whiteness"—antiblack and antiself—rather than to restore them to a self-defined state in political, physical, and cultural terms. It was not until the civil rights movement that black people redefined themselves on their own terms by heightening their race consciousness and taking control of those institutions that serve their needs.[6]

Counseling the Black Employee

The element of race may often be used by the black alcoholic to deny an alcohol or drug problem and refuse service. A black's reluctance to be referred to a competent black counselor should be openly challenged as should a refusal to accept the services of a competent white counselor, who he or she may feel is insensitive to the black culture. If alcoholism, drug addiction, and other problems among blacks are to be combatted in an effective way, influential cultural practices and economic and behavioral factors must be considered when assisting black employees. Significant knowledge about the characteristics of the black population must be gained, since blacks, as well as other ethnic groups, suffer from pressures not experienced by nonminority members of society.[7]

Perhaps the most crucial area of minority counseling is that of counselor training. A person who counsels black alcoholics must be keenly attuned to the social, economic, and cultural differences between blacks and whites, as well as to the black experience as it relates to counseling and training programs. The problem has been stated this way:

> Black clients are not well served by the helping professionals, particularly white professionals. Several writers suggest that the inability of whites to transcend the parameters of their own cultural reference points is the main problem. Other scholars suggest that black clients must change their attitudes if counselors are to be effective. The implication is that when black clients are able to submerge their negative feelings about whites and to perceive each prospective helper as an individual, better counseling interactions will occur. Still other writers minimize the race variable and insist on an egalitarian approach to therapy. They insist that human beings reflect a core of universal feelings and intrapsychic phenomena, which can be handled by any competent therapist regardless of race, color, or class. In order to bring some clarity to the overall question, and to avoid the either/or stance, new approaches to psychological theory appear necessary.[8]

Counselors of black alcoholic employees must be knowledgeable in the following areas:

1. Background of the black experience (for example, the cultural differences between the black African American and the black West Indian American).
2. The black family.
3. Service delivery systems and the counseling process in relation to blacks as clients.

It is only when this knowledge is apparent that the EAP counselor can become an agent to create change.[9]

The EAP field still has a long way to go in modifying its predominantly white cultural perspective. If we reverse the picture and look at how many white people go to black counselors, black lawyers, or black physicians, we can see the hypocrisy in saying that a black person is rationalizing when he or she wants a black counselor. The EAP field is severely underrepresented by black administrators and counselors, and blacks are not utilizing facilities in proportion to their representation in the workforce.[10] As the field grows, it can no longer ignore this special population that comprises such a large percentage of the workforce.

HISPANICS

Unavailability of Resources

In 1978, in an attempt to obtain some references on industrial alcoholism programs for Hispanics, I conducted several computerized literature searches. The computer data center at Boston College was used to search out related topics. Inform and Social Science Citation Index were used as data bases. Inform contains approximately 10,000 documents produced by Abstracted Business Information, including 280 business and financial journals, covering the period 1971–1978. Social Science Citation Index has worldwide journal coverage, including over 300,000 records; coverage was from 1972 to 1976. Not one single reference was provided by the search. Next, occupational alcoholism and Puerto Ricans, Mexican Americans, and Spanish Americans were cross-indexed. Again, not one citation was found. Discussions with various Hispanic experts on alcohol abuse, including the executive director of the National Spanish-Speaking Commission on Alcoholism as well as the Hispanic Office for Program Evaluation in Boston, confirmed that there was no material on this subject.[11]

It is clear that the emerging EAP field has done virtually nothing for Hispanics. Only recently has a trend emerged to design alternative models of mental health service delivery (not EAPs) that recognize the differences in the cultural backgrounds of clients. This includes models that reach out to people in need, that are geographically and psychologically accessible, that take advantage of naturally occurring psychosocial support systems (such as families, ethnic communities, religious affiliations, and employment contents), and that are in harmony with the fabric of the consumer population, respecting its members' human dignity, regardless of race, sex, ethnic background, or belief system.[12] The EAP field would do well to study some of these mental health approaches and assess their possible application to EAPs.

Statement of the Problem

Community mental health care, which focuses on alcohol, drug, and mental health problems, does not meet the needs of Hispanics, who, as a group, probably receive the least amount of care. Statistics seriously underestimate the frequency and severity of mental health problems among Hispanics. In addition, the care they receive tends to be of poor quality. The major factors that account for this critical situation can be grouped into five categories: (1) an inadequate data base; (2) cultural heterogeneity; (3) institutional policies and practices; (4) personnel needs; and (5) inadequate research and evaluation.[13]

Inadequacy of the Data Base

It is generally agreed that Hispanics constitute the second largest ethnic minority in the United States today. In the near future, it is expected to be the largest. Most recent estimates indicate that there are approximately 16–23 million Spanish-speaking people in the United States, making it the country with the fifth largest Spanish-speaking population in the world. Puerto Ricans are a minority of the overall population of New York, yet, along with blacks, they comprise the majority of people who are most affected by drug use and abuse. They do not have a voice in the policies and planning of treatment services, which is a function carried out by middle-class professionals with little substantive knowledge about the Hispanic or black cultures.

Current estimates of the incidence of alcohol, drug, and mental health problems among Hispanics are based on extrapolations from studies that fail to take into account the distinctive cultural values and unique familial and social structures that have a direct bearing on a person's perception of his or her own state of mental health. The inadequacy of basic demographic data also stems from the lack of standard criteria for identifying the Hispanic community at large as well as the various groups within it. The outcome of this inadequacy, besides the lack of appropriate treatment facilities, is a loss to the Hispanic community of millions of dollars in federal funds distributed on the basis of population counts.[14]

Cultural Heterogeneity

The U.S. Hispanic community is culturally heterogeneous, comprised of three readily identifiable groups of diverse origins— Mexican-Americans (Chicanos), Puerto Ricans, and Cubans. However, it is a common practice to lump together all Spanish-speaking people, thereby glossing over the multiple differences among and within groups. The question of delivery of EAP services is critical in this multicultural Hispanic context, since the effectiveness and accessibility of these services depends on acknowledgment of the cultural differences.[15]

Institutional Policies and Practices

The destructive forces of cultural stereotyping, institutional racism, and professional elitism are evident in the EAP field. As E. F. Torrey points out in the manuscript "Psychiatric Services for Mexican Americans," mental health services in this country:

> . . . are sharply bound by both class and cultural values. . . . The vast majority of services, delivered by highly trained professionals stressing insight and autonomy, evolved to meet the needs of upper class America. . . . The resulting lack of class and cultural perspectives produces services for minority groups that, when they exist at all, are both illogical and irrelevant.[16]

Mental health services dominated by traditional intervention models neglect the Hispanics' struggles with problems of self-esteem and attempts to gain strength and dignity. The concept of mental illness in the Hispanic culture is one filled with stigma and suspicions. According to several Hispanic administrators I met on a recent trip to Puerto Rico, even the use of a psychologist or psychiatrist in a program may produce an adverse reaction, whereas a social worker may prove more readily acceptable.

Personnel Needs

Systematic affirmative action efforts to recruit Hispanics into training programs have yet to be mounted. Hispanics are underrepresented among the consumers of mental health services and among the professionals who staff the programs. Less than 1 percent of the professional workforce in mental health programs is Hispanic. The sensitization of white professionals to Hispanic culture has received insufficient attention,[17] as has the need for professionals to know Spanish if they will be working with Hispanics.

Inadequate Research and Evaluation

Inadequate research of the Hispanic community is evident in the scarcity of material on the mental health problems of Hispanic people. As one survey of the literature concluded:

There is a severe paucity of mental health research on the SSSS (Spanish-speaking, Spanish-surnamed). What little there is, unfortunately, is of execrable quality. We have pursued studies based on unwarranted assumptions; we have encountered the questionable use of statistical tests; we have complained of the absence of adequate controls or adequate matching of subjects or other indices of low quality research [which] results in contradictory or incompatible findings.[18]

The Hispanic experience must be further investigated so that mental health, alcohol, and drug services may be delivered in the most efficient and accessible manner. Only after such an investigation can the lack of basic knowledge of Hispanic health and of the cultural heterogeneity of the population be remedied.

Considerations for the Future

Many questions with respect to alcohol and drug taking as well as mental health problems among Hispanics still need to be raised. For example, is alcoholism among Hispanics associated with acculturation and stress or with other causes? Are alcoholism and drug rates among Hispanics related to low socioeconomic conditions or to other conditions prevalent among the population?

The following plan of action is recommended for use at the federal, state, and industrial levels:

- Special emphasis should be given to studying the drinking patterns of Hispanic women, a virtual unknown.
- A special national effort should be made to request research funding from the Alcohol, Drug Abuse, and Mental Health Administration (ADAMHA) for researching some of the questions already raised, ascertaining what studies related to Hispanics have been funded by ADAMHA, and making their results available to the EAP field.
- The use of EAPs by Hispanics is virtually nonexistent, yet it may offer the most hope for Hispanics with alcohol problems. If alcohol is found to be a major problem among Hispanics, as the facts are beginning to indicate, then priority must be given to reaching this population at the workplace through EAPs.
- Several issues need close scrutiny in the industrial area. Are Hispanics being served by EAPs in proportion to their numbers in the workplace? What are their special needs? Are there any

Spanish-speaking alcoholism counselors in industry? Hispanic counselors should be recruited and trained.[19]

The issues are very complex, since little has been done on a national scale to investigate and support the types of service delivery models that are effective in addressing the cultural differences of the Hispanic community. In addition, the training of Hispanic personnel needs to be improved and expanded to increase their availability to serve at all levels of service delivery and research.[20]

NATIVE AMERICANS

Prevalence of Problem

Estimates of drinking problems among Native Americans are derived from statistics concerning trouble with the law, disruption of family life, high suicide rates, high cirrhosis rates, and drug and alcohol abuse among Native American youths. Five of the ten major causes of death among Native Americans are directly related to alcohol abuse: accidents, cirrhosis of the liver, alcoholism, suicide, and homicide.[21] In 1980, Representative Daniel Peadres (R-Arizona) stated that alcoholism had reached "epidemic proportions" among the 150,000 Navajo residents of the nation's largest Indian reservation. Although liquor is forbidden on the reservation, bootlegging is a widespread, largely uncontrollable, multimillion-dollar business.[22] In 1977 approximately 30 percent of Cheyenne and Navajo adults aged 25–44 came to Indian Health Service (IHS) facilities one or more times experiencing a health problem in which the heavy use of alcohol played an important role. Their diagnoses were either alcoholism, DTs, or alcoholic hallucinosis. In 16 percent of the cases, the life-threatening complication was alcoholic cirrhosis.[23] Alcohol abuse is seen as a major problem by Native Americans themselves. In fact, the prevalence of drinking among Native Americans affords numerous opportunities for both direct and indirect social reinforcement. The example portrayed to youths is that drinking is socially acceptable and condoned, which in turn reinforces drinking practices among the young.[24]

There is a great diversity in the health status and needs of the Native American population, which includes members of over 200 independent tribes that live in urban, rural, and reservation settings throughout the United States. In general, Native Americans suffer from a greater prevalence of health problems than the population as a whole. Health problems of special concern to them include obesity, diabetes, accidents, environmental hazards, alcohol-related illnesses, and mental health problems. High unemployment, poor housing, and other economic and social difficulties contribute to these health problems and must be addressed. In addition, Native American health care services suffer from inadequate resources. Efforts are being made to improve this, but often the use of available resources could be better planned and coordinated by the federal agencies involved.

Cultural Aspects

Lewis E. Patrie, of the Oklahoma City area IHS, sees among Native Americans pervasive feelings of depression, helplessness, and futility, mixed with resentment over past and present injustices, and a wish to have these wrongs righted.[25] The poorest IHS facilities exist in this western Oklahoma location, as do the most serious health problems. The people experience the highest unemployment rate of Native Americans in the state—80 percent. The way of life has changed drastically for this population. Unemployed men tend to drink, and women tend to drink with their menfolk. Many children do not receive adequate parenting and often copy their parents' drinking habits. The educational level is low; more than 50 percent of students drop out of school between first and twelfth grades. Nuclear families have become common, with less attention paid to the older people and to traditions. Prejudice against Native Americans is widespread and has created a vicious circle. Unemployment, misunderstanding, and lack of communication leads to lowered self-esteem and increased feelings of rejection, which leads to further self-destructive behavior, which reinforces prejudices.

Research and Demonstration

Native Americans are skeptical of the usefulness of previous research and anthropological studies, and are more interested in program and protocol development than basic research. They therefore should be included in the planning of all projects concerning Native Americans, whenever possible. It is necessary to consider relevant cultural differences in all phases of project planning and implementation, which should focus on programs at the local, tribal, and national levels. Research is especially needed in the following areas:

- Factors contributing to the high rates of diabetes and alcoholism among Native Americans.
- Cultural relevance and effectiveness for Native Americans of educational materials and behavior change strategies.
- Appropriateness of traditional Native American physical and mental health care for today's health problems.
- Health needs of the rural (nonreservation) population.

These recommendations, among others, were considered in the development of the final drafts of "Objectives for the Nation," the ten-year plan for health promotion strategies in the United States. They increased the attention being given to disease prevention and health promotion for specific populations, including Native Americans, while providing a direction for such prevention.[26]

Occupational Alcoholism

In August 1980, I visited the Oklahoma City IHS office and three facilities in New Mexico and Arizona—the Window Rock IHS, the Lupton Alcoholism Treatment Service in Gallup, and the IHS Hospital in Santa Fe. As I drove through one Navajo reservation with the medical director of the IHS, I saw a great many wrecked automobiles piled on an off-the-road site. "That's the result of alcoholism," the director told me. And what had been done about the problem? The road had been widened. Clearly, this is an inadequate response to the pervasive alcoholism among Native Americans.

The following are my observations in regard to the incidence of the problem and the need for the occupational alcoholism model to be developed for the Native American population:

- The IHS personnel office at one site stated that it fires or suspends 50 percent of the Native Americans it hires. (Alcohol is usually involved in these cases, although it is deteriorating job performance that directly causes the firing or suspension.)
- The average life expectancy of the Native American male is 44 years.
- From what several recovered alcoholics told me it was evident that the occupational model had not been tried and that they

165

believed that such a program should be implemented on a test basis, using the threat of job loss as leverage.

- Alcoholism is rampant. There is hardly a Native American family that is not affected by it.
- Window Rock had neither a detoxification center nor a 28-day treatment program. This lack of medical coverage presented a real problem since alcoholism rehabilitation at the IHS hospital was almost nonexistent. What passed for a treatment center consisted of one trailer miles away, which often held 35 people or more although its capacity was 10. The trailer's staff were recovered alcoholics and impressively dedicated to their work, but even so, running an alcoholism program with almost no money is clearly impossible.
- Beatings of women by alcoholic spouses, boyfriends, or fathers is common and must be addressed in any alcoholism program. Women often missed work, according to the IHS personnel officer, because of such beatings.
- The recovered alcoholics to whom I spoke did not think it was mandatory that the head of the program be a Native American, and the recovered alcoholic women did not feel it was important to have a woman counselor. The main concern was to have a qualified, empathetic person administer the program, which everyone agreed was desperately needed. AA and Al-Anon were viewed as possible alternatives because of their strong spiritual orientation.[27]

The Navajo Tribal Utility Authority is starting an EAP. In addition, some coal companies are developing strip mining in the area. Subsequently, there is a more diverse number of employers of Navajos that might be interested in developing EAPs. The DHHS response has been to try to establish an ECS program for the IHS. This plan would include specially trained staff appointed by the IHS district office responsible for the development of the program.

THE HANDICAPPED

Definition of Handicapped

The primary purpose of the Rehabilitation Act of 1973 was to strengthen the federal effort in the area of vocational rehabilitation.

The 1973 act departed from earlier legislation by prohibiting discrimination against handicapped people in federally assisted programs and by requiring federal agencies and contractors to institute affirmative action programs for hiring and promoting the handicapped. The act contained a single definition of the term *handicapped* that was applicable to all sections of the act, including the antidiscrimination and affirmative action sections. According to a 1975 supplement that was added to this act to clarify it, a person was considered handicapped for all purposes under the act if he or she (1) had a physical or mental disability that impaired his or her employability, and (2) could be expected to benefit in terms of employability from the vocational rehabilitation services under the act.[28] In a further clarification, Attorney General Griffin Bell concluded that "persons suffering from alcohol and drug addiction are included within the statutory definition of 'handicapped individuals.' "[29]

The Labor Department regulations define a *qualified handicapped individual* as a person who is "capable of performing a particular job with reasonable accommodation to his or her handicap." Ward McCreedy, associate director of federal contract compliance programs, states that the regulations ban institutional or systematic exclusion of handicapped people solely on the basis of the particular handicap and that the key to affirmative action is the word *qualified*.[30] He referred to a Labor Department letter of explanation that includes the following:

> The government is not insisting on job opportunities for irresponsible workers. Rather, we are saying that a person's handicap—regardless of its origin—should not be the sole basis for refusing employment. Obviously, a person whose dependency on alcohol and drugs interferes with acceptable behavior or ability to meet normal job requirements is not qualified for employment.[31]

It is important to realize that this discussion focuses on two groups of employees—the physically handicapped and the drug-abusing or alcoholic employee. The EAP field has given little attention to the former. All employees have the potential of developing a physical handicap. An accident, heart attack, or stroke can render a healthy employee handicapped in a matter of minutes. EAPs need to realize that many handicapped individuals were not born with their handicap, and for those who become handicapped in adulthood and while working, the adjustment can be very difficult and the resulting stress inordinately high. Those born with a handicap may find as well that adjustment to the work site is stressful.

Reasonable Accommodation

Regulations on nondiscrimination for handicapped people require that agencies make reasonable accommodation to the known physical or mental limitations of a handicapped applicant or employee unless it can be shown that the accommodation would cause undue hardship on the agency. Reasonable accommodation is a logical adjustment made to a job or work environment that enables a qualified handicapped person to perform the duties of that position. The value and nature of a particular accommodation may be clarified by considering such questions as the following:

- Is the accommodation necessary for the performance of duties?
- What effect will the accommodation have on the agency's operations and the employee's performance?
- To what extent does the accommodation compensate for the handicapped person's limitations?
- Will the accommodation give the person the opportunity to function, participate, or compete on a more equal basis with co-workers?
- Would the accommodation benefit nonhandicapped as well as other handicapped individuals?
- Are there alternatives that would accomplish the same purpose?[32]

The responsibility of employers to provide accommodation does not end when the disabled person is hired. It is important to ensure that the EAP program is accessible to them. For example, consider paralyzed employees: Does the location and the accessibility of the counselor meet the special needs of these people? Other types of actions required in connection with reasonable accommodation are as varied as the needs of the people involved. They may include:

- Modifying written examinations.
- Modifying work sites.
- Making facilities accessible.
- Adjusting work schedules.
- Restructuring jobs.

- Providing assistive devices.
- Providing readers, interpreters, and people who are proficient in sign language.
- Adopting flexible leave policies.
- Reassigning and retraining employees.
- Eliminating transportation barriers.[33]

These are some of the innovative approaches to reasonable accommodation that have been taken by many federal agencies. Perhaps as more experience is gained, new types of action will be added to the list.

Reaching the Handicapped with EAPs

The EAP is an effective way of improving the coordination of employment and community resources designed to meet the varied needs of handicapped people. A disability, if severe enough, can precipitate a host of other problems, such as medical and health care concerns; a need for rehabilitation services; a need for job accommodations or restructuring; financial and legal problems; personal and family problems; a need for child care or care of dependent adults; and a need for homemaker services. To meet the special needs of the handicapped, the EAP strives for early identification and appropriate action to prevent further hardships.

The case manager or counselor maintains an active and aggressive role by seeking out the client and thoroughly exploring the problems at the earliest possible stage. The key to the successful implementation of this approach is the counselor's role in enabling the client to think through the possible implications of his or her disability. The counselor performs four primary functions: (1) assessment of the client's problems and needs; (2) development with the client of strategies to solve particular problems; (3) provision of actual services to the client, including referrals to the appropriate helping resources; and (4) provision of follow-up services to ensure that the client and appropriate resources have taken the mutually agreed upon action.

The work site intervention provided by the EAP allows the counselor to monitor and consult with the employee and to determine what kinds of services may be needed as well as to encourage the recovery process when the handicap is temporary. Special changes may be warranted, such as a change in work hours or even a change in the job itself. In order to assess the need for possible intervention, the counselor and employee need to review a full description of the present work situation, medical data to clarify the nature of limitations, and responses to questions about work-related problems (for example, What can the client no longer do? What kind of changes would be best?).[34]

The Merit Systems Protection Board

The Merit Systems Protection Board (MSPB), as the administrative authority charged with adjudicating federal employee appeals from a variety of employer-initiated actions, may hear defenses raised by employees in which allegations of handicap discrimination are made.[35] The following two decisions by the MSPB provide important guidance to federal agencies on what does and does not constitute the requisite reasonable accommodation in cases involving alcoholism. Although they concern federal employees, they are applicable also to private sector programs.

In determining what constitutes reasonable accommodation for alcoholism or other drug abuse, the board relies in part on the provisions of the Comprehensive Alcohol Abuse and Alcoholism Prevention, Treatment and Rehabilitation Act of 1970 (for example, implementation of an EAP),[36] as well as on OPM's rules implementing that act in the Federal Personnel Manual.[37]

The first case is an example of how employees may potentially view employers who do not support their alcohol treatment efforts and instead take punitive action. *Felten* v. *Department of Labor* (*DOL*) involves a safety specialist with the Occupational Safety and Health Administration (OSHA) who was charged with eight grounds of misconduct by the agency. The presiding MSPB official sustained seven of the eight charges. The employee did not challenge this finding, but instead raised the affirmative defense that his removal constituted discrimination on the basis of alcoholism, a handicapping condition,[38] and that the agency had failed to "reasonably accommodate" his condition as required by applicable regulations.[39]

For the following reasons, the board found in favor of the employee and therefore granted the petition for review and reversed the previous decision of the presiding official. During approximately two years prior to the employee's dismissal, agency officials informed him of the existence of alcoholism rehabilitation programs and suggested that he attend. It was not until the employee received a notice that he was about to lose his job, however, that he decided to enroll in a program and requested that a decision on the action be stayed while he attempted to rehabilitate himself through program attendance. The deciding official agreed to this, and the employee was given advance sick leave to attend the program. Upon completing the four-week program, he returned to the job; three weeks later he was fired.

It was clear to the board that the agency had promised to forestall action as long as the employee was seriously attempting rehabilitation and, by implication, had agreed that it was reasonable to allow him the opportunity to overcome his problem. There was no evidence that indicated resumption of drinking after the program ended. By proceeding with plans to fire him, despite the fact that he was apparently no longer drinking and was functioning adequately on the job, the agency had arbitrarily withdrawn the accommodation. The board concluded that the agency had thereby discriminated against the employee because of his handicap.[40] Accordingly the board ordered that the employee be reinstated.

In the case of *Ruzek* v. *General Services Administration (GSA)*, the agency planned to fire the employee, a guard, for sleeping on duty. The employee admitted to the charge, but said it was related to his alcoholism, a problem he subsequently brought under control in AA. A fellow AA participant also wrote to the agency on the employee's behalf. The agency, nevertheless, fired the guard, taking into consideration his past record. He appealed, claiming handicap discrimination. In the hearing, the guard's supervisor testified that, during a conversation with the employee in connection with an earlier disciplinary action, the supervisor had mentioned the employee's drinking problem and told him that the agency would be willing to help him. The supervisor and his witnesses, including a psychiatrist, testified that they believed the employee was an alcoholic. The presiding official concluded likewise and that the agency had met its obligations by telling the employee that assistance was available.

It was this decision that the employee appealed to the MSPB, which responded:

> Thus, we find that, in order to afford reasonable accommodation to an employee who is handicapped by alcoholism, an agency must offer the employee rehabilitative assistance and allow him an opportunity

to take sick leave for treatment if necessary, before initiating any disciplinary action for continuing performance or misconduct problems related to his alcoholism. If offering rehabilitative assistance, the employee's supervisor need not confront him with the supervisor's belief that the employee has a drinking problem, but he must make the employee aware in general terms that the supervisor suspects the employee has a problem affecting his performance or conduct, and that the supervisor recommends that the employee participate in a particular rehabilitation or counseling program which is available to him.[41]

The board found the agency's "weak attempt at counseling" did not constitute reasonable accommodation and that, in light of the supervisor's drinking history and in light of the information given the agency about his participation in AA and his success at overcoming the drinking problem, the agency should have canceled the proposed firing and given the employee another chance. In other words, a supervisor must do more than simply suggest participation in or indicate the availability of a rehabilitation or counseling program. The board concluded that the agency had committed handicap discrimination and reversed the initial decision of the presiding official and the agency action.[42]

It is important to recognize that while these two decisions deal with alcoholism, the provisions apply equally to drug abuse, physical handicaps, and any psychological disorder, such as mental retardation, organic brain syndrome, mental illness, and specific learning disabilities. The agency's obligation to provide reasonable accommodation applies when any such condition substantially limits one or more major life activities—caring for one's self, performing manual tasks, walking, seeing, hearing, speaking, breathing, learning, or working.

CONCLUSION

Although I do not support the labeling of a program as strictly for minorities, I believe that the program should record the numbers and types of groups that it serves. This documentation is important (1) to prevent a group from being scapegoated; and (2) to determine whether the company's services are reaching diverse populations. This includes proportionate numbers of women, racial minorities, and handicapped employees, with the appropriate accommodations when necessary.

Counseling Minorities and Handicapped in the Workplace

Programs must be modified to address the unique concerns of minority groups. Areas that employ a large minority population must emphasize the training of counselors in the appropriate language and aspects of the minority culture, while encouraging the integration of minority counselors in treatment resources and in program administration and staffing. In addition, the needs of the handicapped must be adequately addressed. Handicapped people should be encouraged to join the EAP field, since they can provide valuable input to alert others to sensitivities and unique problems of the handicapped. Programs must then be adapted and special adjustments must be made to deal with these particular groups. As part of the human services industry, EAPs must accept the responsibility of demonstrating appropriate concern for them.

REFERENCES

1. Joseph A. Califano, Jr., "The 1982 Report on Drug Abuse and Alcoholism," Report to Governor Hugh L. Carey, State of New York, June 1982, p. 84.

2. Dale A. Masi, "Reaching Minority and Handicapped Employees" (Unpublished paper, 1981).

3. Frederick D. Harper, ed., *Alcohol Abuse and Black America* (Alexandria, Va.: Douglass Publishers, 1976), p. 1.

4. Ibid.

5. Cited in George Davis and Gregg Watson, *Black Life in Corporate America* (New York: Anchor Press/Doubleday, 1982).

6. Preston Wilcox, "Positive Mental Health in the Black Community," *Racism and Mental Health*, Willie, Kramer, and Brown, eds. (Pittsburgh: University of Pittsburgh Press, 1973), pp. 466-470.

7. Fred T. Davis, "Counseling the Black Alcoholic," *Alcohol Abuse and Black America*, Frederick D. Harper, ed. (Alexandria, Va.: Douglass Publishers, 1976), pp. 85-86.

8. W. Banks, "The Black Client and the Helping Professional," *Black Psychology*, R. Jones, ed. (New York: Harper & Row, 1972).

9. Creigs C. Beverly, "Toward a Model for Training Black Alcoholic Counselors," *Alcohol Abuse and Black America*, Frederick D. Harper, ed. (Alexandria, Va.: Douglass Publishers, 1976), pp. 88-96.

10. W. F. Roseman, "Working with Unions from a Black Perspective" (Paper presented at NIAAA Skills Development Workshop—Agenda for Black Alcoholism Programs, Jackson, Miss., July 15-17, 1981).

11. Dale A. Masi, "Occupational Alcoholism: An Area of Action for Hispanics," *Mental Health, Drug and Alcohol Abuse: An Hispanic Assessment of Present and Future Challenges*, José Szapocznik, ed. (Washington, D.C.: COSSMHO, 1979), p. 81.

12. José Szapocznik, ed., *Mental Health, Drug and Alcohol Abuse: An Hispanic Assessment of Present and Future Challenges* (Washington, D.C.: COSSMHO, 1979), pp. ix–x.

13. A. Anthony Arce, "Mental Health Policy and the Hispanic Community," Paper cited in Masi, "Occupational Alcoholism: An Area of Action for Hispanics," pp. 30–31.

14. Ibid.

15. Ibid.

16. E. F. Torrey, "Psychiatric Services for Mexican Americans" (Unpublished manuscript, 1968).

17. Arce, "Mental Health Policy and the Hispanic Community," pp. 35–37.

18. A. M. Padilla and P. Aranda, "Latino Mental Health: Bibliography and Abstracts," DHEW Publication No. (HSM) 73–9144 (Washington, D.C.: Government Printing Office, 1974). This was reprinted in 1976 as DHEW Publication No. (ADM) 76–317.

19. Masi, "Occupational Alcoholism," pp. 80–82.

20. Szapocznik, *Mental Health, Drug and Alcohol Abuse*, p. x.

21. J. M. Andre, "The Epidemiology of Alcoholism Among American Indians and Alaska Natives" (Albuquerque, N.M.: Indian Health Service, 1979).

22. Cited in *The Arizona Republic*, August 18, 1980.

23. John R. De Luca, ed., "Fourth Special Report to the U.S. Congress on Alcohol and Health from the Secretary of DHHS" (Washington, D.C.: National Institute of Alcoholism and Alcohol Abuse, January 1981), p. 85.

24. De Luca, "Fourth Special Report to the U.S. Congress," pp. 85–86.

25. Lewis E. Patrie, "Overview of Mental Health Needs in Western Oklahoma" (Paper presented to a public hearing of the President's Commission on Mental Health, Oklahoma City, July 18, 1977), pp. 1–4.

26. Lawrence W. Green, Introductory remarks delivered to conference on "Strategies for Promoting Health for Specific Population: American Indians" (Washington, D.C., May 1980), pp. 12–16 of proceedings of conference.

27. Dale A. Masi, "Meeting Summaries for IHS Trip," August 18–19, 1980, pp. 2–3.

28. Rehabilitation Act, U.S.C. 706(5), 1975 Supp.

29. Griffin B. Bell, "Opinion of the Attorney General of the United States," Vol. 43, Op. No. 12, April 12, 1977, pp. 3–10.

30. Cited in "Alcohol Rights Discussed by Labor and HEW Officials," *The Almacan*, Vol. 7, No. 9 (October 1977).

31. Cited in ibid.

32. "OPM Handbook of Reasonable Accommodation," O-318-947 (Washington, D.C.: Government Printing Office, 1980), p. 2.

33. Ibid., pp. 4–6.

34. Industrial Social Welfare Center, Columbia University School of Social Work, "Preventive Rehabilitation Service Delivery: A Manual," 1976, pp. 1–9.

35. Robert A. Maroldo, Jr., "MSPB: Review of Handicap Discrimination Cases," *General Merit System Reporter*, Vol. 82, No. 6 (July 1982).

36. 42 U.S.C. 454(a)(8) and (b)(4); 42 U.S.C. 4561(a)(c)(1) and (d).

37. FPM Supp. 792-2, Subchapter 51-2(1); FPM Supp. 792-2, Subchapter 55-1(a) and (b).

38. 29 U.S.C. S 791.

39. 29 C.F.R. S 1613.704(a).

40. 5 U.S.C. SS 2302(b)(1)(D) and 7701(c)(2)(B).

41. MSPB Docket SLO75209017, August 20, 1981.

42. Ibid.

Chapter 11

International Employee Counseling

This chapter focuses on the development of international employee counseling and addresses the areas of (1) Americans employed overseas and (2) European human services in industry, which in turn is subdivided into the European industrial social work field and the recent development of EAPs in Europe.

I first began working in the field of international employee counseling when I left the United States in December 1967 to live in Italy (where my ex-husband was stationed in the U.S. Air Force) with my three children. The tour lasted for five years, including three years spent in England. I witnessed firsthand the alcohol problem of military, government, and multinational employees and their families. Drugs were widely available in the American teenage community, and severe emotional problems were pervasive. Because of this personal experience I continue to have a strong commitment to overseas Americans.

While in Italy, I worked under the auspices of several different organizations. I studied the community development projects in northern Italy and was awarded a year's postdoctoral grant from the American Association of University Women (AAUW). Concurrently, I held a consultantship with NIMH, Office of the Director, which enabled me to complete reports on mental health programs at Pordenone, Gorizia, Rovereto, and San Vito, Italy. I was then appointed a Senior Fulbright Scholarship for the academic year 1969–1970, which resulted in the publication in 1972 of the monograph *Exploring Italian Social Work: Columbus "in Reverse."* My work with NIMH included a major study of day-care nurseries throughout Italy, many of which were associated with work organizations. My work in England included the continuation of NIMH consulting for

176

mental health facilities as well as teaching social administration in a British college.

My international background and demonstrated commitment to the problems of overseas employees led to my invitation to assist in the development of the International Occupational Program Association (IOPA) in 1977, for which I subsequently served as executive vice-president. This was a not-for-profit association that planned for the development of programs and services for overseas employees and their families who were undergoing problems, whether they were due to alcohol, drugs, or emotional adjustment. I was sent to six foreign countries in the summer of 1978, to visit the companies' employees and treatment facilities before making my recommendation to the corporations.

Since 1975, I have also lectured extensively at many international conferences, including the World Congress on Alcoholism in London and several international congresses on EAPs in Vienna, Zurich, Iraq, and Bangkok. As a lecturer and faculty member of the Caribbean School of Alcohol Studies in the Virgin Islands, I worked with Michael Beaubrun, director, in addition to developing EAP training sessions under the auspices of the Pan American Health Organization (PAHO) in Trinidad and Barbados. My current activity includes the development of consortiums in Puerto Rico and the Virgin Islands.

Counseling has existed in industry in Europe for many years, but it is very different from the EAPs in the United States. European social work in industry is more like traditional American social work. It is nondirective and relies on self-referrals. A great deal of work is done with families, but the problems of alcoholism and drug addiction are not emphasized. The job performance model is used only infrequently.

The division between traditional European social work in industry and the development of EAPs in Europe must be reconciled by the merger of these two systems and the direction of resources to the development and implementation of EAPs. The European industrial social work field provides human resources that could be given the proper training to staff EAPs. Failure to do so will result in an unnecessary repetition of the mistakes that stemmed from the heavy emphasis on alcoholism without an appropriate professional staff that characterized the early occupational programs in the United States.

I will now turn to a discussion of the particular problems of

Americans employed overseas and will show how these problems tie in with EAPs. I will then explore the related topic of the European industrial social work system.

AMERICANS EMPLOYED OVERSEAS

Americans overseas are often a forgotten population. EAPs have not yet moved to provide services for this group of employees. However, Americans employed abroad are becoming increasingly important to companies, because companies are becoming aware of their high employee turnover rate, the subsequent excessive cost, and the difficulty in obtaining people willing to work overseas. This special population is faced with culture shock; a lack of appropriate services and of a comprehensive alcohol, drug, and mental health system to address its needs; and the inadequacy of family orientation to the new country. Today there is the added stress of terrorism.

Culture Shock

Culture shock is experienced by almost everyone who lives overseas, regardless of education or status. Because of the lack of preparation and the denial by the employer that culture shock occurs, the troubled person feels isolated. This often results in destructive behavior, such as the release of aggression and hostility through drinking, drug taking, crime, and other bizarre symptoms.[1]

It is estimated that 30–40 percent of families request or require evacuation from overseas duty prior to expiration of the contractual period.[2] This is in contrast to the 1.4 percent for graduates of the Business Council for International Understanding, a training program affiliated with Washington's American University that assists people in preparing for the overseas living situation.

Today the effects of culture shock are perhaps more seriously considered in the private sector than in the public sector. Such corporations as Mobil Oil and General Motors have been quick to realize that it does not pay to send an American on an overseas assignment before each member of the family is trained for the difficulties of living in another culture. For example, Mobil plans to send about 2,000 families to Saudi Arabia at a relocation cost of $50,000 to $210,000 per family. Because they realize that it is simply good business to protect that investment, Mobil and other corporations have begun to offer programs at overseas training centers around the country that are designed to assist a family's adjustment.[3]

Everyone recognizes that a mild form of culture shock takes place in any change of social scene. However, there are qualitative differences in a move to another country. An interesting phenomenon that accompanies culture shock overseas is the change of value structure. Being out of one's native country sometimes results in a loosening of the usual code of conduct. What would be considered unacceptable behavior in the United States is seen as possible overseas, and social conditions may be so different that they require a whole new set of coping mechanisms. The employee experiences anxiety that is affected by the location of the new assignment, his or her economic situation, and the changes in standard of living. In addition, the family of the employee is similarly affected by financial, cultural, professional, and academic readjustment in a foreign setting.

The following excerpts from my own experiences living abroad highlight a few of the differences that cause this sense of dislocation:

> When I think of Italy, not only do I think of the artistic accomplishments but also of having to carry our drinking water because of the threat of hepatitis.

> For two years we did not have a telephone. Medical facilities except for an outpatient dispensary were located three hours' driving time away.

> The hospital and specialists were located in Germany. Several wives went through pregnancies in Germany because of complications while husbands remained in Italy with the other children. Untold stresses resulted when medical problems combined with inadequate care.[4]

Given these differences, it is not surprising that people experienced difficulties. The cries for help were apparent:

> The installation in England was tiny—no recreational facilities, no medical facilities—but there were four clubs with bars.

> Because of the lack of facilities and the security which existed, I heard problems which wives were afraid to express to others. One pilot's wife, whose husband was an alcoholic, was in terror each time he took up the jet—she finally fled to the U.S. Another civilian wife slashed her wrists; no mental health facilities were available. Tranquilizers

flowed freely because they were the main available sedation for women.

Physicians and dentists were often known to drink heavily. Drinking was so heavy that constant chauffeur service was available at the Officer's Club for both civilian and military.[5]

James Julius, a psychiatrist who staffed the first mental health consortium of companies in Iran, maintains that, in addition to the culture shock that everyone experiences in a foreign country, some people, when removed from the security of a familiar setting, regress to past inabilities to cope with a situation. A person often works through an emotional difficulty, yet when faced with the instability of living in a new environment, the previous problem will resurface. Inability to cope with problems, in addition to the culture shock, could pose numerous problems for Americans relocated in an overseas environment.[6]

Lack of Services

In addition to the problems due to culture shock, the Americans' situation is further aggravated by a lack of services. In my travels I found that U.S. employees and their families overseas faced significant problems of alcoholism and alcohol abuse, legal and illegal drug use, and emotional crises, and that employees, spouses, teenagers, and young children were experiencing pressures due to the radical changes in lifestyle. Personnel directors both in the United States and abroad were handling problems for which they were unprepared and unskilled. They spoke of attempted suicides, of teenagers incarcerated for the possession or sale of heroin, and of alcoholic employees—all without available treatment resources. The personnel directors, although they were well meaning and caring people, understandably did not have the training for handling the emotional problems that their employees were facing. Also, apparently no company or government was tracking the incidence of problems. There was no way of knowing how many addiction problems, suicide attempts, battering incidences, and depressions were occurring, because no statistics were available. However, it was an accepted fact that heavy drinking and alcoholism were prevalent, and drug abuse and pill taking were excessive among women and teenagers.

Another problem was lack of employment opportunities for employees' spouses. This was particularly a problem of the spouses of those employed in government as well as those employed by multinational corporations. Such problems became managerial concerns because spouses (usually wives) would become restless and would return home when they could not find employment. Families experienced difficulties, and managers were often put in the role of counselors because there was no one else for the employees to turn to for help. This put managers in a position they were not trained for and could not handle. Norman Sartorius, director of the Mental Health Division of the World Health Organization, acknowledged in a meeting with me in June 1978 that this is a critical worldwide problem among overseas Americans. Many problems also existed for children with learning difficulties and physical handicaps. School officials maintained that parents were led to believe before they left the United States that there were special schools for such children abroad, when in fact these children often lost years from their educational development because of the lack of educational facilities.

Treatment facilities, although available in Europe, were not appropriate unless the person was fluent in the native language. Facilities in England might have been used for some alcoholism referrals, but they were already at capacity with their own clientele. To compound this difficulty, AA is not as available in Europe as it is in the United States, and English is not spoken at AA meetings.

Issues and Recommendations for Companies

EAPs overseas must be designed differently from those in the United States, relying more heavily on in-house staff and providing more extensive counseling. The key to implementing any recommendations depends on the commitment of a company to solve its own problems and to work cooperatively with other companies. Another major overall recommendation is clearly that a multinational alcohol, drug, and mental health treatment system be established to serve the needs of overseas employees and their families. I designed such a system, with the assistance of James Julius and Joseph Pursch, for the Office of Drug Abuse Policy at the White House. The system covered a plan for providing services on an outpatient, emergency care, and inpatient basis in the Mideast and Europe, including England. Because of a change in administrations, the system has not been put into effect. However, I feel it is still viable and strongly needed.

In addition, a systematic cross-cultural education effort must be designed to prevent or minimize the culture shock that employees and their families often experience. The social, economic, ethnic, religious, cultural, and travel barriers that tend to separate human beings from each other are beginning to crumble. American workers need to learn the skill of dealing with differences, especially in people. "Apart from the humanitarian consideration of providing such training to lessen culture and future shock, there are pragmatic reasons why organizations should undertake 'cross-cultural education' for their employees."[7] This form of education focuses on the factors that give people a sense of identity and distinction. It includes the analysis of what a person outside the majority group should understand and do to facilitate communication with people of the other culture.

The following are a few of my recommendations for change, included in my report to the International Occupational Program Association:

- A comprehensive program from screening for overseas employment to repatriation programs should be implemented by each company.
- Personnel directors need special training in all mental health areas, especially alcoholism; medical directors and other key personnel should also receive special training.
- Companies should do more to employ women and should include in their contracts that they will help wives find employment in the host country.
- Consideration should be given to the employee's family. A company should provide at least one professional counselor in each overseas location per 1,000 Americans there; the figure of 1,000 includes family members overseas. Because of the severity of problems and the lack of referral sources, 1 counselor per 1,000 Americans is actually a very conservative estimate.
- Serious consideration should be given to screening wives and teenagers. Individual interviews should be held before departure to ensure that families have a full understanding of the situation.
- Treatment for emergency care, such as detoxification centers

and mental health facilities for attempted suicides, is badly needed.

- Appropriate inpatient facilities are also needed for both alcoholics and the mentally ill.
- Facilities should be located so that their services can be used cooperatively by a number of companies.

A coordinated plan among international companies and government departments is required if these recommendations are to be successfully implemented. The alternatives to not providing such services are increased turnover rates, dissatisfaction among employees at overseas locations, and a higher cost in meeting contract commitments. These costs are escalating at a rapid rate—companies are reporting the cost of replacing one employee who must return home because of an emotional or addiction problem at approximately $100,000.

Inadequate Family Orientation

Overseas assignments are, unfortunately, always thought of in terms of the employee, who is usually assumed to be male. Families are often viewed by the State Department as "excess baggage," and it is assumed that they will travel wherever the husband or father is sent unless the employer decides otherwise. As a result, the stresses on the family are probably far greater than those experienced by the employee; the stability of the family is shaken, and the strains on them present other serious consequences. This continues even after the family returns to the United States. Since such cases are not unique, a company needs to think very seriously about the families that it sends overseas.

Particularly hard hit are the wives of overseas employees. One article describes the situation in relation to the wives of those employed in the military and in multinational organizations:

> What can be more sexist than identifying a woman exclusively in terms of her dependent status as a wife and an individual who must be sponsored? The military establishment and the feminist movement are tugging the service wife in two directions.[8]

In his book *Corporate Wives—Corporate Casualties?* psychiatrist Robert Seidenberg further explained the trauma and loss of identity:

Evidence is mounting to substantiate the observation that moving has a deleterious effect, particularly on women. . . . For the corporate wife serving abroad, integration into the multinational corporation means that her job, in addition to managing the household and her children, is to entertain indigenous company officials and traveling executives. . . . Personal interests or activities apart from the corporation are strictly no-nos in a foreign land, where possible involvements are always subject to controversy, misinterpretation, or both. . . . But living in an enclave, separated and alienated from all but other employee families and their servants, eventually wears down the soul. A person's humanity diminishes under such conditions of actual and spiritual segregation. As the need for free participation in a social or political community is thwarted, atrophy inevitably sets in.[9]

Proposals for Employers to Assist Employees

The following are suggested strategies designed to reduce the stress and culture shock that a family may experience when uprooted from its home and resettled in a foreign atmosphere.

Companies need to screen families going overseas. Besides the husband's eligibility for a job, the family's ability to adapt to overseas living needs to be considered. For example, teenage children are particularly susceptible to emotional distress if they must leave high schools to move overseas. One alternative might be to have the teenager remain in school in the United States.

Overseas departments need to have personnel who have lived overseas. One international vice-president of a large company told me that the extent of his company's screening was to tell the employee that if he or she (or his or her family) had problems, then they should not go overseas. Employers must understand that people may develop problems once overseas because of the nature of the situation.

Orientation to the foreign country should take place in the United States over a period of time and should include training in customs, language, and cultural values. Families who have already been to that country should be present to answer questions. If a company has more than one family going to a particular country, these families should meet during the orientation. The anxiety of moving to a foreign land can be greatly reduced if people see familiar faces upon arrival.

The company needs to assume responsibility when sending an employee overseas. If the company commits itself to helping make the transition easier, it can allay fears. Many families suffer in silence because they think that if they reveal any problems they will all be sent back to the United States and the husband/father will lose his job. Problems, particularly alcoholism, then become more severe than they would otherwise have been. The company needs to stand behind its employees.

Companies should try to help wives find jobs. As a result of the women's movement, more and more wives are apt to refuse to move because of their husbands' career unless there is an equal opportunity for them. Future generations of spouses will be neither submissive nor obstructive. Individual human beings will maintain attitudes and behavior consonant with their own personal growth and fulfillment. Corporate decision makers will be faced with the bittersweet necessity of taking the achievement motivation of both mates into account when recruiting or transferring employees. And the employee will need to screen the company to see whether it can give opportunities to both the husband and wife.[10]

EUROPEAN HUMAN SERVICES IN INDUSTRY

In 1978, I interviewed Swiss and French industrial social workers and was also able to obtain material written by German industrial social workers. These materials, in addition to the data I accumulated while living and working overseas, allowed U.S. social workers, EAPs, and businesses to get a glimpse of the social work services offered at the job sites in Europe and to note the similarities with and differences from those in the United States. The fact that EAPs have not been developed in other countries to the extent that they have been in the United States is due to many factors, including (1) a misconception by other countries of the nature of alcohol and drug abuse and a minimization of their incidence; (2) a strong stigma attached to alcoholism, which prevents the introduction of a program in the workplace; (3) a difference in the definition of alcoholism (in Europe alcoholism is often diagnosed only after it has resulted in physical deterioration and the person has lost his or her job and/or family); (4) the difference in the uses of industrial social workers, who in Europe work primarily with the family and with financial aid for employees; and (5) the lower prestige of social workers in Europe.

European Industrial Social Work

The following describes the social work picture in Italy, the Netherlands, Germany, and Switzerland as examples of European human services in industry. Questions raised by European social workers are also discussed.

It is increasingly important to clarify European systems of social work education. The meanings of terms used in social work are not necessarily the same in other countries as they are in the United States. *Trained,* for instance, is a word that causes confusion. To an American, this word, when applied to a social worker, means that the person has a master of social work degree. To an Italian, it means that the person has had three years of schooling in social work, not university affiliated.

> It may be useful to explain that the profession of social work in Italy is not clearly defined by law as almost all professions are. Several laws concerning juvenile delinquency, schools and hospitals require social work activities, but nowhere is there a legal definition of what social workers are. The University schools of social work, sanctioned by decree of the President of the Republic, gave them some kind of legal basis. Of course, this directly concerns only the few dozens of social workers graduated from those schools, but it is hoped that, in some way, the seven or eight thousand social workers existing in Italy will find some kind of legal qualification and professional safeguard.[11]

In a meeting I had with him, Dean Nervo of the Padua School of Social Work said that a person cannot work in a social agency without graduating from a school of social work. Students attend for three years, enrolling directly after high school—the average age of students is 15–20 years. Faculties of all the schools I visited expressed grave concern about their lack of university status, their precarious financial position, and the lack of social planning internships.[12]

The Netherlands has a specialization in schools of social work called "personnel social work." For this specialty, which begins in the sophomore year, a ten-week experience as an unskilled worker and an eight-month field placement in a personnel social work setting is required. The fourth year (comparable to a U.S. college's senior year) includes more intensive study in social work, psychology, and psychiatry.[13]

A different approach is evident in Germany. Schools of social work provide only a basic education and very limited specialization. New students are seldom interested in social work in industry because they do not want to work in a capitalistic structured company, yet there has been a history of social workers employed in industry.

Part of the problem is that the goals of social work in industry have not been clearly defined.[14]

Some firms in Europe, as in the United States, have their own social workers; some chain stores (for example, Hema in the Netherlands) have a central office that provides essential management operations and encourages the use of personnel social workers in coping with internal management and supervisory problems. The division of social work is part of the personnel department, and its activities are coordinated with those of the other divisions by the director of personnel.[15]

In Switzerland, a central service is offered upon which business and industries may draw; it is known as the SV service (*Schweizer Verband Volksdienst*). On its fiftieth anniversary in 1942, it published a booklet outlining its social work standards and services. It specifically addressed workers in industry. The service is

> in charge of allocating and educating the social workers, of adopting the functions to changing circumstances, of formulating working contracts, and of interpreting new methods of social work. It also provides statistics about the work done. . . . Delegating the overall management of the social services to SV means for the company to delegate the responsibility to experts in the field.[16]

In 1972, the SV service contracted with over 80 companies in the German part of Switzerland.

Although European services may vary by policy, hiring arrangements, social work standards, and the capabilities of individual social workers, certain generalities may be drawn. By and large, social services are centered on job-related and family problems. Individual problems that require intensive therapy, ongoing casework services, or family involvement, and problems for which other services are available, are usually not served by job-site social workers.[17] The transition to the EAP model of confronting employees whose job performance is deteriorating would seem natural for European practitioners. In the United States, EAPs were started to deal with alcoholism, then they moved into productivity issues. The reverse may be the process in Europe.

Specialized, comprehensive, and advanced training in EAPs and in counseling alcoholics could enable social workers to staff EAPs in Europe. In addition, this training could be part of an overall educational effort to modify the conception of alcoholism in these countries. If such efforts are not made, the same mistakes that were made in the United States will probably be repeated in Europe before any progress and development occurs. In the United States, professionals were not originally welcome in the occupational arena. Today, because of liability issues and the natural professionalization of the field, EAPs in the United States are increasingly being staffed by social workers. It would seem ironic for other countries not to benefit from our experience.

EAPs in Europe and the West Indies

This section discusses the current EAP movement in England, Scotland, and Trinidad and Tobago. The trend, which is a direct response to the transition from occupational alcoholism programs to EAPs in the United States, clearly cannot be limited to only these locations. However, they are representative of the programs in the forefront of international EAP development.

England

Following heart disease and cancer, alcoholism is England's third most devastating illness. As a disrupting force in the national economy, the illness has few equals. It is the most common cause of absenteeism, job loss, inefficiency, waste, and breakdown in morale and effective supervision. British industry has only recently recognized that alcoholism is a widespread and serious illness, and that positive intervention can help valued employees recover from alcoholism. It was partially due to this realization that Broadway Lodge, an alcoholism treatment center in Bristol, England, was established in 1974. The methods are based on the highly successful Hazelden treatment center in the United States and include intensive group therapy, individual counseling, educational lectures, and medical and physiological evaluation. The goal of the treatment is to ensure that the person leaves free of dependence on alcohol or drugs. The encouragement and support of employers and families is important both during and after the treatment period.

The basic difference between the treatment at Broadway Lodge and many other British alcoholism centers is that the former insists that no drugs whatsoever be used. Broadway's philosophy is that the alcoholic must face reality before recovery can start. Philip Golding, medical director for Broadway Lodge, believes that British industry is very neglectful in its attitude toward alcoholism. In comparison to U.S. standards, the amount of research and help on alcoholism in the

United Kingdom is minuscule. The enormous pressures on National Health doctors to deal with more easily treated illnesses means that the alcoholic often does not receive the amount and quality of attention that he or she invariably needs. AA has established guidelines for the treatment of the disease but is not as visible in England as it is in the United States. "It is ignorance," claims Golding, "which is the main reason why so many alcoholics remain untreated. Medical students are not taught about alcoholism in their training, so when they become GPs, they do not spot the warning signs."[18]

Scotland

Like England and many other European countries, Scotland only recently called attention to the problem of alcohol abuse in the employment setting. The misguided focus and analysis of the high incidence of alcoholism is revealed in the following quotes:

"If we stopped every man who smelled of alcohol going through the gates on the night shift, the place would be empty."

(Views of plant managers of a large heavy steel company in Scotland, 1977)

"An alcoholic shop floor worker is treated differently from an alcoholic who is a member of management where it can be hidden ... with the shop floor workers it is often too late to do something and he has to be dismissed."

(Extracts from an address by the Scottish Secretary of the Transport and General Workers Union at a luncheon in Glasgow, 1977)

"We fire 100 alcoholics a year."

(Comments by personnel officers of Scottish shipbuilding companies, 1975 and 1976).

Alcoholism is so prevalent that it has been customary either not to try to deal with it or to fire the employee. Clearly, both approaches are mistakes, and in response to them, the Scottish Council on Alcoholism concluded in 1977 that the answers to the problems of alcoholism are to be found in a joint union–management approach to alcoholism recovery programs (ARPs) at an individual company or organization level. The council states that places of employment provide the setting not found elsewhere for overcoming the major obstacles unique to alcoholism because it has been conclusively demonstrated that the work performance of every alcoholic deteriorates, even in the early stage of the illness. The primary objective of an ARP is "to provide effective help and treatment to those employees suffering from alcoholism and hence to overcome the problems unique to alcoholism which continue together to encourage people to conceal or deny the existence of a drinking problem and to resist treatment."[19]

The council crossed a crucial barrier, which many other Europeans have yet to overcome, in acknowledging that problems related to alcoholism also affect work performance. "There will be some [cases]," it states

> which involve problems of alcohol abuse (as distinct from alcoholism itself), and problems other than, or in addition to, those related to alcohol. Examples of non-alcohol related causes of unsatisfactory job performance are use of other drugs, marital, family, financial, legal and emotional problems or other health problems. Although this program is primarily concerned with the effective handling of alcoholism, these other problems require to be resolved. Thus, ideally, and in the long term, an ARP should be a part of a wider concept of an EAP designed to help employees with any health or social problem which impairs their work performance, and to aid them in gaining assistance before their condition renders them unemployable.[20]

Trinidad and Tobago

A rough indication of the size of the alcoholism problem in Trinidad and Tobago can be obtained by looking at the results of a study conducted in 1979 by Rampersad Parasram, vice-president of the Trinidad and Tobago National Council on Alcoholism (NCA). He found that 47 percent of the male medical admissions to the Port of Spain General Hospital during that year were for alcohol-related illness (not alcoholism alone).[21] In response to this alarming statistic, the NCA encouraged the joint efforts of both labor and management to promote the understanding of alcoholism as an illness and of the alcoholic as a sick person who, with help, has excellent chances for recovery. The union and company, through the development of constructive programs for the alcoholic, seeks not only to improve the health and self-confidence of the alcoholic but to reduce absenteeism and job loss. As an editorial in the Trinidad *NCA Bulletin* of March 1982 states:

> In order to successfully achieve our goal, we look forward to an agreement between the company and the union to cooperate at the plant level in encouraging employees afflicted with alcoholism to undergo a coordinated program directed to the objective of their rehabilitation.[22]

It was in response to this resolution of joint labor–management cooperation that the NCA developed the EAP seminar where I was the guest lecturer in March 1982. The Honorable Ronald Williams, minister of the state enterprises for Trinidad, stated in his greeting address at the seminar that "all employees of labor in both the private and public sectors should seek to create Employee Assistance Programs aimed at the early identification of problems in their workers and at providing human services especially in the area of alcohol and drug problems." He continued that the problem is not so much the advanced alcoholic but the man or woman who develops the problem gradually and manages to conceal it while making bad decisions and creating problems at work. He acknowledged the need for more employee assistance training seminars to help locate these people.[23]

Trinidad perhaps represents the forerunner in alcoholism treatment in the West Indies and is rapidly moving its concentration on alcoholism to the broader EAP field. Under the auspices of the Pan American Health Organization, I conducted a three-day EAP training session for approximately 80 businesspeople in March 1983. In addition, a three-day training session was conducted in Barbados for approximately 35 participants. Plans are in process for a consultant to be sent to Trinidad to continue the EAP development in the West Indies. Also, a West Indian professional (with an M.S.W. and an M.P.A.) will be sent to the United States to work with me at the University of Maryland on special EAP design and implementation strategies that can be utilized in Trinidad.

CONCLUSION

The field of international employee counseling is in the very beginning stages of development. The addiction and the mental health needs of Americans employed overseas (and of their family members) present unique problems and challenges for employers. At the request of employers, workers have uprooted their families from familiar ties and environments; they have been thrust into cultures and value systems different from and often opposed to their own. They have given up the support systems of friends and families, and professional help for emotional problems is either lacking or woefully inadequate. Since the employer is the common denominator for all the families, and since it stands to lose greatly from personnel problems, it behooves the employer to pay attention to the needs for services by the employee and his or her family members.[24]

The social work services in Europe are underdeveloped in a unique way that focuses on family and financial areas. In a separate realm, EAP awareness and training is just beginning to surface in European countries and the West Indies, despite an overemphasis on alcoholism. The EAP represents an effective and humanistic method of addressing the wide range of alcohol, drug, and mental health problems that result in a loss of productivity for the employer. It is critical to reconcile the division between traditional social work and the development of EAPs, or else the U.S. mistake of overemphasizing occupational alcoholism will be repeated.

REFERENCES

1. Dale A. Masi, *Human Services in Industry* (Lexington, Mass.: Lexington Books, 1982), pp. 128–130.

2. Catherine McCrane Keating, "Culture Shock, America: Can You Leave It and Love It?" *The Washington Post Magazine*, June 18, 1978, p. 2.

3. Ibid., pp. 2–3.

4. Dale A. Masi, *Exploring Italian Social Work: Columbus "in Reverse,"* DHEW Publication No. (HSM) 72-9025 (Rockville, Md.: National Institute of Mental Health, 1972), pp. vii–x.

5. Dale A. Masi, "Family Perspectives in Being Assigned Overseas" (Paper presented at the International Conference on Alcoholism in Multinational Corporations, Boston, April 1977), p. 1.

6. James Julius, "Mental Health Problems of Overseas Americans" (Unpublished paper presented at meeting of ALMACA International Division, Washington, D.C., October 1980).

7. Philip R. Harris and Dorothy L. Harris, cited in Masi, *Human Services in Industry*, pp. 125–128.

8. "Feminism Changing Wives' Role?" *Air Force Times*, November 22, 1976, p. 27.

9. Robert Seidenberg, *Corporate Wives—Corporate Casualties?* (New York: AMACOM, 1973), pp. 29-31, pp. 153-155.

10. Ibid., pp. 153-155.

11. Aldo Visalberghi, "Structure of University Education and Education for Social Work in Italy," *Journal for Education for Social Work*, Vol. 6, No. 1 (Spring 1970).

12. Masi, *Exploring Italian Social Work*, pp. 30-31.

13. Elise de Vries, "Personnel Social Work in the Netherlands" (Speech delivered to a group of representatives from private industry and government, March 26, 1970), p. 1.

14. Christina Stahl, trans. Christine Neghli, *Social Worker in Industry*, Blätter der Wohlfahrter Pflege, 124 (Stuttgart, Germany: July 1977), p. 147.

15. M. Gumfler, "Social Work in Industry—A Model of Social Work in Industry When the Social Worker Is Not Directly Hired by the Company" (Switzerland: Schweizer Verband Volksdienst, 1942).

16. Cited in de Vries, "Personnel Social Work in the Netherlands," pp. 3-4.

17. Masi, *Human Services in Industry*, pp. 204-205.

18. Cited in "Broadway Lodge," reprinted from *Bristol and West Country Illustrated*, October 1977, pp. 20-21.

19. Geoffrey Isles, "A Joint Union-Management Approach to Alcoholism Recovery Programs" (Scottish Council on Alcoholism, Advisers to Industry, 1977), pp. 3-7.

20. Ibid.

21. Michael H. Beaubrun, "President's Message," Trinidad *NCA Bulletin*, Vol. 3 (March 1982), p. 3.

22. Trinidad *NCA Bulletin*, Vol. 3 (March 1982), p. 5.

23. The Honorable Ronald Williams, "Draft of Notes for the Speech of the Prime Minister of State Enterprises to Open Seminar on Employee Assistance Programs," March 18, 1983, pp. 2-6.

24. Masi, *Human Services in Industry*, p. 133.

Chapter 12

Evaluation

Evaluating a functioning EAP cannot be the same as pure research. Evaluation is constrained by time and money in the workplace, issues of confidentiality, and access to employees. All these factors limit the sophistication of the research design. What is important for the evaluator to know is how to conduct applied research that results in sound, reliable data—a method that is possible within the structure of the EAP. (Evaluation is also distinct from an audit, which is an accounting system used to monitor whether a program is spending its money in the ways it claims to be.)

Most comprehensive evaluation studies in the past have focused on the treatment of alcoholism problems in industry; very few have addressed the broad-based EAP concept or the numerous other problems from which an employee may suffer such as drugs and emotional, financial, and marital problems. Similarly, the evaluation of mental health programs addressed only the treatment aspect of those particular problems. The focus on measurable goal attainment scales as a framework permitted a study of the efficacy of different treatment modes, but they proved insufficient and incomplete since they emphasized only treatment outcome and had no relation to cost or work performance. It was due to this partial nature of the occupational alcoholism and mental health evaluation models that new methods for EAP evaluation have recently emerged to document program effectiveness in dealing with a wide range of employee problems.

The EAP evaluation model recently developed by the DHHS ECS evaluates on both a cost-benefit basis and a cost-effectiveness basis that utilizes control groups, unlike any other ECS in the public sector. It is the most comprehensive and systematic method yet in use for evaluating an EAP.

This chapter will discuss the importance of evaluating EAPs, the concepts of cost-benefit analysis and cost-effectiveness analysis, the DHHS ECS evaluation model, and the importance of confidentiality.

THE IMPORTANCE OF EVALUATION

The importance of evaluating an EAP cannot be overestimated. Many programs must be evaluated to justify their existence to some external authority. Even if this is not the case, an EAP should be evaluated to ascertain the extent to which it is reaching its objectives, and to find ways to improve the effectiveness of its performance.

The field of human services, like any other field, must be held accountable for its actions. A quantitative evaluation system is an organized method for measuring a program's activities and process in relation to their impact and outcome and targeting the areas that require modification. This type of program evaluation serves as a feedback mechanism that monitors the EAP's performance in relation to a control group matched for age, sex, payroll class, and geographic location. If the program is not monitored, or measured, then it cannot be evaluated accurately.

The first step in evaluation is to specify particular program objectives to be evaluated. Without clearly defined objectives, evaluation cannot proceed, since it would be impossible to judge whether objectives are being met. The specific objectives to be evaluated will vary over time, depending on the developmental stage of the program, the particular problems being faced, and the availability of data.

Although evaluation is an important element in any program, certain conditions must be satisfied for the evaluation to measure the impact or outcome of the program accurately:

1. The program must establish clear goals and direction.
2. The program decision makers must agree on what the program is intended to do.
3. The organization itself must be supportive of the evaluation.
4. Sufficient funds and a qualified staff must be available to conduct an adequate evaluation.[1]

When these conditions are not met, an evaluation should not be considered.

195

Evaluation will serve different purposes for different people at different times. Some of the factors that might be assessed are:

1. *Effort.* What is the size of the evaluation task? How much time, money, and human effort are required?
2. *Effectiveness.* Is the program reaching its goals? Is it serving the intended clients? Is it saving the company money? Is it really doing what it is intended to do?
3. *Accountability.* Is the program accomplishing something worthwhile? Are the expenditures of resources justified?
4. *Goal definition.* Are the goals clarified and defined? Are the means of goal attainment being checked?
5. *Documentation.* Can data be provided that will demonstrate to outside groups the effectiveness of the program?
6. *Underlying assumptions.* Can this kind of program really make a difference? Is it being realistic? Are the methods and techniques successful?

COST-BENEFIT ANALYSIS (CBA)

A cost-benefit analysis addresses the question of whether an organization can expect a reasonable return for its investment of resources in a program in terms of identifiable cost reduction. The evaluation estimates a dollar value for the benefits the EAP provides to the organization. CBA measures the direct and indirect costs, including program operational expenses and costs attributable to the employee's problem(s), in order to determine the total dollar expenditure for implementation of the program as compared to the cost that would be incurred without the program. These two amounts are weighed to evaluate whether the program, given its estimated cost, can be justified economically.

As discussed earlier in this book, direct costs to industry include absenteeism, medical expenses, disability payments, early pension payments, and supervisory time required for discipline. Several studies have developed estimates of savings in direct-cost categories that may result from the establishment of a program. For example, Allis-Chalmers Company reported annual savings of $80,000 as a result of reduced absenteeism among problem drinkers.[2] A study of the Illinois Bell Telephone Company program reported another category of direct costs—that of disability payments. The company program resulted in a reduction of sickness and disability cases for savings of $459,000.[3]

Indirect costs, however, are more difficult to measure, and reports on such costs usually rely on estimates rather than on actual cost measurements. These costs include increased accidents, inefficiency of alcoholic workers, inefficiency of fellow workers, deterioration of morale, added sick-pay costs, and costs of replacing trained workers. In one study, suspected problem drinkers were found to be 16 times as costly to insurers as other employees. Thus, problem drinkers have been found to be significantly more costly (than non-problem-drinking employees) to themselves, to their companies, and to insurers.[4]

One example of a cost-benefit analysis was described by Alander and Campbell, who evaluated the results obtained by General Motors' Oldsmobile division. The objective of their project was to demonstrate whether or not an alcohol rehabilitation program pays off by reducing overall company costs, lost person hours, disciplinary actions, accidents, sick leaves, and sickness and accident benefits. The subjects were 117 hourly workers (111 men, 6 women) who had actively participated in the GM rehabilitation program. An unmatched control group consisted of 24 male employees, known to have alcohol-related problems, but who had not volunteered to participate in the program after an initial interview. The project results were impressive in all performance areas. The pre-program total wage loss for those in the study group was approximately $463,520 whereas the total wage loss after involvement in the program was $237,176. Alander and Campbell reported average treatment (not program) costs of $105 per participant in the GM program.[5]

COST-EFFECTIVENESS ANALYSIS (CEA)

Like a CBA, a cost-effectiveness analysis quantifies program outcomes, most likely in dollars, and compares this with the available program costs. But unlike the CBA, it does not require a projection of intangible or future savings for various types of programs. A CEA addresses whether a program is being conducted at an acceptable level of effectiveness, in terms of optimum return per dollar expended. A cost-effectiveness study could be used to show the ratio of dollars invested to decreases in absenteeism, without necessarily showing the actual monetary costs of absenteeism (which are very difficult to determine). In addition, cost-effectiveness evaluation can be used to compare alternative EAP strategies against a common outcome, and can represent a viable alternative to the more complex and problematic CBA.

Program costs for the federal civil service program, for example, are estimated at $5 per employed person ($15 million annually), with potential cost savings estimated at between $135 million and $280 million annually.[6] James T. Wrich's cost estimate (based on a series of assumptions and estimates concerning problem prevalence, expected penetration rates, and other variables) is $67,220 for the first year of running an EAP in a company with 1,000 employees; the long-term cost over a 25-year period is estimated at $426,740.[7]

THE DHHS ECS EVALUATION MODEL

The DHHS ECS model evaluates the process used by an EAP, the impact of the program, and its outcome. All three aspects are evaluated on the basis of employees' job performance, rather than treatment mode. This method of EAP evaluation is flexible enough to assess a program's ability to deal with a wide range of employee problems that cause work productivity to deteriorate. In addition, the efficacy of the EAP in meeting the needs of the troubled employees and restoring them to full productivity may be measured in economic terms that provide a basis for program modification where necessary.

Design of the System

The final design of the DHHS ECS evaluation system was the result of an intensive ECS staff review of the literature, in addition to interviews of lead evaluators in the field and preparation of a position paper. This was followed by the convening of a team of experts, who would design an appropriate plan. The need to focus significant efforts on the evaluation of ECS programs was apparent: In the public sector, no broadly based ECS had been evaluated that demonstrated both cost-effectiveness and cost benefit. Most private sector evaluations had concentrated on alcohol and drug problems only, and few had used control groups.

The team of experts from DHHS who designed the evaluation system included two evaluators of health programs from the Office of the Assistant Secretary for Health, statistical and planning experts assigned from the Office of Planning and Evaluation, two attorneys from the Office of the General Counsel, a computer expert, and the ECS staff members, who coordinated the entire effort. The group met for a period of one year, and the final plan was presented to the joint staffs of the Office of the Assistant Secretary for Planning and Evaluation and the Office of the Deputy Assistant Secretary for Health, where approval for funds were granted. With the help of the DHHS Contracts Office, the evaluation plan was incorporated into a request for proposals and culminated, in September 1982, in a 30-month contract with Development Associates, Inc., which has now assumed responsibility for implementing the entire system. The Stufflebeam model* was selected as the model for the ECS evaluation.[8] All 16 units, in addition to the five DHHS demonstration projects, fall within the evaluation purview. The three components of the model being used include process evaluation, impact evaluation, and outcome evaluation.

Process evaluation provides program decision makers with information needed for anticipating and overcoming procedural difficulties, making administrative program decisions, and interpreting program outcomes. Data for use in this phase are obtained quarterly from each unit through the use of a Unit Quarterly Report. Information on supervisory training, employee orientation sessions, outreach activities, contract and agreement activities, and employees who use the program are provided in this report. In addition, process data enable the EAP administrator to determine whether appropriate numbers of alcohol, drug, and emotional cases are being seen; it is important to ensure that the program is reaching different categories of employees in proportion to their numbers in the company.

The Unit Quarterly Report reflects both administrative and counseling activities. In addition, staffing and budget information and management-by-objectives plans will provide baseline data for this component of evaluation. A periodic review of these data will assure quality control of what is reported. Other instruments addressing the special demonstration projects may be necessary.

Impact evaluation is operationally defined for this plan as changes in participating employees relative to personal problems as a result

* The Stufflebeam approach emphasizes feeding the evaluation results back into the system as they are being determined. This makes evaluation practical, helpful, and immediate, because one does not have to wait years for an evaluation to be completed to find out what could be done to better the program.

of the program and not due to other work conditions, such as pay raises and transfers of supervisors. The impact data will not be available until 18 months following the start of the evaluation. This is because of the varying stages of development in each unit as well as the need for time to pass before treatment can be evaluated.

The contractor will be expected to develop the impact data instruments based on the emphasis of the different units. Goal attainment scales will not be used, and program staff will be consulted regarding the instruments. The ECS director's office will review and comment on any instruments developed. Measures must be taken to ensure confidentiality of the data. Interviewing supervisors is a possible means of collecting this information.

The most critical aspect of the model is outcome evaluation. Outcomes for the purpose of this evaluation are to be measured in terms of reductions in administrative costs to DHHS. Certain worker performance or personnel items as well as certain health cost items were carefully selected as areas where administrative costs to the department should be reduced. They, therefore, will be examined in this phase of the evaluation. The personnel items include sick leave used, sick leave balance, sick leave advanced, annual leave used, annual leave balance, annual leave advanced, leave without pay, and absent without leave; the health items include health insurance claims, sick benefits payments, number of accidents claimed, accident benefits paid, number of outpatient alcoholism and mental health visits before and after treatment, and number of inpatient alcoholism and mental health days before and after treatment.[9]

The ECS staff have been trained to use the departmental computer terminals to retrieve the personnel items on each employee. The computer system has been designed to remove all personal identification from the information. No one other than ECS staff will have access to client names, social security numbers, or code numbers that could be linked to any individuals.

The retrieval of health cost items will follow a model developed by NIMH. Confidentiality will be assured by using another federal agency, OPM (Benefits Division), as the conduit for collecting information. Data will be sent from the health insurance carriers in aggregate form to OPM for transmittal to the DHHS ECS evaluation contractor. An analysis of both sets of data will be conducted to link them to the total program cost and to the cost of individual ECS units. The contractor will then conduct a cost-benefit and cost-effectiveness analysis of the data. In order to reach an unqualified conclusion that positive changes in any or all of the variables are attributable to the ECS program, the use of a comparison group is imperative. Employees who use the ECS program will be compared to the total DHHS employee population in each unit, using the same kinds of data items described above. Comparisons will also be made by grade level, age, sex, and agency (if desired).

As the number of clients at each site increases, it will be possible to compare the programs in terms of cost-effectiveness. Using the data generated via the various phases of the evaluation process, the cost benefits of the program can be calculated. Selection of the most cost-effective and cost-beneficial features for transport to the other programs will be the responsibility of the ECS staff. Complete data will be provided in the summary reports to allow judgments to be made.

Several final observations and conclusions should be made regarding the development of the DHHS ECS evaluation model. One major consideration is the accomplishment of a project like this in an incredibly large bureaucracy such as the federal government. This is no small task; the operational time frame for a large bureaucracy is much longer than what might be considered normal in other industries. The formation of the evaluation team was time-consuming and took a major coordination effort because of the number of different offices involved. The role of an inside advocate at a high departmental level, specifically the Assistant Secretary for Personnel Administration (ASPER), was absolutely essential for the final implementation of the plan. As an advocate, the ASPER was able to resolve major conflicts, gain top-level support for both the idea of evaluation and the funding, and provide solutions to other problems that arose. One of the most important reasons for the success of the system's implementation was the development of a balance of political acumen and evaluation expertise throughout the entire process. It proved essential that the evaluation expertise not be compromised while satisfying the political issues. In the end, the evaluations results and methodology will be more valid.[10]

THE IMPORTANCE OF CONFIDENTIALITY

Confidentiality can be the most important issue faced in the development of an evaluation system. Each component, data collection form, and procedure has to be closely examined for its compliance with all confidentiality regulations. The entire evaluation system was reviewed and approved by the Office of the General Counsel. It was found that the entire system was in accord with the Privacy Act and alcohol and drug regulations.

Because of the inherent sensitivity of the ECS program, some procedures were developed and determined to be legally correct, yet were later abandoned. The original plan called for the retrieval of personnel data by requesting permission from employees to use their social security numbers and then forwarding these numbers so that the information could be centrally collected. Although the procedure was deemed appropriate and legal by the attorneys, it met with a great deal of resistance since there were too many people handling the data. The idea was abandoned, and it was agreed that only ECS staff, who had the right to such information, would obtain it and make it available anonymously to the contractor. This new system required reprogramming the DHHS computers so that the output would have no identifying information. This settled the confidentiality issue for this part of the system and eliminated the remote possibility that an ESC counselor might inadvertently forget to remove such data before they were sent to the contractor.

The issue of confidentiality was overriding the development of other procedures, including who would keypunch the computer, how supervisors would be interviewed, and how the health insurance data would be transferred. It is absolutely essential that any ECS carefully consider all confidentiality ramifications before starting an evaluation. The reputation of the program could be destroyed if the employees perceive the evaluation negatively. Strict adherence to the principle of confidentiality in some ways limits the amount of data an evaluator can obtain, but it preserves the integrity of the employees and the ECS program.

The inherent sensitivity of the confidentiality issue also became apparent in another component of the system. Impact evaluation was initially to be measured by the use of goal attainment scales. It was determined that such scales, although legal, did not measure the intake and referral assessment. Rather, they measured treatment and were not included in the evaluation. Although goal attainment scales were an accepted method in the field of human services, it was decided that the contractor would develop this stage of the evaluation.

Confidentiality can also be used as a defense against having an evaluation system. People can be threatened by the thought of being evaluated and will try to think of reasons why an evaluation of a human services program cannot be done. This is characteristic not only of EAPs but of the entire human services field. A major battle emerges between those who apply pressure for the program to demonstrate its effectiveness and those who claim that documentation is impossible. Unfortunately, providers often do not realize that evaluation can help them "sell" their programs. In many cases, they are providing valuable, needed services and evaluations can help them demonstrate this.

CONCLUSION

It is becoming evident that companies must develop comprehensive and systematic evaluation procedures to assess the effectiveness of their programs while demonstrating the organization's accountability. The documentation of cost-effectiveness is a crucial element in the evaluation design and provides the necessary justification for viewing the EAP as an economically viable alternative. In addition, the evaluation design must look at such areas as absenteeism, accident rate, and work performance for the study group as compared with a control group of similar age, sex, and number of years of service to the company. Health care costs are a major consideration.

Additional issues are crucial to the implementation of an effective evaluation plan. Confidentiality is a sensitive issue and must be respected. The backing of unions and company management is necessary as a support system. It must be proved that the EAP is a source of benefit to the individual and to the organization. The decline in health insurance costs with EAP implementation must be documented. And extensive research, perhaps with university and EAP personnel, must be conducted to supplement the evaluation. As Erfurt and Foote stated:

> Individual programs will always need to carry out periodic overall evaluation of their success. But as evidence becomes clearer about how best to set up and carry out an occupational program, EAPs can focus less attention on detailed analysis about the effects of their services, and more on simply whether or not the programs are providing the services that have been identified as most effective.[11]

Occupational alcoholism and mental health programs evaluation models have proved inadequate because of their limited scope on the treatment (impact) mode of the system. Their inability to address the diversity of employee problems in the workplace, in addition to their exclusion of work performance as a measure of program effectiveness, paved the way for the EAP evaluation model to provide a clearer and more comprehensive approach.

REFERENCES

1. C. R. Jones, "Evaluation of Occupational Programs: An Application and Some Observations" (Paper prepared for and delivered at the annual meeting of the Alcohol and Drug Problems Association of North America, September 26, 1977), pp. 5-7.

2. William E. Schlenger and B. J. Hayward, "Assessing the Impact of Occupational Programs" (Raleigh, N.C.: Human and Ecology Institute, October 31, 1975), pp. 4-6.

3. Ibid.

4. Ibid.

5. R. Alander and T. Campbell, "One Organization's Approach: An Evaluative Study of an Alcohol and Drug Recovery Program," Prepared for General Motors Corporation—Oldsmobile Division (East Lansing, Mich., Michigan State University, School of Labor and Industrial Relations, December 1973).

6. Schlenger and Hayward, "Assessing the Impact."

7. James T. Wrich, cited in ibid., p. 2.

8. Daniel L. Stufflebeam and Egan Gula, "Strategies for the Institutionalizing of the CIPP Evaluation Model" (Address delivered at the Annual PDK Symposium on Evaluation Research, Columbus, Ohio, June 24, 1970).

9. Dale A. Masi and Lisa Teems, "DHHS ECS Evaluation System: Designs, Issues and Conclusions," *Evaluation Journal*, July 1983.

10. Ibid.

11. John Erfurt and Andrea Foote, *Occupational EAP for Substance Abuse and Mental Health Problems* (Ann Arbor, Mich.: Institute of Labor and Industrial Relations, 1977), pp. 26-30.

Chapter 13

Case Studies

It is appropriate that the last chapter of this book describe some unique applications in the EAP field. As the field grows, an entire case study manual may be written to accompany a book like this one. In the meantime, I have selected these three as examples of real efforts taking place. I hope they will inspire other EAP administrators to attempt new directions in their programs, as the fledgling EAP field develops into a full-grown profession.

Case Study 1

MODEL FOR AN EVENING AND
WEEKEND TREATMENT PROGRAM*

The idea for the evening and weekend treatment program (E&WTP) originated in Boston, where I served as the administrator for several EAPs. I perceived the need for a special alcoholism program because of six major concerns:

- *The individuality of alcohol cases.* The diversity and range of alcohol problems in the workplace demonstrated the inapplicability of a standard treatment program for all cases. The 28-day treatment was not necessary for everyone, yet once-a-week therapy with AA was insufficient for some.
- *The insufficiency of annual sick leave.* Most employees with alcohol

---

* This material originally appeared as an article by Dale A. Masi entitled "A Model for Evening and Weekend Treatment for Alcoholism in the Workplace." It is reprinted, with permission, from *Labor-Management Alcoholism Journal*, Vol. 12, No. 5 (March/April 1983). © 1983 by the National Council on Alcoholism, Inc.

problems exhausted their annual or sick leave, preventing further inpatient treatment. Federal regulations made this especially difficult for government employees who had already used their advanced leave.

- *The question of reentry.* The notable absence of an employee who participated in the 28-day treatment led concerned co-workers to inquire about the nature of the absence and to offer their assistance. Such concern, although natural, threatened the confidentiality of the individual.
- *Insurance coverage.* The escalating costs of the 28-day treatment programs concerned the insurance companies that provided employee coverage.
- *Children of single parents.* Even sophisticated treatment facilities did not provide accommodations for children. The costly alternative of private arrangements for day-care services for 28 days posed difficulties for the single parent who needed treatment.
- *The interdependence of the EAPs and the treatment programs.* This led the treatment sector to depend on the EAPs for their referrals and, likewise, led the EAPs to adjust their referrals and mechanisms to the treatment facilities. EAPs needed additional consideration of their special needs by treatment facilities. For example, the unique role of the supervisor needed to be considered.

In acknowledging these concerns, I consulted with Joseph Purcsh, a psychiatrist specializing in the treatment of alcoholism, who was supportive of the concept of an evening and weekend program and suggested a six-month treatment period. The program would address the diverse needs of the working person and allow the EAP to provide input as to what these needs are.

Program Design

The DHHS ECS, chosen as a model program for the federal government, included the development of special programs to address the diversity of alcohol, drug, and mental health problems in the workplace. The development of the conceptual framework for the evening and weekend program resulted in a decision to explore the possibility of a special project in this area. Because of its special mandate, the DHHS program was the appropriate

EAP to launch such an effort. What followed was a quest to secure the financing system, the proper location, the necessary clients, and the appropriate treatment facility. Each of these items is described below.

- Meetings with Blue Cross/Blue Shield in an effort to obtain insurance coverage for participation in the treatment program spanned a two-year period. They expressed an interest but would provide coverage only if the program was to be tested and not if it was to be offered as an open-ended treatment or service. Since DHHS recognized the importance and the necessity of a comprehensive evaluation system, the plans for the development and implementation of the E&WTP proceeded.
- The assistant secretary for personnel administration at DHHS originally suggested the work site as the ideal location for the E&WTP. Hospital rooms were not necessary, and the offices and conference rooms, otherwise not used in the evenings, could be put into operation as a cost-saving alternative.
- To secure a sufficient number of participating employees, a meeting was planned with OPM, which as the overall personnel agency is responsible for the entire federal government's EAP effort. In support of this program, OPM hosted several meetings to encourage the participation of other federal agencies in the D.C. area.
- A panel composed of the Department of Defense, the Treasury Department, OPM, and DHHS was formed to select the appropriate treatment facility from a host of interested parties. After meeting with several facilities, Atlantic Counseling/Melwood Farm was selected to provide the service. In September 1982, Fairfax Hospital assumed the treatment responsibilities because of corporation changes at Melwood. Child care is available through the DHHS nursery. Special arrangements are made for a nursery school teacher to work in the evenings. The service is available for children up to age 12.

Program Description

In April 1982, an agreement was signed by DHHS, the Blue Cross/Blue Shield Federal Employee Program, and Melwood Farm to specify the respective responsibilities of each agency. The agreement was based on the assumptions that (1) the project include at least 65 participants to provide sufficient data for a thorough evaluation after 12 months, and (2) the evaluation segment of the project be funded by DHHS.

The comprehensive E&WTP is administered over a 26-week period to clients from diverse government agencies, the majority of whom are referred by the federal EAP. The hours for the first month of treatment are 5:30 P.M. to 9:30 P.M., Monday through Friday, with additional hours on Saturday from 9:00 A.M. to 1:00 P.M. and on Sunday from 1:00 P.M. to 5:00 P.M. After the first month, the client's treatment is scheduled on Tuesday, Friday, and Saturday for the remainder of the program, reducing the weekly hours from 28 to 12. The program focuses on the goal of total abstinence from alcohol, which is pursued through group therapy, education, and AA. The program schedule is designed to encourage the groups to deal with the immediate problems of the group members and to provide educational and other structural experiences.

A majority of the staff are professionals with experience treating alcoholics. The director of treatment is highly experienced and respected in the field of alcoholism. It is not difficult to obtain counselors in the evening, since it is an opportunity for extra employment, so the program has access to a variety of highly skilled practitioners.

Evaluation Questions

Development Associates is the consulting firm contracted by DHHS to conduct its EAP evaluation. The three questions to be examined for the E&WTP are:

1. Does the program provide a cost-effective approach to treatment in terms of improving worker performance?
2. Does the evening and weekend strategy provide effective alcoholism treatment?
3. Does the evening and weekend strategy provide a cost-effective treatment approach in terms of reducing overall health care treatment costs?

The methods for assessing these three areas are described below.

Supervisor job performance ratings, conducted at intake, at the completion of treatment, and six months after the completion of treatment, comprise the primary method of assessing the impact of the program on job performance. The client is rated as exhibiting desirable and undesirable work traits (punctuality, absenteeism, accident rate, attentiveness, employee relationships) on a more-than-average, average, or less-than-average basis. Each of the three ratings use the same criteria to rate the work performance of the client.

Treatment effects directly related to alcoholism recovery are primarily assessed in terms of successful completion of the six-month treatment program and continued abstinence from alcohol for six months following the completion of treatment. Observable traits of alcohol- and drug-free behavior, regular attendance during treatment, and self-report measures obtained by client intake and follow-up interviews are also assessed in the E&WTP evaluation.

The Blue Cross/Blue Shield federal EAP assesses the treatment approach in terms of cost-effectiveness related to health care costs. An analysis of the increase or decrease of such costs relative to the use of DHHS employee coverage for the E&WTP (and for a control group of federal employees enrolled in the 28-day treatment program in 1980–1981) is the basis for this assessment. Other relevant considerations include a comparison of the two groups in the number of health claims filed and the expense of health care before, during, and after treatment.

The first results of the E&WTP evaluation have not been released as of this writing.

Conclusion

The E&WTP represents an innovative approach to treating the alcohol problems that affect the work productivity and the mental and physical health of the employee, and the cost-effectiveness of the employing organization. The evening and weekend program, in addition to offering the convenience of the work site setting and the wide range of therapeutic strategies, provides a viable alternative that focuses on the individual needs of each client.

At this time, over one-half of the 65 needed clients have been referred into the program. Child care has not been used, probably because of the 40+ age of the majority of patients. There have been some dropouts, and the first two groups have successfully completed the program. An aftercare program has been initiated. At this rate cost-effectiveness and cost-reduction data for the completed program will be available sometime in 1984.

Case Study 2

MARIJUANA USE IN THE WORKPLACE*

General Motors Corporation (GM) initiated its joint corporate-wide union–management substance abuse program in 1972. It is supported by the highest levels of the corporation and the United Automobile Workers International Union. All the other major unions representing GM employees have similar joint labor–management programs available to salaried employees and nonrepresented hourly employees.

The program was initially designed to provide assistance to employees whose alcoholism interfered with their work performance. However, it later was expanded to provide assistance to employees who abused substances other than alcohol. It, therefore, became known as the Substance Abuse Program. A joint union–management approach was used from the beginning. It was recognized that neither management nor the local union could on its own provide the level of motivation required to get alcoholic employees to accept help for their problem. Prior to initiation of the joint program, it was not unusual for management and the union to be aware of cases where alcoholic employees used both parties, playing one against the other, to perpetuate their alcoholic behavior on the job. The joint program enabled both union and management to work together to encourage an employee to accept help; it thus discouraged an employee's continued use of self-destructive behavior to the point where he or she had to be fired.

Because of the increased awareness that employees have problems apart from substance abuse that interfere with their job performance, GM has made its EAP more comprehensive. The program provides evaluation and referral assistance not only to employees with substance abuse problems but also to those with such other difficulties as emotional, marital, family, and financial crises. The expansion of this program, like that of many others, addresses the full range of employee problems adversely affecting job performance, thus making it more useful to troubled employees. Continuous review of its operations is necessary to ensure that it effectively helps the substance abusers for which it was initially designed.

* This case study was prepared by Daniel Lanier, Jr., D.S.W., in collaboration with Linda J. Brown, M.A.

Program Dynamics

The role of the union–management program is to accomplish essentially three things:

- Provide for the early identification of employees having job performance problems that are generally associated with alcoholism, drug abuse, and other medical–behavioral problems, including the use of marijuana on the job.
- Promote the referral of identified troubled employees for proper evaluation and treatment, so that their disease and/or personal problems can be addressed. Employees will have an opportunity to alter their behavior and to improve their job performance before they become unemployable.
- Provide for a combination of aftercare, follow-up, and reintegration into the workforce following a period of treatment that may have required the employee to spend time away from the work site.

The local plant medical director maintains professional responsibility for the conduct of the program at each work site. The director provides medical evaluation, problem identification, and referral and supervises medication. He or she has supervisory responsibility for the substance abuse program. Day-to-day operational activities are generally carried out by the appointed union and management representatives. The general management representative provides evaluation of the troubled employee, problem identification, referral, follow-up, aftercare, and educational and training programs for supervisors, committee persons, and other plant personnel. He or she monitors treatment resources in the community and absenteeism reports of employees, and provides liaison to and education of community treatment facilities personnel. The union representative assists with problem identification and evaluation of employees, accepts employees for referral, and assists in referrals to community treatment facilities. He or she monitors job performance and follow-up after treatment, and acts as a liaison to the local union. Some locations have a full-time professional management representative with clinical skills who works with the union representative to direct the program's activities.

This case study presents a summary of 13 programs with full-time management and union representatives. Although these representatives generally see employees having a wide variety of problems that interfere with job performance, this case study concentrates only on that part of the program activity dealing with marijuana use and abuse. Marijuana occupies a precarious position in our society. Although it has been decriminalized in many states, it is still an illegal drug. Although its use can be dangerous in the workplace, it has not generally been considered a major problem in this location.

Why the Concern with Marijuana?

GM has established shop rules that define standards of conduct for the employee on the job. The shop and safety rules are generally concerned with the safety of the employee. Among these are rules governing the use of marijuana and other dangerous drugs:

> Committing any of the following violations will be sufficient grounds for disciplinary action ranging from reprimand to immediate discharge, depending upon the seriousness of the offense in the judgment of Management:
>
> (Shop Rule 32)
> Possession of, or consumption of liquor or any alcoholic beverage, narcotics, or dangerous drugs on company property at any time is prohibited, as is reporting for work under influence of alcohol, when suffering from alcoholic hangover, or in any unsafe condition.
>
> (Shop Rule 33)
> Use, possession, distribution, sale or offering for sale, of narcotics or dangerous drugs including marijuana or any hallucinogenic agents, on company property at any time are also prohibited, as is reporting for work under the influence of narcotics or dangerous drugs.[1]

Although these rules were developed by management to express its concern for safety in the workplace, there also are other reasons why the corporation is concerned about the use of marijuana on the job. These were stated very succinctly by Robert G. Wiencek, GM's director of occupational safety and health:

> The use of marijuana in the plant also has an impact on Labor Relations actions in terms of the number of grievances filed, the tension produced among employees and union as a result of the grievance, the cost of adjudicating grievances, and the cost of umpire decisions as the result of employees using marijuana on the job. . . . The use of

marijuana on the job also interferes with productivity in another way. It requires that a drug culture be maintained in the place of employment. The drug culture is a place where illegal drugs can be obtained and dispensed, where money can be exchanged for the drugs, and is an atmosphere which permits the use of illicit drugs without fear of being reported, apprehended, reprimanded, or dismissed.[2]

The use of marijuana in the workplace presents a danger for other health and safety reasons. Its use has been known to cause anxiety reactions, it impairs the judgment of the user, and it causes time–space distortions. It is now an established fact that the regular use of marijuana causes both psychological and intellectual impairment. Its use also affects perception, motor coordination, and memory as well as impairing learning ability.[3] There is increasing evidence of physical damage from long-term use of marijuana similar to that resulting from cigarette smoking—for example, laryngitis, bronchitis, coughs, and cellular change.[4] All these result in additional health costs and present additional health hazards in the workplace. They add to the concern for having a workplace that is free of mind-altering drugs.

Extent of Marijuana Use in Plants

A stratified random survey was made of 13 GM plant facilities to determine the extent of marijuana use by employees on the job. The selection of the plants was based on specific criteria, including the following:

1. Full-time union and management representatives were assigned to the EAP.
2. The program had been operational for at least five years prior to the time the survey was taken.
3. Records were available for at least five years indicating numbers of employees referred to the program and the types of problems that precipitated the referral.
4. The EAP personnel were aware of what happens to employees who use marijuana on the job.

The EAP personnel of the 13 plants selected to participate in the survey were asked to respond to the following questions:

- What was the extent of marijuana use at their plant locations?
- How many employees were seen by or referred to the EAP dur-

ing the (a) past year, (b) past two years, and (c) past five years for the use of marijuana?

- What disciplinary action was taken with employees who were apprehended smoking marijuana on the job?
- What observed incidents came to the plant's attention as a result of marijuana on the job?

The last question was designed to obtain information regarding accidents, aggressive behavior, or other unusual events related to marijuana use in the workplace.

The survey covered a total of 145,490 employees. Geographically, the plants were located in the midwestern states of Ohio, Michigan, and Indiana. The plant populations ranged in size from fewer than 5,000 employees to 17,000 employees. The median plant size was 10,500 employees. Only one plant had fewer than 13,000 people; four plants had more than 13,000 but fewer than 15,000; and the remaining plants had more than 15,000 employees. The vast majority of the sites, therefore, consisted of large industrial plants.

Classified by type of industrial organization, the surveyed plants included light, medium, and heavy industrial operations. Several of the plants included the complete line of manufacturing operations from stamping through assembly, as well as sales and marketing operations.

The overall corporate workforce at the time of the survey was approximately 17 percent female and 83 percent male. Approximately 18 percent of the workforce was black, 4 percent Hispanic, and 78 percent white. It included 89 percent hourly (blue collar) employees, with the remaining percent being salaried (white collar) employees. Although data regarding the racial, gender, and compensation characteristics of the workforces at the locations covered by the survey were not collected, these factors were not believed to be significantly at variance with those for the overall corporate population.

An analysis of the data indicated a keen awareness on the part of the EAP personnel regarding marijuana use within the plant. Nine of the program survey participants described marijuana use on the job as being heavy; one described it as heavy to moderate; two described it as moderate; and one described it as light.

The extent of marijuana use reported represents a subjective evaluation by the EAP personnel. The best indicator of the meaning of the term *heavy* is from those EAP personnel who used it to describe a situation in which 10–15 percent of the employees were regular users. Several of the respondents used this percentage in describing heavy use. The only location at which a respondent used the term *light* to describe the use was a very light industrial site with a large number of clerical, engineering, technical, and professional personnel. It should also be noted that in one location, which had a larger percentage of female employees (55 percent) than male employees, the respondents indicated "moderate" use of marijuana.

Disciplinary Action

The penalty for use of marijuana on the job appeared to be fairly consistent. All locations indicated that an employee found using marijuana was disciplined according to the provisions of the shop and safety rules. Respondents generally indicated that employees were written up for violation of either Shop Rule No. 32 or Shop Rule No. 33.

Respondents also indicated that a "progressive" disciplinary procedure was generally used. Progressive discipline usually meant that the penalty for the first offense was less severe than that for subsequent offenses. It was customary to apply the principles of progressive discipline for shop rule violations involving the personal use of marijuana in the plants. However, the selling of marijuana in the plants was considered a dischargeable offense. Among those plants surveyed, there was only one location that had primarily professional, technical, clerical, and engineering employees and where most workers were not represented by a union.

Discussion

There was near unanimity among respondents about the degree of marijuana use at their plant locations. Twelve of the 13 respondents indicated that use at their locations was either heavy or moderate. Respondents also indicated that there were adequate provisions at the work site to deal with this problem. All respondents indicated an awareness of the shop and safety rules and the progressive disciplinary system in dealing with employees who use marijuana at work. However, there was an incongruence in that very few employees were actually disciplined and therefore referred to the attention of the EAP personnel as a result of marijuana use. In all except three locations, either the number of employees referred to the program was extremely small or the statistical data were unavailable regarding the actual number referred. Even at the plant that had the highest referral rate, only 1 out of every 136 employees referred used the program; at the plant that had the lowest rate, only 1 out of 4,765 saw the program staff.

Conclusion

One then is left to ask why, despite the generally low number of employees actually referred, a perception continues that marijuana use is heavy among industrial workers in those plants surveyed? Several tentative reasons may be advanced to explain this inconsistency. The adjective (*heavy, moderate*) that was used to describe the number of marijuana users at a location may actually have described the number referred to the EAP. If the reported frequencies of use were correct, then large numbers of employees who used marijuana apparently were not being referred to the program. This suggests that there is a lack of knowledge that marijuana users have behavioral or medical problems that the EAP could address. Do supervisers lack knowledge about how to address the problems of marijuana users, and does this survey therefore indicate a need for further training focused on this problem?

Comments made by Wiencek earlier in this case study raise a different question—Is the drug culture in the industrial setting so pervasive that the smoking of a marijuana joint is an accepted and expected part of the behavior of the industrial worker? If it is, an EAP must overcome this attitude to encourage the referral of marijuana users in the workplace. This also suggests that the traditional structure of the EAP, designed to provide assistance to employees who exhibit deteriorating job performance over a period of time, may not be appropriate to deal with the marijuana user. Since this type of deterioration may not be as readily apparent among marijuana users, supervisors may indeed think that they do not have sufficient justification for referring employees who are marijuana users.

Supervisors and EAP personnel, however, must be made aware that the marijuana-dependent person possesses the same set of sociopsychological problems as abusers of other mind-altering substances. Therefore, they should be readily referred by supervisors and should be treated in the same manner by EAP personnel as other drug-dependent people. The low number of referrals, despite the incidence of drug use at the 13 locations studied, suggests that additional efforts could be very productive in meeting the needs of this underserved segment of troubled employees.

Case Study 3

MEMBERS HELPING MEMBERS: THE AFA EAP AS A PEER REFERRAL MODEL THAT WORKS*

The Association of Flight Attendants (AFA) is the largest flight attendant union in the world, representing more than 21,000 flight attendants, employed by 14 airlines. The membership is 87 percent female, and the average age is 31 years; 52 percent of the members are married, and 17 percent have children. An attrition rate of only 6 percent reflects the increasing stability of the workforce.

AFA was established as an autonomous organization in December 1973, with the majority of members at that time being represented by the Air Line Pilots Association (ALPA) Steward and Stewardess Division. Although AFA maintains a close affiliation with the AFL–CIO through ALPA, autonomy has allowed the union to concentrate efforts in areas other than collective bargaining and to provide a variety of important services to the professional flight attendant. High on AFA's list of priorities is the overall health and well-being of its membership.

During the 1950s and 1960s, many young women became flight attendants because they were attracted by the glamour, travel, adventure, and excitement of flying. They remained on the job for an average of 18 months. Then civil rights and equal opportunity laws as well as later case decisions eliminated restrictions on marital status and age. Both women and men were becoming flight attendants and planned to remain in the profession, not for a year or two, but for an entire career. By 1974, the average seniority was seven to nine years, quite a change from only ten years earlier.

In the mid-1970s, AFA began actively to seek out information on the question of stress-related problems on the job and their effects on members. In April 1974, AFA attended hearings conducted by the House Committee on Government Operations Special Studies Sub-

* This case study was prepared by Barbara Feuer, M.S., Director of the Association of Flight Attendants Employee Assistance Program.

committee, which examined the occupational alcoholism programs then in existence and focused on alcohol abuse by federal civil service employees.

During the spring of 1975, AFA distributed a preliminary survey to all members to assist in identifying health concerns common to flight attendants. Two years later, a more in-depth membership survey was developed. Additionally, the executive board was queried to determine whether the individual member airlines had occupational alcoholism treatment programs.

Liza Eatinger, a Western Airlines flight attendant, and Jim Naccarato, a United Airlines flight attendant and the current EAP coordinator, were appointed by the union to study EAPs. After extensive research and participation at numerous seminars and conferences, they submitted a report to the board of directors in 1978 on the feasibility of an EAP for the association. Their report received unanimous support, and funds were approved to prepare a grant application to the National Institute on Alcoholism and Alcohol Abuse (NIAAA). The grant application was timely because it complemented a commitment from NIAAA's Occupational Branch to look more carefully at the problems of women in the workplace. In addition, the association's EAP would be dealing with a predominantly female, highly mobile, and irregularly supervised membership. The Association of Flight Attendants Employee Assistance Program (AFA-EAP) officially began operations in July 1980, with a demonstration grant from NIAAA, to provide services to members and their families experiencing emotional/psychological, alcohol/drug, marital/family, financial/legal, and other stress-related problems.

Designing the Model

In designing a program model, it became clear to AFA that a supervisory model EAP, which relies primarily on supervisors to recognize signs of impaired job performance, would not be most effective in meeting the needs of the membership. Flight attendants are a highly mobile workforce, with irregular hours of duty, who do their work with a minimum of supervision.

For example, a flight attendant's work schedule may vary from as many as 22 to as few as 10 days a month, while the workday can range from 3 to 17 hours within a 24-hour period. Trips may last from one to five days, and rest periods are taken wherever and whenever the work assignment is completed. Flying partners usually change from month to month.

Daily job supervision in this high-stress, service-oriented profession is virtually nonexistent. It is not unusual for supervisory contact to occur only once during a three-month period, with the contact consisting solely of a 15-minute appearance evaluation. Under these circumstances, the probability of identifying and intervening with a troubled employee is not very likely.

On the other hand, flight attendants not only work together in a confined space but lodge, eat, and socialize with other crew members during rest periods. These combined personal, professional, and social relationships often place flight attendants in a unique position to observe potential problem behavior in their flying partners. The association capitalized on this unique environment and developed a program model that recognizes the importance of peers as potential catalysts for change and takes advantage of the inherent supportive relationships that exist among flight attendants. This concept was further reinforced by an in-depth study of the flight attendant subculture conducted by the EAP during the spring of 1982.

When the EAP first began training committee members in the fall of 1980, Joan Volpe, the program's research consultant, was hired to do an evaluation of the seminars and their effectiveness in training participants in the skills necessary to intervene with troubled co-workers. As a participant–observer at trainings during the next two years, Volpe became increasingly aware that the participants had a cohesiveness that transcended individual members. Informal conversations revealed we–them distinctions that went beyond the typical industrial group identity. As an anthropologist, Volpe, as well as the EAP staff, was intrigued and began seriously to question whether a subculture of flight attendants existed.

When research funds became available for an investigation of the effectiveness of the AFA EAP peer referral model, Volpe was asked to research the flight attendant lifestyle by doing an ethnographic study of the flight attendant subculture. Since the work environment is such an important factor in job performance for this population, the idea of exploring the context of the flight attendants' work life was strongly encouraged. The study was done with the hopes of tapping into the flight attendant identity with the intent of learning more about the membership so that the EAP would truly reflect its needs. The finished product, the only study of its kind on flight attendants, far exceeded the association's expectations, and the positive response and acknowledgment from the membership validated the accuracy and authenticity of Volpe's work.

The foundation of the AFA EAP is the EAP committee and its members. These full-time flight attendants are volunteers who have been chosen by their union leadership because they possess the qualities necessary to be effective in helping troubled co-workers and in administering the EAP for their respective airlines. Many of the 70-plus EAP committee members have held previous union committee positions; some have backgrounds in the helping professions, while others are recovering alcoholics or Al-Anon members. All have been carefully chosen because they are respected, trusted, and well-liked by their peers. They understand and abide by the strict confidentiality that plays an important role in the acceptance and use of the EAP by the membership.

The EAP committee members assume primary responsibility for recognizing signs of problem behavior and referring troubled co-workers to help. They oversee the majority of program activities carried out at their home bases, with full support from the national office staff in Washington, D.C. EAP committees have been established in all the states where members live. EAP committee chairpersons for each member airline have also developed operating procedures for their respective committees to ensure efficient, effective, and consistent program operations at the local level and system-wide. The program model is constantly being reviewed and refined so that it can most effectively meet the needs of AFA's diverse population.

EAP committee member responsibilities include but are not limited to:

- Promoting understanding of the EAP and the on-the-job effects of emotional/psychological, alcohol/drug, marital/familial, legal/financial, behavioral/medical, and stress-related problems.
- Intervening (informally and formally) with a troubled member whose personal problems are affecting his or her work. This also includes monitoring the progress of those members involved in treatment and aftercare for at least a year.
- Maintaining accurate, confidential case records on all clients.
- Promoting the EAP at his or her base. Marketing efforts include developing and disseminating educational materials; conducting

local EAP seminars for other union committees, management, and the general flight attendant population; publicizing the EAP and its services in newsletter articles, at local union council meetings, and during recurrent training; and conducting local workshops on EAP-related topics.

- Researching local community treatment resources and self-help groups in his or her city of residence and developing treatment resource directories. Sharing resource information with EAP committee members from other member airlines located in the same city.
- Keeping the necessary union leadership apprised of EAP activities and program operations.
- Contacting other union committees to advocate for EAP-related issues relevant to the membership (negotiations, grievances, safety, and insurance committees).

In addition, the EAP chairperson is responsible for:

- Developing a policy statement regarding use of the EAP on his or her respective airline that is approved by appropriate union officers.
- Working with management personnel and/or company EAP representatives in assisting flight attendants, according to the policy on that airline.
- Developing specific operating procedures for use by all EAP committees on his or her respective carrier to ensure efficient, effective, and consistent program operations at the local level and system-wide.

Training: A Necessary Ingredient

More than 100 EAP committee members have received an average of 108 hours of training. EAP training seminars are divided into basic, advanced, and postadvanced modules, which were developed by the national office EAP staff. The comprehensive programs include presentations by EAP and other in-house staff and by consultants who are recognized authorities in their respective fields. Role-plays, films, videotaping, small-group work, and experiential exercise complement the lecture–discussion format.

Because individuals troubled by alcohol-related problems are not likely to self-refer for help, the basic training focuses on teaching

EAP committee members how to recognize signs of problem behavior. Presentations on understanding the dynamics of alcoholism, treatment issues for women, and the importance of aftercare are also included. Preintervention planning strategies are practiced, using simulated case studies that give all participants hands-on experience. Other important content areas include basic listening and communication skills, presentations on confidentiality, developing community resources, record keeping, and preventing burnout.

The advanced and postadvanced training is more comprehensive than initial training in focusing on the many other problems that affect a troubled employee's on-the-job behavior. Topics covered include continuing sobriety, crisis intervention and suicide prevention, working with rape victims, domestic violence, eating disorders, working with the adult children of alcoholics, fear of flying, cocaine abuse, and managing stress. Additionally, the training concentrates on program promotion, case management issues, interfacing effectively with other union committees, and advanced communication skills. All training also stresses the importance, in order to function most effectively, of understanding the concepts of detachment and the committee member's responsibility to but not for a troubled coworker.

Since the EAP is the "new kid on the block," integration of the program into the existing organizational structure, both at the national office and in the field, is a high priority. One of the objectives of the AFA EAP is to work cooperatively with those airlines that already have company EAPs. Consequently, the AFA EAP has participated in several joint training sessions for EAP committee members and their management counterparts. The first such training, held in September 1982 with United Airlines, emphasized the ways in which the AFA EAP and the United EAP could work cooperatively to assist troubled flight attendants. This training, an industry first, has been followed by local joint training planned and carried out by EAP committee members with Western, Alaska, Frontier, and Republic airlines management personnel.

Education and Program Promotion

Education and prevention have continued to be critical elements in promoting the program in the field. To make the program consistently visible to the membership, the national office has written educational brochures on relevant EAP-related topics. During the first three years of operation, members have been mailed brochures on such topics as recognizing when to get help from the EAP, dealing with tension, coping with the stress and strain of the holiday season, prescription drugs, and anger. A detachable list of names and phone numbers of EAP committee members is often included with the mailings.

Information about the EAP and its many services is prominently displayed on union bulletin boards, in newsletters written by local EAP committees, in local union council newsletters, at union meetings, during yearly recurrent flight attendant training, and in *Flightlog*, the association's quarterly membership magazine. Presentations on the EAP are also included in leadership training for union officers conducted at the national level. EAP committee members in different cities have jointly coordinated seminars for flight attendant members on depression and loneliness, alcohol and drug abuse, nutrition and self-care, and stress management.

Developing Community Resources

Treatment resource information for every state is on file in the national office. Information is available on clinicians who specialize in all types of counseling and therapy, including alcohol and drug addiction diagnosis and treatment. Extensive information on in- and outpatient treatment facilities, and other services, including legal and financial assistance, is also available. EAP committees interview local service providers and assess the scope of services they provide. They are also responsible for keeping up-to-date resource files at their respective local offices.

Program Evaluation—A Critical Component

Does the AFA peer model EAP really work? From October 1980, when the EAP began serving members, through June 1983, more than 1,000 flight attendants and their family members received assistance.

During the summer of 1982, the program evaluation consultant began a comprehensive analysis of approximately 500 cases—51 percent were referred for chemical dependency problems; 25 percent requested assistance for emotional/psychological problems; 8 percent sought help for job-related problems with no behavioral/medical origin; 10 percent were experiencing marital or family problems; 4 percent were involved in situations of domestic violence or rape; and 2 percent had financial problems.

Overall, 47 percent of the cases were peer referrals—a clear demonstration that the AFA EAP is successful in helping troubled members get help for themselves. Thirty percent were self-referrals and the remainder were referred by management (13 percent) or family members (10 percent). Another indication of program success is that the often adversarial barriers that exist between management and the union come down in order to help the troubled member/employee.

Although 43.2 percent of the emotional problems were self-referrals, only 18.4 percent of the chemical dependency problems were. Troubled employees experiencing alcohol- and drug-related problems were referred by their peers in 56.3 percent of the cases, by the company in 18.4 percent of the cases, and by a family member in 6.8 percent of the cases analyzed. In the first two years of operation, 73 percent of the cases analyzed were referred for help, another demonstration that the union's prototype peer referral model does indeed work.

As the program began its fourth year, plans were to broaden its emphasis to encompass all members, not only the troubled flight attendant. By focusing on overall health and well-being in its educational efforts, the program may help prevent the development of problems that might require a referral to the EAP.

REFERENCES

1. "Shop and Safety Rules," *Shop Rules and Regulations* (Detroit: General Motors Corporation, 1981), p. 209.

2. Robert G. Wiencek, "Marijuana in the Work Place," *Drug Abuse in the Modern World: A Perspective for the Eighties* (New York: Pergamon Press, 1981).

3. *Addiction and Substance Abuse Report* (New York: Grafton Publications, April 1980), pp. B1–B2.

4. George K. Russell, *Marijuana Today* (New York: The Myrin Institute for Adult Education, 1976), pp. 17–43.

Index

Index

Index

Index

Index

Nervo, Dean, on Italian social workers, 186

Netherlands, social work in, 186

NIAAA, *see* National Institute on Alcohol Abuse and Alcoholism

NIMH (National Institute of Mental Health), 16

"Objectives for the Nation," 165

occupational alcoholism programs
confrontational approach to, 11
in federal agencies, mandating of, 12
limitations of, 5–6, 8–9, 13
during 1940s, 6–8
during 1950s, 9–11
during 1960s, 11–12
during 1970s, 12–14
supervisory identification approach to, 8–9, *see also* supervisory referrals
union support of, 54–56, *see also* union–management programs
see also alcohol abuse programs

occupational alcoholism programs, examples of:
Allis-Chalmers Manufacturing Company, 7–8
evening and weekend treatment program (E&WTP), 16, 205–209
Kemper Insurance Development Program, 88–90
Malden-Medford Consortium, 69–71
Taunton-Brockton Industrial Consortium, 67–69

occupational segregation, 146–149

Office of Disease Prevention and Health Promotion, 136

Office of Drug Abuse Policy, 181

Office of Personnel Management (OPM), 15, 16, 61–63, 207

Oppenheimer, Valerie Kincade, on pink collar professions, 147

Pan American Health Organization, 191

Parasram, Rampersad, on alcoholism in Trinidad, 190

Parker, Frank J., 35n

Peadres, Daniel, on alcoholism among Native Americans, 163

Peele, Stanton, on alcohol addiction, 78

peer referrals, 219

Perlis, Leo, on industrial alcoholism programs, 10–11, 56

personnel costs, 2

Pitochelli, William, support of consortiums by, 62

Planners Studio (PS) study, on women and occupational alcoholism, 86–87

"Policy and Program in Alcoholism," 8

policy statement, 26–29
on drug abuse, 105–106
employee education through, 57

"Positive Mental Health in the Black Community" (Wilcox), 157

privacy, right of, 37, 119
see also confidentiality

Privacy Act (1974)
and DHHS ECS Case Maintenance System, 32–33
referral memo and, 52

problem drinkers
cost of, to employers, 197
description of, 73
identification of, 13–14
see also alcohol abuse programs; alcoholism; occupational alcoholism programs

productivity loss, 1–4
see also job performance

public safety, 102–104, 212–213

233